Contracting with Citizens

This book demonstrates that contracts, community intermediaries, and participatory processes are closely interlinked, and they can change urban politics.

In participatory processes, residents negotiate with policymakers about the future of their neighborhood. In the last few decades, this happened increasingly in co-creation sessions where citizens are deemed to have an equal position vis-a-vis developers and civil servants. The goal of this book is to understand and theorize how these negotiations affect collective action. The book will scrutinize the role of contracts, community intermediaries, and participatory processes in development projects and planning policies. Using a comparative case study of Amsterdam, Hamburg, and New York, this book reveals how seemingly fresh and novel planning practices are used to justify processes of capital accumulation and reveals how morals, politics, and law can create institutional change.

The book presents a novel theoretical approach to studying urban politics, putting emphasis on (private) law and the material arrangements of participatory processes. It will be of interest to researchers and students of planning, geography, sociology, public administration, and law and will provide valuable lessons for practitioners interested in understanding the effects of contractual governance on neighborhoods.

E.W. (Michiel) Stapper has a position as an assistant professor at the Department of Geography, Planning, and International Development Studies at the University of Amsterdam, the Netherlands. His research interests lie in the intersection of cities, society, and the law. In 2020, he was awarded a Horizon Europe project as PI, investigating how the European Green Deal affects and involves marginalized communities. In 2023, he was awarded a Dutch Starter Grant for a project that conducts a socio-legal study of large-scale climate plans in the United States, European Union, Japan, and Korea.

Routledge Research in Planning and Urban Design

Routledge Research in Planning and Urban Design is a series of academic monographs for scholars working in these disciplines and the overlaps between them. Building on Routledge's history of academic rigour and cutting-edge research, the series contributes to the rapidly expanding literature in all areas of planning and urban design.

Rebuilding Urban Complexity
A Configurational Approach to Postindustrial Cities
Francesca Froy

The Protection of Green Spaces for Climate Change Adaptation
Planning Systems, Policies and Instruments
Edited by Maciej J. Nowak

Exclusion in Smart Cities
Assessment and Strategy for Strengthening Resilience
Izabela Jonek-Kowalska and Radosław Wolniak

The Green Belt, Housing Crises and Planning Systems
Charles Edward Goode

Displaced Urbanism
Edited by Gihan Karunaratne

Resilient Urbanism
Edited by Gihan Karunaratne

Contracting with Citizens
How Morals, Politics, and Laws Shape Cities
E.W. (Michiel) Stapper

For more information about this series, please visit: www.routledge.com/Routledge-Research-in-Planning-and-Urban-Design/book-series/RRPUD

Contracting with Citizens

How Morals, Politics, and Laws Shape Cities

E.W. (Michiel) Stapper

Routledge
Taylor & Francis Group
LONDON AND NEW YORK

Designed cover image: Photograph by E.W. (Michiel) Stapper.

First published 2025
by Routledge
4 Park Square, Milton Park, Abingdon, Oxon OX14 4RN

and by Routledge
605 Third Avenue, New York, NY 10158

Routledge is an imprint of the Taylor & Francis Group, an informa business

British Library Cataloguing-in-Publication Data
A catalogue record for this book is available from the British Library

ISBN: 978-1-032-71282-6 (hbk)
ISBN: 978-1-032-71283-3 (pbk)
ISBN: 978-1-032-71284-0 (ebk)

DOI: 10.4324/9781032712840

Typeset in Times New Roman
by Apex CoVantage, LLC

Contents

Tables

Acknowledgments

This book began as a PhD project in 2016. Saying it has been a long journey might sound cliché, but it truly was. I am deeply grateful to everyone I met along the way. Above all, I owe so much to the people who work tirelessly to improve their neighborhoods. Their dedication and service to their communities continue to amaze me. This book exists because they shared their experiences, insights, and ideas. Thanks to them, I can now share what I've learned about cities and urban politics. A special thanks to Mike Brantjes, Marjora Carter, Dominic Berg, Cathrin Zengerling, and Veronika Hilberman for showing me how residents shape cities.

I could not have written this book without the unwavering support of my family. Research is a process of trial and error, and my family gave me the confidence to stumble and the encouragement to keep going. Thank you for letting me be distracted and inconsistent in my attention. I love you to the moon and back: Airen, Astrid, Arjo, Fedde, Jochem, Kim, Renée, Sophieke, and Yves.

To my dear family, friends, and colleagues, your love and support kept me grounded and motivated. I wasn't the brightest student and often struggled in school, so the fact that I've written an academic book would likely surprise my primary school teachers. I still remember my sister Renée telling me I could become smarter by performing a ritual of stepping on our floor tiles in a specific sequence. I followed her instructions religiously—it's up to fellow sociologists to decide whether that ritual led to this moment. Perseverance, too, was a lesson I learned from being tackled daily by my oldest sister, Kim. Thank you, Dad, for insisting to the high school director that I was smart enough to go to HAVO. Thank you, Branta, for loving me, taking care of me, *pacarku yang manis*.

To my colleagues at the University of Amsterdam, thank you for your constructive criticism and thought-provoking discussions. A special thanks to Fenna Smits and Anastasiya Halauniova for our deep conversations about rotten cities and devaluation, and to Tuna Taşan-Kok, Danielle Chevalier, and Tobias Arnoldussen for the pizza nights and academic debates. I'm also grateful to my PhD supervisors, Jan Willem Duyvendak, Leonie Janssen-Jansen, and Menno van der Veen, for their guidance. And to my former colleagues at Tilburg Law School, thank you for our engaging conversations about the nature of law.

Lastly, I dedicate this book to my mother. After she passed away, we found a note where she wrote, *maak al je dromen waar*—make all your dreams come true.

This book is for you because, while I couldn't have imagined going to university, you believed I could. You always told me to be happy and cheerful and to laugh often. Over these past eight years, I've been able to learn from others, ask countless questions, explore cities, and build new friendships. This dissertation is the result of the joy I've found in doing research.

1 Urban ordering

It is a cloudy evening in New York City's Lower East Side as I rush to the community board meeting of Manhattan's third district. At these meetings, political representatives give updates, residents can ask questions, and board members vote on land use, budgets, and community services. A neighborhood resident uses his speaking time to complain about the construction work around the subway stations. Animated, he waves a document in the air—the request for proposal (RFP) for Essex Crossing. The RFP outlines the development project's requirements and forms the basis for a contract between the parties. Although it is not yet a contract, it forms the basis for one and includes the criteria formulated by residents through a participatory process. The man reminded everybody that the community board guaranteed in the RFP that the subway stations would remain accessible during and after construction. This was not the case, and he now wanted to know who would enforce the agreement.

On the other side of the Atlantic, in Amsterdam, I talked with three residents who had met during the participatory process for the Oostenburg-Noord development project. They aimed for the project to include a community center, hoping to bring people together in their gentrifying neighborhood. Their proposal, lacking a financial plan, was initially rejected because the developer thought it was unprofessional. The residents then hired a planning consultant. When I asked how they paid for the consultant, they laughed and said: "We are not yet a legal person, but we have already found subsidies!" Their new, more professionally presented plan led to signing a letter of intent with the developer.

In yet another Atlantic harbor city, Hamburg, I met a coordinator working for Q8, an organization that aims to make Hamburg accessible to all of its residents. She tells me that one of their greatest achievements was making Neue Mitte Altona—a development project of 1,600 housing units—barrier-free for people with disabilities. She explains that Q8 succeeded by tabling 30 recommendations, translating them into contractual terms, and lobbying for their implementation. But whereas Q8 was successful, another group of residents, the Koordinierungsgremium, boycotted the participatory process for Neue Mitte Altona, arguing that their recommendations were not taken seriously and were used as window-dressing.

These vignettes all portray residents using contracts and agreements to have their goals incorporated into urban development projects. A particular configuration

DOI: 10.4324/9781032712840-1

of contracts and agreements is at stake in all three participatory processes. The vignettes also show the increased importance of contracts, community intermediaries, and participation in urban politics. Moreover, the vignette from Hamburg portrays that the goals of some residents are seen as more worthy of inclusion than others, showing how the participatory process can draw moral boundaries between citizens.

Urban politics is increasingly ordered through negotiation processes. This increases the importance of contracts, community intermediaries, and participation. This has been explained within urban studies as the by-product of neoliberalism and market-oriented reforms (Raco, 2013; Swyngedouw et al., 2002) or the result of good urban governance (Fagotto and Fung, 2006; Torfing et al., 2019). Studies show that contracts are used to circumvent public processes and advance the goals of urban elites (Raco, 2013). However, research also shows that contracts can be designed to enhance democratic accountability (Janssen-Jansen and van der Veen, 2017; Tasan-Kok et al., 2019). Community intermediaries are described as helping their neighborhoods flourish (Fagotto and Fung, 2006) and potentially undermining democratic processes (Levine, 2016). Participation is hailed as giving residents a say about their neighborhood (Albrechts, 2012; Torfing et al., 2019) and as window dressing (Walker et al., 2015). These mixed research results lack a clear explanation.

This book sets the critical capacity of urban dwellers as the center of urban politics. Those actors are shaped and constrained by processes related to class, gender, and race but never determined by them. There is resistance everywhere. This research highlights how critiques from residents, developers, politicians, and civil servants lead to changes in urban politics. Some of those critiques are displaced, and some of them are institutionalized. They crystalize in new moral, political, and legal arrangements. In the past, neighborhood meetings where civil servants discuss their plans have been criticized as too static and top-down. Therefore, they have been increasingly replaced by co-creation sessions. Co-creation is the idea that citizens should actively participate in urban development processes and come up with creative solutions. Those who actively participate are seen as worthy residents. Community intermediaries—consultants or community workers—often replace politicians as neighborhood representatives in decision-making processes since politicians are seen as out of touch or untrustworthy. Contracts increasingly replace public laws as the main steering tool in planning because public laws lack flexibility.

This book offers an explanation for those changes through the lens of sociology of critique (Boltanski and Chiapello, 2005; Boltanski and Thévenot, 1991) and pragmatism (Dewey, 1927; Young, 2000). Both traditions see actors as creative agents who have the capacity to critique institutions. This book presents three main arguments. First, the critical capacity of urban actors has led to the increased use of participation, community intermediaries, and contracts. Second, although actors have the capacity to critique institutions, the process of capital accumulation (Boltanski and Chiapello, 2005) and barriers related to race, gender, and class (Young, 1990, 2000) constrain their abilities to shape urban politics. Third, this book will highlight how interactions between urban actors are deeply embedded in materialities. Objects are drawn in for support in public disputes (Boltanski and Thévenot, 1991) and hold "particular institutionalized patterns of power and authority" (Winner, 1980, p. 134). Objects afford capacities to certain actors and constrain the ability to act for other actors (Yaneva, 2009). This materially embedded and embodied tension between the critical capacity of urban actors and structural barriers explains institutional changes in urban politics.

I employ the tools provided by sociologists of critique such as Luc Boltanksi, Laurent Thévenot, and Ève Chiapello to analyze how urban actors organize collective action in uncertain situations. I especially make use of their concept of pragmatic registers, a set of principles, valued actors and objects, and practices that are strongly associated with each other. These registers are strongly ingrained in society and structure the behavior of actors. However, they differ from discourses in the sense that they are less restrictive. Registers can be omnipresent but never omnipotent. Therefore, different registers have to compromise with each other, creating very specific local constellations that are able to coordinate collective action. They are threads woven through the social fabric, supporting the individual critiques of actors and transforming them into a collective critique. Whereas Luc Boltanski, Laurent Thévenot, and Ève Chiapello focus on the moral and political aspects of registers, I add a legal aspect. Adding the legal aspect is important, because legal tools—such as contracts, public laws, or agreements—play a central role in coordinating collective action.

Thus, pragmatic registers are specific constellations of morals, politics, and laws. Morals help actors navigate uncertain situations: what ought to be? Politics help actors to arrange what kind of actions will be undertaken: who decides? Laws help actors stabilize relations: what rules will be in place? It is important to underline that those pragmatic registers emerge through the critiques and interactions of urban actors until they transcend local particularities and become reproduced on a large scale. Thus, pragmatic registers are not outside forces that determine actors' actions.

Pragmatic sociologists distinguish between reality and the world, between "everything that is the case" and what is considered with uncertainty (Boltanski, 2011, p. 57). In this book, I present pragmatic registers as deeply embedded within the social fabric of cities and embodied through urban actors and objects. Thus, pragmatic registers are not external drivers but work through actors and objects.

In theory, the number of registers is infinite; however, there are only a limited amount of registers that can transcend space and time and be reproduced throughout large areas of the world. The sheer mobilizing power of those pragmatic registers is what makes them pragmatic registers. They can be recognized by actors living in different geographies and with different positions in society. A compromise between the different registers—often mediated through objects—can bring together diverse actors such as community activists invoking the right to affordable housing through a manifesto and investors calculating the profitability of affordable housing through Excel sheets.

In addition, pragmatic registers are useful concepts to show how the clash between processes of capital accumulation and the democratic practices in North

America and Europe are deeply embedded and embodied within materialities. Protesters use their bodies to prevent the demolition of a building or gentrification processes in a neighborhood. Buildings themselves are complex entities of use and exchange values. Pragmatic registers are not merely linguistic devices but embedded and embodied in and between actors and objects.

In the next paragraphs, I briefly discuss different aspects of participation, community intermediaries, and contracts, and I show how different institutional orders emerged in cities in Europe and North America.

1.1 Participation, community intermediaries, and contracts

This book focuses on participatory processes and the role community intermediaries and contracts play in those processes. In this section, I describe the different academic discussions around those concepts within urban studies. As this section will show, urban politics is always evolving, never linear (Le Galès and Vitale, 2013).

In 1969, Arnstein defined participation as "it is the redistribution of power that enables the have-not citizens, presently excluded from the political and economic processes, to be deliberately included in the future" (Arnstein, 1969). She introduced the famous 'ladder of citizen participation' in the same article, which is a scale to analyze to what extent citizens have control over decision-making processes. The scale ranges from nonparticipation to degrees of tokenism to degrees of citizen power (Arnstein, 1969, p. 217). Whereas Arnstein defined participation as the redistribution of power, later definitions relate participation mostly to communication and deliberation efforts such as "respectful discussion within and between discursive communities" (Healey, 1993, p. 242) and "engagement enables people to achieve a fuller expression of their interest by debating and sharing ideas with others" (Lowndes et al., 2006, p. 238). In this book, I use a broad definition of participation, relating to all efforts to involve residents in decision-making processes. The involvement can range from consultation to having decision-making power.

In this study, I use the term 'community intermediaries' to refer to those actors who act as 'go-betweens.' In the literature, they are often described as actors who have networks in the neighborhood and who interact with other actors, such as governmental agencies and developers (Kim et al., 2021; Shea, 2011; Vivier and Sanchez-Betancourt, 2020). They collect the interests, needs, and desires of residents through talking with residents, networking in the neighborhood, and/or participatory processes. From those engagements, they create a set of coherent and unequivocal needs for the neighborhood—although the needs and interests of residents in practice can be very contentious and contradictory. I will refer to those needs as the residents' principles.

I make a distinction between two types of community intermediaries: actors that are linked to neighborhood organizations and actors that are linked to commercial consultancy bureaus. Neighborhood organizations are organizations that provide several services to residents of a neighborhood, ranging from health- and social care to cultural activities. Leaders of those neighborhood organizations can often function as spokespersons of the neighborhood; they assume a position in which they can speak for the residents. In recent decades, those leaders have gained legitimacy as spokespersons at the cost of elected officials (Levine, 2016). Moreover, neighborhood organizations are important actors in urban redevelopment projects, as they often partner with governmental agencies and developers to design and implement those plans (Kort and Klijn, 2011; Swyngedouw, 2005; Tasan-Kok, 2010).

The other type of community intermediary is commercial consultancy bureaus. Because a wide variety of actors are involved in urban planning, the ability of consultants to solve problems related to cooperation and coordination is regarded as valuable (Grijzen, 2010). Consultants can act as mediators between actors by understanding their interests and the organizational contexts in which they operate (Caloffi and Gambarotto, 2017). They are increasingly hired to organize participatory processes and inquire what the needs of residents are (Stapper et al., 2020). So, in contrast to leaders of neighborhood organizations, consultants do not represent residents. However, the consultants act as intermediaries between the residents, governmental agencies, and commercial parties. Although consultants work for commercial bureaus, it is important to note that the increased role of consultants in urban planning is not only related to market-oriented reforms. Local administrations wish to implement collaborative and communicative planning policies, and consultants are deemed to have expertise that civil servants do not have (Raco et al., 2016; Stapper et al., 2020).

Next to community intermediaries, this book will examine the role of contracts as tools of urban governance, focusing especially on how contractual relations between residents, developers, and government agencies within participatory processes. Contracts are often seen as written documents with a set of fixed agreements that regulate transactions. However, empirical research has shown that contracts are flexible tools that can be adjusted when circumstances change (Macaulay, 1963; Van den Hurk and Tasan-Kok, 2020). Moreover, agreements do include both written and oral commitments of contractual parties (Eisenberg, 2018; Smits, 2014).

In order to understand contractual relations, it is important to understand that all contracts are agreements, but not all agreements are contracts (see Eisenberg, 2018). The distinction between contracts and agreements comes down to whether the contractual parties have the intention to be legally bound to their promises (Eisenberg, 2018; Smits, 2014). Generally understood and studied as mechanisms to govern business relations, contracts have been studied less as tools of governance to achieve public policy goals (Janssen-Jansen and van der Veen, 2017)). The research on contracts used in governance suggests that contracts are rigid tools that make public policy opaque and inflexible to new political realities: "any shift towards contractual private provision is often inflexible and limits the ability of welfare service providers, and by extension local communities, to reform public services to meet new demands" (Raco, 2013, p. 50). Savini similarly argues that "development contracts signed between government and private sector developers under the regime of private law are more rigid than zoning plans in changing circumstances" (Savini et al., 2016, p. 460). However, Van den Hurk and Taşan-Kok note that "both public and private actors prefer to seek solutions rather than strictly follow a contract" (Van den Hurk and Tasan-Kok, 2020, p. 16). Contracts can also be used to enhance democratic accountability when they are designed for that purpose (Janssen-Jansen and van der Veen, 2017; Tasan-Kok et al., 2019). In this book, contracts are analyzed as a set of contractual relations on a continuum, ranging from enforceable to less enforceable agreements.

1.2 Institutional change in Amsterdam, Hamburg, and New York

The argument of this book is that the increased importance of participation, community intermediaries, and contracts can be understood as the emergence of the so-called entrepreneurial register since the 2010s. The entrepreneurial register was increasingly invoked to deal with uncertain situations because there was a growing critique in society of bureaucratic and rigid government agencies and profit-seeking commercial parties. The entrepreneurial register provided justifications for the embrace of the creativity and innovations of self-organization in planning practices. To understand how the entrepreneurial register has restructured urban politics since the 2010s, I start with understanding the different waves of registers that have captivated urban politics since the 1960s. I describe these waves as an interplay between social movements that actively criticize urban politics and urban actors that benefit from processes of capital accumulation.

Governments in North America and Western Europe have encouraged citizen participation in urban development since the 1960s. Since then, participatory processes have become an important part of urban politics. Nevertheless, the aims of participation and how it is organized have seen many changes over the years (Fagotto and Fung, 2006; Innes and Booher, 2004; Uitermark and Duyvendak, 2008; Walker et al., 2015). Baiocchi and Ganuza (2017) distinguish between three periods: those of public administration, new public management, and public governance. Community intermediaries have played a role in participatory processes since the 1960s but became increasingly important in the 1980s due to market-oriented reforms and privatization policies (Levine, 2016; Saint-Martin, 1998). The same goes for contracts; while they have always played an important role in urban development, they gained importance due to privatization policies in the 1980s (Vincent-Jones, 2007).

The post-war period of the 1950s and the 1960s has been characterized by top-down planning and modernist ideas on building the ideal city. Urban renewal programs demolished impoverished (inner) city neighborhoods and built new high-rises to accommodate a growing housing demand. This can be described as an industrial register, aiming to order cities efficiently and functionally through goal-maximizing and scientific research (see Boltanski and Thévenot, 1991, p. 185–93). During the 1960s and the 1970s this led to growing resistance in cities. The idea that cities can be ordered through top-down plans without the influence of residents was heavily criticized. In Amsterdam, Hamburg, and New York, this led to (violent) clashes with the police and the introduction of new ideas to organize urban development.

In Amsterdam, the 'provo' movement launched plans to promote squatting and end the speculation of housing as a response to modernist city planning practices in the 1960s (Owens, 2016; Provo, 1966). The provo's tried to actively mobilize youth to take control of empty houses in Amsterdam (Provo, 1966). They painted doors of vacant buildings as a sign that they could be squatted. The rationale behind this plan was that everybody "has the right to a just distribution of (collective) housing" (Provo, 1966). The practice of squatting grew until it peaked in the mid-1970s. The tactic also had an international impact; people from across Europe came to Amsterdam to learn how to squat (Owens, 2016). Another way activists voiced their critique of municipal planning practices was the violent clash between activists and the police around the demolition plans of the Nieuwmarkt neighborhood. The municipality planned to demolish this neighborhood to build a metro line. Several demonstrations were organized, but the municipality continued with its plans. In 1975, residents barricaded the neighborhood to stop the construction workers from continuing their work (Gemeente Amsterdam, 2020). In turn, the municipal government decided to break the occupation by sending the police to the square. This led to massive riots, known as the 'battle for the Nieuwmarkt,' which continued for 15 days (Gemeente Amsterdam, 2020; Owens, 2016).

In Hamburg, activists started to squat in empty buildings in the early 1970s. They often created public facilities—with support from neighborhood residents—such as co-housing or youth centers (Scheller, 2020; Templin, 2016). A famous example is the Fabrik, a cultural center founded in an old machine parts factory. The new approach to using old industrial space and transforming it with cultural activities was imitated across the world (Fabrik, 2024). However, not all the initiatives were embraced by the authorities. In 1973, activists squatted a building in Hohenfelde to create a house for students and migrants. The police used 500 agents to remove the squatters from the building (Michels, 2010).

In New York, Jane Jacobs famously resisted urban renewal programs (Jane Jacobs, 1961). But that period is also characterized by the Stonewall riots, where the queer community claimed the right to be treated equally in urban spaces (Andersson, 2015), and the civil rights movement that fought against racial discrimination. For example, the Brooklyn chapter of the Congress of Racial Equality (CORE) laid bare the racially motivated negligence of housing conditions in Bedford-Stuyvesant (Purnell, 2007). In the same neighborhood, Black organizers founded the first community development corporation to improve the lives of the residents (Williams, 1985). Other pioneering community development corporations were located in Brooklyn and the Bronx (Angotti, 2008). Community intermediaries such as community development corporations offered various services to neighborhood residents, ranging from job counseling to education and cultural activities (Williams, 1985). Community development corporations spread to many more neighborhoods across the world.

The critiques that were voiced as a response to modernist planning practices crystallized in new pragmatic registers to organize urban development. From the 1960s to the 1980s, during the period of public administration (Baiocchi and Ganuza, 2017, p. 52), increasingly participatory processes were organized to consult residents on issues of spatial planning. Scholars of the period—for example, Jacobs (1958), Davidoff (1965), and Arnstein (1969)—understood participation as the process to give residents access to decision-making power and an important part of democracy. Jacobs, whose work on urban life greatly influenced urban planning and public participation, argued that "residents should decide how cities will be built" (Jacobs, 1958, p. 131). Davidoff similarly held that planners should champion the interests of residents and that "choices about policy should be taken through public debate and participation" (Davidoff, 1965). In Arnstein's "ladder of citizen power," citizen control is participation's highest aim: "participation of the governed in their government is, in theory, the cornerstone of democracy" (Arnstein, 1969, p. 216). In this book, I refer to the aim of giving power to citizens—working for the public good and strengthening democratic procedures—as the civic register, which I borrow from the work of Boltanski and Thévenot (1991). Largely organized through public procedures, the goal of civic participation is to organize collective action and to emancipate and empower citizens (Boltanski and Thévenot, 1991).

This period also witnessed the installation of citizen advisory boards and review and comment procedures (Baiocchi and Ganuza, 2017). In Amsterdam, new national regulations gave residents the ability to review and comment on plans (Verlaan, 2016). Moreover, a new planning paradigm was introduced, called 'bouwen voor de buurt,' or building for the neighborhood. Instead of the demolition of old neighborhoods and top-down planning, urban renewal projects were introduced to improve neighborhoods through consultation with residents (Pruyt, 1985).

In Hamburg, the mayor of Hamburg held a famous speech called 'Die unregierbarkeit der Städte,' or the Ungovernability of Cities 1975. He analyzed the problems of Hamburg and unpacked why cities appeared to be ungovernable. Hamburg and other cities seemed to have to deal with social unrest, increasingly empty inner cities, and a declining industrial presence. This led to problems in city budgets and diminished the possibility of city governments intervening directly in urban development. The solution was increasing democratization and participation. However, he noted that democratization and participation are not only meant for residents to ask requests from the government; citizens also have a responsibility to take care of their neighborhoods (Klose, 1975).

In New York, a wave of regulations gave more influence to residents in the 1960s and the 1970s. Community boards are committees of appointed representatives of neighborhoods. There were 59 boards established in 1963 (City of New York, 2024). The famous ULURP procedure—uniform land use review procedure—was introduced in 1976 (City of New York, 2024). The ULURP procedure gives community boards the ability to review urban development projects. Moreover, since federal funding required participation, there was an increase in participatory processes throughout the 1960s (City of New York, 2024).

It should be emphasized that the social movements in the 1960s and the 1970s pushed ideas of participation as empowerment of the people to the forefront of urban planning debates. However, suburbanization processes led to a change in the demographics of cities (Neumann, 2020; Verlaan, 2016; Zukin et al., 2009).

The youth and elderly were those that remained in the cities, whereas people with families moved to the suburbs. Thus, city governments lost an important part of their tax base. This process was coupled with an industrial decline and the oil crises of 1973 and 1979. This severely limited the way city governments could intervene in cities, which made ideas on citizen control more attractive because it meant that residents would start sharing responsibilities. The civic register was invoked to justify the implementation of consultation procedures and the creation of community development corporations. However, the civic register was not omnipotent, and part of the critiques of the social movements were displaced. This resulted in consultation procedures but limited opportunities for residents to have control over decision-making processes. Community development corporations are created—which signals the rise of community intermediaries—but those organizations often have to struggle for funding.

Ideas from new public management entered participatory practices in the 1980s (Baiocchi and Ganuza, 2017). As stated, economic crises led to shrinking public budgets and a new role for citizen participation in urban policy. As government agencies now had to become more efficient and results-oriented (Baiocchi and Ganuza, 2017, p. 56), public-private partnerships—managed through contracts—became the new model to achieve public policy goals (Vincent-Jones, 2007). This led to an explosion of community-based organizations taking over formerly public responsibilities, including affordable housing, economic development, and social policy (Levine, 2016). Planning consultants were increasingly hired to give an aura of credibility to public policies (Saint-Martin, 1998). Baoicchi and Ganuza note that "new public management sought to capture a part of the political imaginary of the 1960s . . . with its ideal of matching its objectives to the needs of citizens" (Baiocchi and Ganuza, 2017, p. 56). The reference to the political imaginaries of the 1960s is also notable in Osborne's work on reinventing government, on how government should adopt more market-like strategies to "do more with less" (Osborne, 1993, p. 350). When results-oriented government agencies work with competitive principles through rules and budgets, the government will be community-owned (Osborne, 1993). Under new public management principles, participation is oriented toward delivering services to customers. "Providers that must compete are constantly trying to lower costs and raise quality. Customers value a choice of services because all have different needs" (Osborne, 1993, p. 354). This market logic assumes that citizens are clients and that policy is 'demand-based' or 'user-based' (Kremer and Tonkens, 2005). In this book, I refer to the focus on growth, competitiveness, and citizens-as-clients as the market register, which I borrow from the work of Boltanski and Thévenot (1991). Private law arrangements are central in market-inspired participation, whose goal is to serve the needs of citizens/customers through efficient and competitive services (Boltanski and Thévenot, 1991).

The participatory structures installed in the 1960s and the 1970s remained largely intact in the period of new public management in Amsterdam, Hamburg, and New York. Consultation processes became common practices for urban renewal and development projects. Although the structures remain in place, the way they are justified has changed. We see that in this period city governments increasingly invoked the market register rather than the civic register to justify the involvement of residents in urban development. Although social movements still put pressure on city governments to adhere to the principles of the civic register, they also started working with city governments in urban development projects. In order to justify these projects, both the market and the civic registers were invoked.

At the beginning of the 1980s, social movements remained dominant in the urban politics of Amsterdam. The clash with the police was often violent. In the Vondelstraat, squatters barricaded themselves in the street, which was eventually broken up through the intervention of military personnel—including tanks and snipers. Although the decade started with heavy conflicts, the squatter movement fizzled out in the 1980s (Van Der Steen, 2024). The movement partly became institutionalized. This happened through the legalization of squatted buildings by the municipality, where the buildings were bought by the municipality, and the squatters received the ownership contracts (Pruijt, 2003). Moreover, residents were increasingly involved in urban renewal projects that were aiming to improve living standards for impoverished neighborhoods. But this does not mean that planning processes become increasingly egalitarian. In the 1990s, the city government allowed housing corporations to sell social housing in those neighborhoods. The goal was to attract higher incomes to the city, by getting in those who were considered to be able to improve living standards in neighborhoods (Uitermark, 2009). Moreover, tenants of housing associations were increasingly seen as 'consumers,' and housing policies became demand-driven (Uitermark, 2009).

In Hamburg, the Hafenstrasse barricade held a grip on urban politics at the beginning of the 1980s. The squatters had massive support throughout Hamburg, from celebrities to university professors and the supporters of FC. St. Pauli (Scheller, 2020). But also, in Hamburg there was a process of institutionalizing social movements. Squatted several times and evicted several times, the buildings became a housing cooperative in 1997. In Hamburg, another driver of institutionalizing was the established of community intermediaries such as the Stattbau and Lawaetz Foundation. Whereas Stattbau was established by activists, the Lawaetz was founded by the municipality, but they both worked on renovation and co-housing projects (Scheller, 2020). In order to prevent direct subsidies to squatters, the organizations functioned as intermediaries—mediated through contracts—between the municipality and activists (Scheller and Thörn, 2018; Stattbau Hamburg, 2024). This aligned with the new motto of the city of Hamburg, '*Unternehmen Hamburg*,' or enterprising Hamburg, to stimulate the economy and attract middle-class and high-income families to the city (Neumann, 2020; Novy and Colomb, 2013; Von Dohnanyi, 1983). It should be noted that not all squatter's movements become institutionalized. The squatted theatre—the Rote Flora—in St. Pauli refused to sign any contract and demanded to be erased from the land use plan (Buchholz, 2016; Scheller, 2020)

In New York, the amount of community development corporations grew quickly (Angotti, 2008). Even some of the squatter movements, such as Banana Kelly in the Bronx, transformed into community development corporations (Pruijt, 2003). They were seen by the city government as good partners in urban renewal projects, being able to mobilize residents and legitimize government policies. They became the main developers in impoverished neighborhoods, building partnerships—governed through contracts—with government agencies, foundations, religious organizations, and private partners (Angotti, 2008). Although the New York City government worked with community development corporations, their main priority was to spur the real estate market (Angotti, 2008). The collaboration of the city of New York with community development corporations was coupled with policies to give developers tax benefits when they coupled 'affordable' housing in new commercial projects (Zukin et al., 2009). This attracted middle-class and high-income families to New York neighborhoods and ignited severe gentrification.

It should be emphasized that the embrace of the market register was not only pushed by city governments. There was also a growing desire in some parts of the social movements to professionalize (Mayer, 2009). Moreover, the success of the activists had brought participation to the forefront of planning practices and had given them much influence on policy. The structures they created benefited mostly those who had the good fortune of living in formerly squatted houses or were leaders of organizations created from the squatting movement (Pruijt, 2003; Scheller, 2020; Uitermark, 2009). This opened the need to justify development projects in new terms—no longer in terms of struggle and empowerment—but in terms of delivering services to clients and competitiveness. Whereas the 1980s still experienced economic stagnation, the 1990s created an economic boom in cities. This boom was positively described as the "triumph of the city" and partially accounted for the new creative and digital sectors (Florida, 2004; Glaseser, 2011).

The economic boom of the 1990s and the early 2000s ended with the financial crisis that started in 2008. There was a growing critique of market-oriented policies and social movements such as the rise of Wall Street in cities across the world. Ascendant since the 2000s, participatory governance was largely a response to new public management's focus on efficiency and results. Participatory governance was less focused on the market and more focused on collaboration with stakeholders (Baiocchi and Ganuza, 2017). "Empowered participation is a third path of reform that takes its inspiration from traditions of civic engagement and participatory democracy rather than public management techniques or competitive markets" (Fung, 2004, p. 9). As political parties and interest groups are often seen as out of touch, participatory governance privileges methods to reconnect with disaffected residents (Baiocchi and Ganuza, 2017).

Participatory governance requires that "both planners and citizens have the capacity to listen sympathetically and share responsibility for problem definition and solution" (Friedmann, 1993). For Albrechts, co-production is the "antidote to the idea that we endlessly need to ask citizens' opinions . . . since citizens are actively involved in the agenda-setting, problem formulation, the shaping of the content of policies, plans, and projects and the delivery as well" (Albrechts, 2012). In a similar vein, Ganuza and Francés argue that "the institutional design of participatory budgets, which aims at the general public, offers a participatory framework that differs from the usual protest model" (Ganuza and Francés, 2012). In participatory governance, there is an emphasis on balancing the power of professionals

(Kremer and Tonkens, 2005). Lay citizens are seen as stakeholders who wish to cooperate with others to create 'win-win solutions,' complementing civil society organizations as partners in urban policy (Baiocchi and Ganuza, 2017, p. 68). The focus is less on empowerment and consumption and more on doing. Public engagement is often organized by consultants because they have experience organizing collaborative and deliberative practices (McCann, 2001). These consultants rely on "business logics and business tools . . . for advancing the moral purposes [empowerment of the people] they seek" (Lee, 2015).

In this book, I refer to the aim of creating innovative solutions, collaborating, and starting new projects as the entrepreneurial register, which I borrow from the work of Boltanski and Chiapello (2005). Entrepreneurial participation aims to create innovative solutions for problems in the public realm. Residents are expected to not rely on government agencies—especially for subsidies—but to set up their own projects. Nevertheless, the projects do not need to be efficient or market-oriented. The experiments of entrepreneurial participation are mostly governed through agreements and contracts. Citizens are stakeholders who enthusiastically work with government agencies and commercial parties to create win-win solutions (Boltanski and Chiapello, 2005).

Although in Amsterdam, Hamburg, and New York the participatory structures installed in the 1960s were still in use in the period of public governance, they were increasingly being supplemented by new participatory modes.

In Amsterdam, there seemed to be a slight revival of active social movements in 2011. The Occupy movement—which originated in New York as a protest against the power of financial institutions—initially had substantial public support (Uitermark and Nicholls, 2012). However, the support dwindled, and the movement failed to be a force in Amsterdam's urban politics. The financial crisis did have a significant impact on Amsterdam. Land prices were declining, the city budget was declining, and investors were hesitant to commit financially. The city government responded by embracing the idea of 'organic urban development' or giving 'creatives' and residents the possibility to sign agreements to use land temporarily (Buitelaar et al., 2018; Savini et al., 2016). The entrepreneurial register was increasingly invoked in order to justify participatory processes and urban development. In an experimental way, lands were developed through small-scale initiatives in the hope of attracting bigger investors (Buitelaar et al., 2018; Savini et al., 2016). Participation, organized by consultants, was thus organized in a co-creative way, with growing responsibilities of residents.

Hamburg—having followed the tendencies of Amsterdam in the decades before—took a different path in the period of public governance. Initially, the city copied parts of the policy of Amsterdam regarding the creative industry (Freie und Hansestadt Hamburg, 2010), but this led to protests and new squatting activities (Novy and Colomb, 2013; Vogelpohl and Buchholz, 2017). While the entrepreneurial register was often invoked to organize participatory processes through co-creation processes, the ownership of property was contested throughout the city (Vogelpohl and Buchholz, 2017). This forced developers and the city government to organize extensive participatory processes and include residents' principles in urban development agreements (Stapper, 2021, 2022). In order to help organize participatory processes in a co-creative way, the Hamburg government created a new agency—Stadwerkstatt—in 2011 (Freie und Hansestadt Hamburg, 2020).

In New York, the Occupy movement set up camp in the financial district and aimed to reclaim public space for the broader public (Dekker and Duyvendak, 2020). The Occupy movement inspired people around the world and quickly became a global phenomenon. With the inauguration of Mayor de Blasio in 2013, new attention was given to affordable housing and involving residents in planning processes. The Office of Housing Strategies was created to promote participatory processes (The City of New York, 2020b). Moreover, neighborhood plans were created through co-creation processes in order to revitalize struggling neighborhoods (The City of New York, 2020a). Next, community benefit agreements—development agreements negotiated between community leaders and developers—were being employed for the first time in New York in this period (Been, 2010). This shows that the entrepreneurial register was gaining traction to justify planning policies in New York. However, activists were quickly disappointed in these new planning practices since they seemed to stimulate gentrification and predominantly serve the interests of developers (Stein, 2019).

This overview has shown the ebb and flood of the pragmatic registers that were activated to justify urban planning processes in Amsterdam, Hamburg, and New York (see Table 1.1). They rose to the foreground through a critique of urban institutions in periods of economic decline or social unrest. But none of the pragmatic registers were omnipotent. They often were activated in a compromise with other pragmatic registers, displacing parts of the critiques that were being voiced. This overview also showed the critical capacity of residents; they were aware of exploitation through capitalist accumulation processes. Moreover, they were aware of social privileges and actively organized to resist social inequalities. However, time and time again, the prevalent strength of capitalism and barriers related to race, gender, and class limit their ability to act. Lastly, the overview showed the deeply embedded urban struggles in materialities. For example, the resistance of residents against municipal policies by squatting houses and barricading neighborhoods. Or the refusal of the squatter group Rote Flora to sign a contract. With their refusal to sign a contract, they criticized commercial real estate processes and prevented losing control of the buildings. Materialities are crucial in coordinating collective action in urban politics. Moreover, the overview has shown that these struggles are embodied in urban actors. The vilification of city officials and developers by activists in the period of public administration or the embrace of the middle class by city officials in the period of public management are examples of how urban politics are embodied in particular actors or groups. They show that pragmatic registers are not forces that structure urban practices from above; they are forces that are embodied and embedded between urban actors and objects. In the next chapter, we show in detail how the different registers influence municipal policies in the three cities.

Table 1.1 Overview pragmatic registers

	Civic register	*Market register*	*Entrepreneurial register*
Main principle	Empowerment	Growth	Innovation
Moral ordering	Citizen-as-activist	Citizen-as-client	Citizen-as-entrepreneur
Political ordering	Democratic practices	Competition and efficiency	Collaboration and starting projects
Legal ordering	Legislation	Procurement and contracts	Agreements

1.3 Overview of the book

This book examines the evolving practices of urban politics, with a focus on participatory processes, community intermediaries, and contracts. Through case studies in Amsterdam, Hamburg, and New York, it reveals how urban actors navigate institutional contradictions and material constraints to influence planning practices. The chapters develop this analysis by addressing specific aspects of these transformations.

Chapter 1 introduces the research puzzle by exploring the increasing prevalence of contracts, community intermediaries, and participatory processes in urban governance. It argues that these changes are not only shaped by institutional critique but also constrained by the process of capital accumulation and barriers related to race, gender, and class. The chapter highlights the tension between urban actors' critical capacities and structural barriers, situating these dynamics in planning practices since the 1960s. **Chapter 2** outlines the qualitative research strategy underpinning the book. It explains how the comparative case study design facilitates an investigation into the interactions between actors, policy documents, and agreements. The chapter ends with an explanation of how contracts should be studied in urban studies. **Chapter 3** focuses on the role of pragmatic registers in municipal planning policies around the 2010s. This chapter illustrates the context in which the different case studies are embedded. It shows how the entrepreneurial register gained prominence, particularly in combination with the market and civic registers, shaping urban policies that emphasize innovation, collaboration, and creativity. The chapter highlights the shift from participation as a right to participation as a responsibility, underscoring the increasing expectation for residents to take an active role in urban development.

Chapter 4 examines the redevelopment of the Esso-Häuser housing complex in Hamburg as a site of contestation between neighborhood residents and developers. This chapter explains the theoretical framework of this book. It introduces the concept of pragmatic registers as constellations of morals, politics, and laws used to navigate institutional contradictions. The case illustrates how property-planning and capitalist-democracy contradictions shape urban development and how registers temporarily resolve these tensions. **Chapter 5** analyzes the K-Buurt redevelopment in Amsterdam's Bijlmer neighborhood, focusing on the role of residents in participatory processes. This chapter highlights how morals shape urban politics. When their needs were excluded from the redevelopment plan, residents staged a participation strike. This chapter examines how actors create guiding principles for collective action and shows how the process of valuing is deeply embedded in materialities and societal structures. **Chapter 6** explores the redevelopment of Essex Crossing in New York as a case study of urban politics organized through long-standing disputes. This chapter explains the role of politics in planning practices. Spanning decades, the struggle between residents, politicians, and the municipality illustrates how participatory processes are shaped by community intermediaries. The chapter shows how critiques can open political spaces but are often displaced, co-opted, or compromised within institutional practices. **Chapter 7** investigates how law shapes urban development by examining cases in Neue Mitte Altona, Oostenburg-Noord, and Kingsbridge Armory. This chapter describes the role of law in urban politics. It argues that law binds actors and objects together, formalizing promises and stabilizing relations. The chapter highlights the interplay between public and private law and how residents' principles are translated into enforceable agreements governing development projects.

Chapter 8 synthesizes the findings of the book. It discusses the consequences of the increasing activation of the entrepreneurial register and the use of contracts and community intermediaries in participatory processes. The chapter emphasizes the reproduction of social inequalities, the worthiness of good residents, and the fragmenting effects of prioritizing contracts over public laws. It concludes by proposing a research and policy agenda to address these challenges.

References

Albrechts, L. 2012. "Reframing Strategic Spatial Planning by Using a Coproduction Perspective." *Planning Theory* 12 (1): 46–63. https://doi.org/10.1177/1473095212452722.

Andersson, Johan. 2015. "'Wilding' in the West Village: Queer Space, Racism and Jane Jacobs Hagiography." *International Journal of Urban and Regional Research* 39 (2): 265–83. https://doi.org/10.1111/1468-2427.12188.

Angotti, T. 2008. *New York for Sale: Community Planning Confronts Global Real Estate.* Cambridge and London: The MIT Press. https://doi.org/10.1080/14649351003759797.

Arnstein, Sherry R. 1969. "A Ladder of Citizen Participation." *Journal of the American Institute of Planners* 35 (4): 216–24. https://doi.org/10.1080/01944366908977225.

Baiocchi, Gianpaolo, and Ernesto Ganuza. 2017. *Popular Democracy: The Paradox of Participation.* Stanford: Stanford University Press.

Been, Vicki. 2010. "Community Benefits Agreements: A New Local Government Tool or Another Variation on the Exactions Theme?" *University of Chicago Law Review* 77 (1): 5–35.

Boltanski, Luc. 2011. *On Critique: A Sociology of Emancipation.* Cambridge: Polity Press.

Boltanski, Luc, and Eve Chiapello. 2005. *The New Spirit of Capitalism.* London, UK: Verso.

Boltanski, Luc, and Laurent Thévenot. 1991. *On Justification: Economies of Worth.* Princeton: Princeton University Press.

Buchholz, Tino. 2016. *Struggling for Recognition and Affordable Housing in Amsterdam and Hamburg.* Groningen: University of Groningen.

Buitelaar, E., E. Grommen, and E. Van der Krabben. 2018. "The Self-Organizing City: An Analysis of the Institutionalization of Organic Urban Development in the Netherlands."

In *Companion to Real Estate Development*, edited by G. Squires, E. Heurkens, and R. Peiser, 169–82. New York: Routledge.
Caloffi, Annalisa, and Francesca Gambarotto. 2017. "Cognitive Distance in Public Procurement and Public—Private Partnerships : An Analysis of the Construction Sector" 35 (5): 765–83. https://doi.org/10.1177/0263774X16680108.
The City of New York. 2020a. "NYC Neighborhood Planning Playbook." https://www1.nyc.gov/site/hpd/services-and-information/nyc-neighborhood-planning-playbook.page.
The City of New York. 2020b. "Office of Neighborhood Strategies." https://www1.nyc.gov/site/hpd/about/office-descriptions.page.
City of New York. 2024. "Step5: Uniform Land Use Review Procedure." https://www.nyc.gov/site/planning/applicants/applicant-portal/step5-ulurp-evolution.page.
Davidoff, Paul. 1965. "Advocacy and Pluralism in Planning." *Journal of the American Institute of Planners* 31 (4): 331–38. https://doi.org/10.1080/01944366508978187.
Dekker, Mischa J.T., and Jan Willem Duyvendak. 2020. "Justifying the Protest Camp: How Occupy Movements' 'Intimate Protest' Challenged Ideas about Legitimate Manifestation." *European Journal of Cultural and Political Sociology* 7 (4): 452–76. https://doi.org/10.1080/23254823.2020.1777441.
Dewey, John. 1927. *The Public and Its Problems*. Ohio University Press.
Eisenberg, M.A. 2018. *Foundational Principles of Contract Law*. New York: Oxford University Press.
Fabrik. 2024. "Die Fabrik: Gestern Und Heute." https://fabrik.de/geschichte.
Fagotto, Elena, and Archon Fung. 2006. "Empowered Participation in Urban Governance: The Minneapolis Neighborhood Revitalization Program." *International Journal of Urban and Regional Research* 30 (3): 638–55. https://doi.org/10.1111/j.1468-2427.2006.00685.x.
Florida, Richard. 2004. *Cities and the Creative Class*. New York: Routledge.
Freie und Hansestadt Hamburg. 2010. *Kreative Milieus Und Offenre Räume in Hamburg*. Hamburg: Behörde für Stadtentwicklung und Umwelt.
Freie und Hansestadt Hamburg. 2020. "Was Will Die Stadwerkstatt."
Friedmann, John. 1993. "Toward a Non-Euclidian Mode of Planning." *Journal of the American Planning Association* 59 (4): 482–85. https://doi.org/10.1080/01944369308975902.
Fung, Archon. 2004. *Empowered Participation*. Princeton: Princeton University Press.
Ganuza, Ernesto, and Francisco Francés. 2012. "The Deliberative Turn in Participation: The Problem of Inclusion and Deliberative Opportunities in Participatory Budgeting." *European Political Science Review* 4 (2): 283–302. https://doi.org/10.1017/S1755773911000270.
Gemeente Amsterdam. 2020, January 12. "De Slag Om de Nieuwmarktbuurt." https://www.amsterdam.nl/nieuws/achtergrond/slag-nieuwmarktbuurt/.
Glaseser, Edward. 2011. *Triumph of the City: How Our Greatest Invention Makes Us Richer, Smarter, Greener, Healthier, and Happier*. London: Penguin Press.
Grijzen, Jantine. 2010. *Outsourcing Planning: What Do Consultants Do in Regional Spatial*. Amsterdam University Press.
Healey, Patsy. 1993. "Planning through Debate: The Communicative Turn in Planning Theory." In *The Argumentative Turn in Policy Analysis and Planning*. Durham, NC: Duke University Press.
Innes, Judith E., and David E. Booher. 2004. "Reframing Public Participation: Strategies for the 21st Century." *Planning Theory & Practice* 5 (4): 419–36. https://doi.org/10.1080/1464935042000293170.
Jacobs, J. 1958. "Downtown Is for People." In *The Urban and Regional Planning Reader*, edited by E.L. Birch, 126–31. New York: Routledge.
Jacobs, Jane. 1961. *The Death and Life of Great American Cities*. Random House.
Janssen-Jansen, Leonie B., and Menno van der Veen. 2017. "Contracting Communities: Conceptualizing Community Benefits Agreements to Improve Citizen Involvement in

Urban Development Projects." *Environment and Planning A* 49 (1): 205–25. https://doi.org/10.1177/0308518X16664730.

Kim, Kon, Blaž Križnik, and Krystallia Kamvasinou. 2021, June. "Between the State and Citizens: Changing Governance of Intermediary Organisations for Inclusive and Sustainable Urban Regeneration in Seoul." *Land Use Policy* 105: 105433. https://doi.org/10.1016/j.landusepol.2021.105433.

Klose, Hans-Ulrich. 1975. "Die Unregierbarkeit Der Städte." https://www.bpb.de/shop/zeitschriften/apuz/archiv/529954/die-unregierbarkeit-der-staedte/.

Kort, Michiel, and Erik-Hans Klijn. 2011. "Public-Private Partnerships in Urban Regeneration Projects: Organizational Form or Managerial Capacity?" *Public Administration Review*, 618–26.

Kremer, M., and Evelien Tonkens. 2005. "Authority, Trust, Knowledge and the Public Good in Disarray." In *Policy, People, and the New Professional*, edited by Jan Willem Duyvendak, Trudie Knijn, and Monique Kremer, 122–36. Amsterdam: Amsterdam University Press.

Lee, C.W. 2015. *Do-It-Yourself Democracy: The Rise of the Public Engagement Industry*. New York: Oxford University Press.

Le Galès, Patrick, and Tommaso Vitale. 2013. "Governing the Large Metropolis. A Research Agenda." https://doi.org/10.31235/osf.io/95zsc.

Levine, Jeremy R. 2016. "The Privatization of Political Representation: Community-Based Organizations as Nonelected Neighborhood Representatives." *American Sociological Review* 81 (6): 1251–75.

Lowndes, Vivien, Lawrence Pratchett, and Gerry Stoker. 2006. "Diagnosing and Remedying the Failings of Official Participation Schemes: The CLEAR Framework." *Social Policy and Society* 5 (2): 281–91. https://doi.org/10.1017/S1474746405002988.

Macaulay, Stewart. 1963. "Non-Contractual Relations in Business: A Preliminary Study." *American Sociological Review* 28 (1): 55–67. https://doi.org/10.4324/9780429494338.

Mayer, Margit. 2009. "The 'Right to the City' in the Context of Shifting Mottos of Urban Social Movements." *City* 13 (2–3): 362–74. https://doi.org/10.1080/13604810902982755.

McCann, Eugene J. 2001. "Collaborative Visioning or Urban Planning as Therapy? The Politics of Public-Private Policy Making." *Professional Geographer* 53 (2): 207–18. https://doi.org/10.1111/0033–0124.00280.

Michels, Goedeke. 2010. "Hamburg Ekhofstrasse 1973." https://www.youtube.com/watch?v=146v6DRIelM.

Neumann, Arndt. 2020. "From Fordist to Neo-Liberal Urban Spaces in Times of de-Industrialization: A Conceptual Frame for a Complex Relationship." *Urban History* 47 (2): 220–35. https://doi.org/10.1017/S0963926819000233.

Novy, Johannes, and Claire Colomb. 2013. "Struggling for the Right to the (Creative) City in Berlin and Hamburg: New Urban Social Movements, New 'Spaces of Hope'?" *International Journal of Urban and Regional Research* 37 (5): 1816–38. https://doi.org/10.1111/j.1468–2427.2012.01115.x.

Osborne, David. 1993. "Reinventing Government." *Public Productivity & Management Review* 16 (4): 349–56.

Owens, Linus. 2016. "Amsterdam Squatters on the Road: A Case Study in Territorial and Relational Urban Politics." In *A European Youth Revolt: European Perspectives on Youth Protest and Social Movements in the 1980s*, edited by Knud Andresen and Bart Van der Steen, 53–67. Palgrave Macmillan.

Provo. 1966, April. "Witte Huizenplan." https://iisg.nl/collections/provo/provo59a-nl.php.

Pruijt, Hans. 2003. "Is the Institutionalization of Urban Movements Inevitable? A Comparison of the Opportunities for Sustained Squatting in New York City and Amsterdam." *International Journal of Urban and Regional Research* 27 (1): 133–57. https://doi.org/10.1111/1468–2427.00436.

Pruyt, Hans. 1985. "Cityvorming Gekraakt: Invloed van Actiegroepen Op Stedelijke Planning in Amsterdam." *AGORA Magazine* 1 (4).

Purnell, Brian. 2007. "Taxation without Sanitation Is Tyranny: Civil Rights Struggles over Garbage Collection in Brooklyn, New York during the Fall of 1962." *Afro-Americans in New York Life and History* 31 (2): 61–88.

Raco, Mike. 2013. "The New Contractualism, the Privatization of the Welfare State, and the Barriers to Open Source Planning." *Planning Practice and Research* 28 (1): 45–64. https://doi.org/10.1080/02697459.2012.694306.

Raco, Mike, Emma Street, and Sonia Freire-Trigo. 2016. "The New Localism, Anti-Political Development Machines, and the Role of Planning Consultants: Lessons from London's South Bank." *Territory, Politics, Governance* 4 (2): 216–40. https://doi.org/10.1080/21622671.2015.1036912.

Saint-Martin, Denis. 1998. "The New Managerialism and the Policy Influence of Consultants in Government: An Historical–Institutionalist Analysis of Britain, Canada and France." *Governance* 11 (3): 319–56. https://doi.org/10.1111/0952–1895.00074.

Savini, Federico, Willem R. Boterman, Wouter P.C. van Gent, and Stan Majoor. 2016. "Amsterdam in the 21st Century: Geography, Housing, Spatial Development and Politics." *Cities* 52: 103–13. https://doi.org/10.1016/j.cities.2015.11.017.

Scheller, David. 2020. "Hamburg: Housing Movements and Local Government." In *Contemporary Co-Housing in Europe: Towards Sustainable Cities?*, edited by Pernilla Hagbert, Henrik Gutzon Larsen, Håkan Thörn, and Cahtrin Wasshede, 57–74. Routledge.

Scheller, David, and Håkan Thörn. 2018. "Governing 'Sustainable Urban Development' Through Self-Build Groups and Co-Housing: The Cases of Hamburg and Gothenburg." *International Journal of Urban and Regional Research* 42 (5): 914–33. https://doi.org/10.1111/1468–2427.12652.

Shea, Jennifer. 2011. "Taking Nonprofit Intermediaries Seriously: A Middle-Range Theory for Implementation Research." *Public Administration Review* 71 (1): 57–66. https://doi.org/10.1111/j.1540–6210.2010.02306.x.

Smits, J.M. 2014. *Contract Law A Comparative Introduction*. Cheltenham: Edward Elgar Publishing Limited.

Stapper, E.W. 2021, September. "Contracting with Citizens: How Residents in Hamburg and New York Negotiated Development Agreements." *Land Use Policy* 111: 105743. https://doi.org/10.1016/j.landusepol.2021.105743.

Stapper, E.W. 2022. "Private Ordering of Public Processes: How Contracts Structure Participatory Processes in Urban Development in Amsterdam and Hamburg." *Urban Studies* 59 (9): 1872–88. https://doi.org/10.1177/00420980211024144.

Stapper, E.W., M. Van der Veen, and L.B. Janssen-Jansen. 2020. "Consultants as Intermediaries: Their Perceptions on Citizen Involvement in Urban Development." *Environment and Planning C: Politics and Space* 38 (1): 1–19. https://doi.org/10.1177/2399654419853583.

Stattbau Hamburg. 2024. "Die Entsehung van STATTBAU Und Die Instrumente Alternativer Sanierung in Hamburg." https://stattbau-hamburg.de/wp-content/uploads/2021/02/STATTBAU-Geschichte-der-Entstehung.pdf.

Stein, S. 2019. *Capital City: Gentrification and the Real Estate State*. London and New York: Verso.

Swyngedouw, Erik. 2005. "Governance Innovation and the Citizen: The Janus Face of Governance-Beyond-the-State." *Urban Studies* 42 (11): 1991–2006.

Swyngedouw, Erik, Frank Moulaert, and Arantxa Rodriguez. 2002. "New Geographies of Power, Exclusion and Injustice Neoliberal Urbanization in Europe : Large-Scale Urban Development Projects and the New Urban Policy." *Antipode* 34: 542–77. https://doi.org/10.1111/1467–8330.00254.

Tasan-Kok, T. 2010. "Entrepreneurial Governance: Challenges of Large-Scale Property-Led Urban Regeneration Projects." *Tijdschrift Voor Economische En Sociale Geografie* 101 (2): 126–49. https://doi.org/10.1111/j.1467–9663.2009.00521.x.

Tasan-Kok, T., M. van den Hurk, S. Özogul, and S. Bittencourt. 2019. "Changing Public Accountability Mechanisms in the Governance of Dutch Urban Regeneration." *European Planning Studies* 27 (6): 1107–28.

Templin, David. 2016. "Beyond the Metropolises: Youth Centre Initiatives in the Youth Revolt of 1980–1981 in West Germany." In *A European Youth Revolt: European Perspectives on Youth Protest and Social Movements in the 1980s*, edited by Knud Andresen and Bart Van der Steen, 67–81. Palgrave Macmillan.

Torfing, J.B., E. Sorensen, and A. Roiseland. 2019. "Transforming the Public Sector into an Arena for Co-Creation: Barriers, Drivers, Benefits and Ways Forward." *Administration & Society* 51 (5): 795–825.

Uitermark, Justus. 2009. "An in Memoriam for the Just City of Amsterdam." *City* 13 (2–3): 347–61.

Uitermark, Justus, and Jan Willem Duyvendak. 2008. "Citizen Participation in a Mediated Age: Neighbourhood Governance in the Netherlands." *International Journal of Urban and Regional Research* 32 (1): 114–34. https://doi.org/10.1111/j.1468–2427.2007.00743.x.

Uitermark, Justus, and Walter Nicholls. 2012. "How Local Networks Shape a Global Movement: Comparing Occupy in Amsterdam and Los Angeles." *Social Movement Studies* 11 (3–4): 295–301. https://doi.org/10.1080/14742837.2012.704181.

Van den Hurk, Martijn, and Tuna Tasan-Kok. 2020. "Contractual Arrangements and Entrepreneurial Governance: Flexibility and Leeway in Urban Regeneration Projects." *Urban Studies* 00 (0): 1–19. https://doi.org/10.1177/0042098019894277.

Van Der Steen, Bart. 2024, January. "Travelling Barricades: Transnational Networks, Diffusion and the Dynamics of 1980s Squatter Conflicts in Western Europe." *Contemporary European History* 1–16. https://doi.org/10.1017/S0960777323000620.

Verlaan, Tim. 2016. *De Toekomst van de Nederlandse Binnenstad 1960–1978*. Universiteit van Amsterdam.

Vincent-Jones, Peter. 2007. "The New Public Contracting : Public Versus Private Ordering?" *Indiana Journal of Global Legal Studies* 14 (2): 259–78. https://doi.org/10.1353/gls.0.0012.

Vivier, Elmé, and Diana Sanchez-Betancourt. 2020. "Community Leaders as Intermediaries: How Everyday Practices Create and Sustain Leadership in Five Informal Settlements in Cape Town." *Leadership* 16 (6): 738–56. https://doi.org/10.1177/1742715020940907.

Vogelpohl, Anne, and Tino Buchholz. 2017. "Breaking With Neoliberalization by Restricting The Housing Market: Novel Urban Policies and the Case of Hamburg." *International Journal of Urban and Regional Research* 41 (2): 266–81. https://doi.org/10.1111/1468–2427.12490.

Von Dohnanyi, Klaus. 1983. "Unternehmen Hamburg." http://www.ueberseeclub.de/resources/Server/pdf-Dateien/1980-1984/vortrag-1983-11-29Dr.%20Klaus%20von%20Dohnanyi.pdf.

Walker, E.T., M. McQuarrie, and C.W. Lee. 2015. "Rising Participation and Declining Democracy." In *Democratizing Inequalities: Dilemmas of the New Public Participation*, edited by C.W. Lee, M. McQuarrie, and E.T. Walker, 3–23. New York: NYU Press.

Williams, Donald E. 1985. "The Nonprofit Corporation and Community Development in Bedford-Stuyvesant." *Washington and Lee Law Review* 42 (4): 1259–84.

Winner, Langdon. 1980. "Do Artifacts Have Politics?" *Daedalus* 109 (1): 121–36.

Yaneva, Albena. 2009. "Making the Social Hold: Towards an Actor-Network Theory of Design." *Design and Culture* 1 (3): 273–88. https://doi.org/10.2752/174967809x12556950208826.

Young, Iris Marion. 1990. *Justice and the Politics of Difference*. New York: Princeton University Press.
Young, Iris Marion. 2000. *Inclusion and Democracy*. New York: Oxford University Press.
Zukin, Sharon, Valerie Trujillo, Peter Frase, Danielle Jackson, Tim Recuber, and Abraham Walker. 2009. "New Retail Capital and Neighborhood Change: Boutiques and Gentrification in New York City." *City and Community* 8 (1): 47–64. https://doi.org/10.1111/j.1540–6040.2009.01269.x.

2 Research strategy

The main puzzle of this book is to understand the increased use of contracts, community intermediaries, and participation. I do not seek to advance general claims about whether residents can influence agreements or the neutrality of for-profit consultants. However, I aim to understand *how* the interests of residents are incorporated into agreements in those cases where residents have been co-negotiators. I aim to scrutinize *how* the supposed neutrality of for-profit consultants changes the context of decision-making in participatory processes. While extant research has addressed agreements that govern public-private partnerships (Raco et al., 2016; Camacho, 2013; Swyngedouw et al., 2002; Tasan-Kok et al., 2019) and community benefit agreements (Baxamusa, 2008; Janssen-Jansen and Van der Veen, 2017), other kinds of agreements also regulate how the outcomes of participation are realized. I thus examine different practices of contracting. I begin with projects where residents have co-negotiated agreements and then explore different kinds of agreements employed in urban development and what role community intermediaries have played (Pickvance, 2001).

2.1 Qualitative strategy

My qualitative research strategy allows me to stay close to actors' own descriptions of the role of contracts and community intermediaries in the participatory process. I study the interactions between actors, relevant policy documents, and agreements and analyze how practices and the activation of registers change over time. While I focus on how actors justify their actions and move from their specific experiences to general judgments (Thévenot, 2002), I do not take positions on the truth claims of actors or see any practice as intrinsically more important than another (Flyvbjerg, 2001).

Since I explore various forms of agreements, this book employs a comparative case study design. Studying multiple cases in several cities allows me to see whether different conditions lead to the same or different contractual relations (Pickvance, 2001). A case study is an in-depth analysis of a specific unit, sensitive to how it is embedded and evolves over time and space (Flyvbjer, 2011). Detailed descriptions are important to explore the specific role of contracts and community intermediaries concerning participation while understanding how actors construct

DOI: 10.4324/9781032712840-2

residents' principles requires seeing the process through their eyes. Formulating the needs of residents and designing agreements takes time; it is therefore important to understand how they develop. Finally, in order to understand the politics surrounding contracts, we need to understand how actors and agreements are embedded in political and social relations.

The dissertation follows the principles of abductive reasoning (Tavory and Timmermans, 2014). Abductive reasoning is focused on theory-building and is distinct from inductive and deductive reasoning. The aim of abduction is to form conjectures about the world that are not explained by existing literature. The deductive analysis starts with a rule, applies that to a case, and observes a result that either proves the plausibility of the rule or falsifies it (Tavory and Timmermans, 2014). Inductive analysis starts by examining a case and poses a universal rule based on those observations (Tavory and Timmermans, 2014). The abductive analysis starts by perceiving observations, relating the observation to other observations with the possibility of unknown causes and hidden effects, and then formulating a theory (Tavory and Timmermans, 2014). Amsterdam, Hamburg, and New York, and the development projects within those cities, are analyzed by relating them to each other to see whether observations in one case are similar or dissimilar to observations in other cases. Thus, in contrast to induction and deduction, abductive analysis does not assume proposition before fact (as with deductive reasoning) nor observation (as with inductive reasoning). Propositions are figured out, presumed after the fact, to explain observations that cannot be fully explained otherwise (Tavory and Timmermans, 2014). The theories described in the first three chapters and explanations of the actors I studied were used to understand and explain observations. The explanations provided by abductive reasoning can be used to formulate deductions and confirmed by inductive research ((Tavory and Timmermans, 2014). At the end of this dissertation, I formulate questions that can be used for further research.

2.2 Selection of cities

Participation has been an important part of urban policy in American and European cities since the 1960s, while the use of contracts as a governance tool has been gaining ground since the 1980s. In order to understand how contracts influence participatory processes, I selected cities that (a) are experimenting with contracts to achieve public goals, (b) have robust participatory structures, and (c) have well-organized groups that act as representatives for residents. The existence of participatory structures and organizations representing residents made it more likely that I would find projects in which residents have co-negotiated agreements in these cities.

The cities of Amsterdam, Hamburg, and New York have been experimenting with participation and negotiating deals with residents through contracts and agreements (Janssen-Jansen and Van der Veen, 2017; Novy and Colomb, 2013; Savini et al., 2016; Vogelpohl and Buchholz, 2017). Moreover, Amsterdam, Hamburg, and New York all have long histories of social movements seeking to influence urban development, making it feasible that there is a political environment that stimulates residents as co-negotiators of contracts (Baiocchi and Ganuza, 2017; Franzén, 2005; Uitermark, 2009).

Amsterdam's strategic plan *Economically Strong and Sustainable* (Gemeente Amsterdam, 2011) announced new ways to steer development in the wake of the 2008 financial crisis, when investors were reluctant to take risks. The municipality sought to attract new forms of investment by working with small-scale initiatives and facilitating self-build schemes by residents (Gemeente Amsterdam, 2011, 94). The strategy—called *organische gebiedsontwikkeling*, which loosely translates as citizen-linked incremental urban development—privileges citizens' initiatives and flexible planning instruments such as temporary functions and contractual agreements and rules instead of fixed land use plans (Buitelaar et al., 2018; Savini et al., 2016). This policy is largely supported by Amsterdam's political class, which by and large has embraced the entrepreneurial discourse on urban change (Savini et al., 2016). Amsterdam has the image of a rebellious city, and the social movements of the 1960s and 1970s led to institutions that installed participatory structures. However, the 1960s and 1970s activists now largely support the entrepreneurial discourse as it aligns with their goals of a less hierarchical state (Uitermark, 2009).

Hamburg's policies for urban development were often inspired by trends in Amsterdam (Freie und Hansestadt Hamburg, 2010, 69–72). The city sought to make planning more flexible and to encourage possibilities for the creative sector and citizen participation (Freie und Hansestadt Hamburg, 2010, 98) and installed a new agency to innovate and promote participation called *Stadwerkstatt* (Freie und Hansestadt Hamburg, 2014). The city of Hamburg also makes widespread use of contractual planning instruments such as urban development measures (*Städtebauliche Entwicklungsmaßnahmen*) and urban development agreements (*Städtebauliche Vertrag*) (Schmidt, 2009). Politically, the city of Hamburg has long been split between right-wing parties supporting pro-market policies and anti-capitalist social movements; the implementation of pro-market policies, such as reducing the lock-in period for rent-controlled social housing and the highest-bidder principle for development deals, sparked demonstrations and protests (Novy and Colomb, 2013; Vogelpohl, 2017). One interviewee told me that artists were central in these protests and in denouncing the municipality's goal of branding Hamburg's creative sector. Several protest groups and citizen initiatives united in the *Recht auf Stadt* (Right to the City) movement (Novy and Colomb, 2013; Vogelpohl and Buchholz, 2017), which enjoyed far-reaching influence. For instance, members of the movement squatted the Gängeviertel complex, which was bought by a developer who wanted to demolish and redevelop the area. The municipality did not evict the squatters and, following negotiations, decided to buy the complex from the investor (Novy and Colomb, 2013). Partly in response to the protests, the municipality introduced the *transparenzportal* (transparency register) in which all contracts and documents the municipality produces are published.

In New York, the Bloomberg administration stimulated real estate development and adopted pro-market policies since 2001. It also experimented with Community Benefit Agreements (CBAs)—deals negotiated between residents' representatives and developers (Baxamusa, 2008; Been, 2010). The results of these CBAs have been mixed. For instance, the CBA of Atlantic Yard was heavily criticized, whereas the CBA of Kingsbridge Armory has been praised as transformative (Janssen-Jansen and van der Veen, 2017; Stein, 2019). With the election of Mayor De Blasio in 2013, government agencies shifted toward creating more affordable housing. The planning approach of the De Blasio administration is participatory: "the City will work with communities to identify areas that can support new development or provide opportunities for preservation" (City of New York, 2014). The city also created the Office of Neighborhood Strategies to organize "meaningful community engagement" (The City of New York, 2020). It works with residents through focus groups, visioning sessions, and workshops to create reports and agreements about future developments. Although these policies aimed to create more affordable housing and work with communities, the outcomes often fell short because the rules of the New York housing market work in favor of speculative developers: "When planners upzone neighborhoods to allow bigger buildings, rent-stabilized landlords will have every reason to sell their properties to speculative developers, who could then knock down the existing properties and build something bigger and more expensive" (Stein, 2019).

2.3 Selection of development projects

I selected two cases for in-depth study in each city. The projects are all critical in that developers negotiated agreements with residents. A critical case is of strategic importance in relation to the general problem (Flyvbjerg, 2001)—in our case, on how contractual relations are formed when residents are co-negotiators. The cases I selected all had (a) an agreement between residents and developers, (b) residents or neighborhood organizations acted independently, (c) community intermediaries played an important role in the process, and (d) were accessible for research.

As stated in the introduction, I view agreements on a continuum: agreements can be more or less enforceable. All agreements outline how an exchange will be organized, providing clarity for all parties that a deal has been reached. To explore different kinds of agreements, I selected cases with more and less enforceable agreements. I searched through local news sites and municipal websites and approached local academics to get a short list of promising development projects in the three cities. I thereafter approached one or two actors connected to each project for an interview. Based on these initial interviews, I decided on whether to continue. As the existence of a contractual agreement negotiated by residents was my main reason for selecting a case, the development projects varied in size and in their participation programs.

In Amsterdam, I ultimately selected the development projects of Oostenburg-Noord and the K-Buurt for in-depth study. Initially I had wanted to study the projects at Havenstraatterrein, Buiksloterham, and Landtong Nieuwe Meer. While Havenstraatterrein had ambitions to experiment with participation and contractual agreements, I learned during my first interview that the municipality intended to suspend these policy goals. I tried to gain access to Buiksloterham, but the actors there had already been interviewed by several scholars and were loath to spend more time on interviews. Landtong Nieuwe Meer also seemed interesting, but there was not yet an agreement with developers. Oostenburg-Noord—developed along the lines of *organische gebiedsontwikkeling*—already had several (tacit) agreements between residents and developers; the plurality of its (tacit) agreements also spoke directly to my research puzzle. I studied the case of Zeeburgerpad in detail, because residents negotiated several agreements with developers. However, I have chosen to focus on two other cases from Amsterdam in this book: Oostenburg-Noord and the K-Buurt. The main group of active residents in Oostenburg-Noord is an NGO seeking to influence urban policy in the eastern part of Amsterdam's city center. In the K-Buurt the residents went on a 'participation strike' to strengthen their position vis-à-vis the municipality. After this conflict the residents developed several contractual relations with the municipality.

In Hamburg, I selected the cases of Neue Mitte Altona and Esso-Häuser for in-depth study. While I also interviewed actors involved in the Gängeviertel project, Neue Mitte Altona and Esso-Häuser had thus far largely escaped academic attention. Neue Mitte Altona is an interesting case as one group of residents (Q8) had succeeded in negotiating an agreement, while another group of residents (Koordinierungsgremium) had boycotted attempts to reach an agreement. Q8 is a foundation to make Hamburg more inclusive; the Koordinierungsgremium was installed by the city to represent the interests of residents. Esso-Häuser is an interesting case because the residents organized the participatory process themselves and negotiated a contract with the developers.

In New York, I ultimately chose Essex Crossing and Kingsbridge Armory for in-depth study. While I had also looked at Sendero Verde, the Peninsula, and Columbia University, the contract at Sendero Verde was negotiated by politicians rather than residents; the Peninsula and Columbia University were interesting as developers had worked closely with residents, but access proved difficult. The case of Essex Crossing spoke directly to my research question as its residents succeeded in organizing the participatory process themselves and worked toward an agreement with the developers; it was recently referred to as a project that "heals civic wounds" in the *New York Times* (Kimmelman, 2019). Kingsbridge Armory was likewise a compelling case as its residents negotiated a contract with developers considered to be transformative (Stein, 2019) (Table 2.1).

2.4 Data collection

The data for this book are mainly drawn from three sources: interviews, policy documents and contracts, and news articles (see Table 2.2).

In total I interviewed 108 actors active in urban development. I held 20 interviews with Dutch consultants on their perceptions of residents' involvement in urban development projects. I further interviewed 25 actors connected to my case studies in Amsterdam, 20 in Hamburg, and 13 in New York. For each project, I sought to interview people representing government agencies, developers, and neighborhood organizations. I also talked to people who were not directly involved in my case studies but who had broader insight into urban development in the

Table 2.1 Characteristics of the projects

	Amsterdam		*Hamburg*		*New York*	
	Oosten-burg Noord	*K-Buurt*	*Neue Mitte Altona*	*Esso-Häuser*	*Essex Crossing*	*Kings-bridge Armory (CBA)*
Project started in	2012	2016	2007	2014	2011	2008
Housing units	1.800	1250	1.600	200	1.000	x
Commercial space	31.000m2	6.000m2	30.000m2	2.500 m2	60.000m2	20.000m2
Agreement	Less en-forceable	More en-forceable	Less en-forceable	More en-forceable	Less en-forceable	More en-forceable
Main resident groups	Eilanden-overleg	Hart voor de K-Buurt	Koordinerungs-gremium, Q8	PlanBude	District board	NWBCCC

Table 2.2 Overview of data collection

	Amsterdam			*Hamburg*			*New York*		
	Oosten-burg Noord	*K-Buurt*	*Citywide*	*Neue Mitte Altona*	*Esso-Häuser*	*Citywide*	*Essex Crossing*	*Kings-bridge Armory*	*Citywide*
Total actors inter-viewed	13	6	38	13	7	6	7	6	12
Total documents	10	1	5	11	4	8	3	3	4
Newspaper articles	5	8	x	36	79	x	43	89	x

three cities. I interviewed 12 such experts in Amsterdam, 7 in Hamburg, and 12 in New York. As gaining access to interviewees in New York proved to be the most difficult, I supplemented interviews with numerous short conversations during academic seminars, participation meetings, and workshops.

In the interviews, I asked about how participation and urban governance were organized in the city, the role of the interviewee in the development project, the crucial moments during the process, who the main actors were, and what the interviewee, looking back on the process, would have changed. I focused especially on how residents' participation was organized, the role of community intermediaries, and how the outcomes of this participation were incorporated into contractual agreements. In the interviews, I sought to create a conversation rather than a cross-examination. I transcribed the interviews and coded them depending on the research question of the individual articles.

Alongside the interviews, I analyzed policy documents and contractual agreements to gain further insight into my case studies. In Amsterdam and Hamburg, the municipality is more active in shaping urban development; they, therefore, produce more policy documents, which I analyzed for their representations of citizens' principles and the development process. Contracts in Amsterdam are not publicly available; luckily, I gained access to some agreements between a developer and residents in the K-Buurt. For Oostenburg-Noord, I had to rely on interviews to learn the most important contractual obligations. Contractual agreements in Hamburg and New York were easier to retrieve—especially in Hamburg, where all contractual agreements must be publicly accessible. By analyzing contractual agreements, I gained useful data on the goals of the project, the goals of the local government, the instruments used to achieve these goals, the obligations of the respective parties, and provisions for delays, non-compliance, financial guarantees, monitoring, and project management, the transfer of rights, termination of contract and the risks and responsibilities of the parties.

I consulted newspaper articles to learn more about the political contexts of the development projects. I used broad search terms with the Nexis Uni database to find as many news articles as possible on my cases in Amsterdam and Hamburg. Since the cases in New York were extensively documented by news outlets, I narrowed my search to articles in the *New York Times*, the *New York Post*, and *New York Daily News*.

I also attended participation meetings in the three cities to get a better feel of the practice of participation. With my limited time, I could only attend one meeting in Hamburg and four meetings in New York; in Amsterdam, I attended 40 participation meetings (mainly in the K-Buurt and for the case of Oostenburg-Noord). City tours also provided valuable information. In Hamburg, a civil servant showed me around Neue Mitte Altona; a friend introduced me to activist spots. In New York, a liaison from the developers showed me around Essex Crossing, while a tour by the Tenement Museum gave me valuable information about the history of the Lower East Side. Alongside such tours, I walked and cycled through Amsterdam, Hamburg, and New York. Marjora Carter and Michael Parkinson pointed me to interesting places in the Bronx; Shin-Pei Tsay, Dominic Berg and Gianpaolo Baoichi in

Manhattan. Cathrin Zengerling and Veronika Hilbermann were both very helpful in pointing out interesting places in Hamburg.

2.5 Notes on studying contracts

Since contracts are often not the focus of research on urban politics, I have written a discussion about how to study contracts best. Contracts are increasingly foundational to the fabric of urban politics. I contrast legal, economic, and sociological approaches to studying contracts.

A legal approach to studying contracts

The legal definition of contracts closely relates to how courts interpret them (Hesselink, 2004). In the doctrinal or legal approach to contracting, a contract has five qualifications, of which the first three are required and the last two are additional. The first qualification is that an offer is made (Eisenberg, 2018; Kötz, 2017; Smits, 2014; Treitel, 2003). Contractual negotiations begin with an invitation to negotiate. In most cases, there is first a period of bargaining, when proposals can be made, adjusted, and refused before an offer is made. An offer is a promise with the intention to be bound by the proposal; it thus contains specific terms by which the offeree is willing to be bound (Treitel, 2003). The offer must be specific; the transaction is coordinated by including clear planning for the exchange. The offeree describes the offer as binding to distinguish it from a mere proposal. When no clear binding offer is made, it depends on how a judge will receive the proposal and who will decide whether a reasonable person would agree that the proposal included a binding offer. For example, when a proposal is sent to several people as an offer—as happens in advertisements—it is considered a proposal. While jurisdictions differ on when proposals are considered offers, most have specific laws to prevent the offeree from being held liable when this is deemed unreasonable (Kötz, 2017). When a governmental agency sets out a tender to purchase a service, this is an invitation rather than an offer. Generally, only the best tender will receive an offer to form a contract. Especially for government agencies, laws regulate how contractual negotiations should take place in order to prevent unfair competition (Treitel, 2003).

The second qualification of a contract is that an offer must be accepted. An offer can be accepted in two ways. The first is the most straightforward: through a declaration to the offeror, where the offer is received and acknowledged, and the offeree declares that she is willing to be bound by the offer (Kötz, 2017). An adjusted acceptance with different terms is not an acceptance but a counter-offer. If a person agrees to buy a house for the proposed amount but adds the condition that she must be able to move in immediately, she is introducing new terms. She is thus not accepting the offer but giving a counter-offer (Treitel, 2003; Smits, 2014). The second way to accept an offer is through conduct. In such cases, it should be clear that there is no need to communicate the acceptance of the offer because the offeror does not need or does not care to know whether an offer is accepted (Treitel, 2003; Smits, 2014; Kötz, 2017; Eisenberg, 2018). For example, when someone enters a taxi, he does not need to articulate that the offer is accepted; the contractual relation comes into existence because he enters the taxi. This is because all reasonable people would agree that they are bound to pay for the ride when they enter the taxi.

The third qualification is that the parties are legally bound by the agreement. Both the offer and the acceptance of the offer are promises. Both promises follow an obligation to act according to the terms of the contract. These obligations are voluntarily accepted obligations, which sets them apart from non-voluntary obligations that follow from the law (Smits, 2014). Once a contract is formed, the contract becomes law (Smits, 2014)—a safeguard for the parties that the exchange will be executed. This means that a court can intervene to force the parties to act according to the terms of the contract. Courts can intervene to enforce both the terms agreed by the parties and the terms that can be reasonably assumed. The principles of good faith, consideration, and estoppel are legal doctrines followed by courts when enforcing contractual relations.

The principle of good faith is the presumption that the parties take each other's interests into account and deal with each other in a fair and reasonable way (Smits, 2014). This principle can be used by courts to fill in the gaps in an agreement. The principle of good faith can be used by courts for law-making and has three functions (Ebke and Steinhauer, 1995). The first is that good faith can give rise to supplementary duties, starting in the pre-contractual phase. For example, parties must be honest about the product being sold, that is, what the product can and cannot do. The second function is that good faith can be used by courts to interpret how reasonable parties would come to an agreement. Through this line of reasoning, courts can fill in the missing parts of a contract. The third function is restrictive. When fundamental changes occur, a reasonable party cannot force a party to honor the terms of the contract, for example in cases of natural disaster or bankruptcy. The principle of good faith plays an important role in Dutch, German, and American contract law. In Germany, this goes back to the economic and political instability of the post–World War II period when courts considered changes to the underlying assumptions of the contractual relationship. A court can decide to reallocate the risks of the contracting parties (Ebke and Steinhauer, 1995). Alongside the principle of good faith, the principle of consideration is important in common law countries such as the United States. Consideration is the idea that courts can only enforce a promise if the other party has promised something in return (Eisenberg, 2018). The quid pro quo principle sets a contract apart from gratuitous promises. Finally, the principle of estoppel means that courts can "estop" parties if they act contrary to earlier behavior (Smits, 2014, p. 84). If a landlord has previously promised a tenant to not raise the rent, a court can intervene to stop the landlord from doing so, even if the landlord is legally allowed to raise the rent.

The fourth qualification of a contract is related to its form. A contract is binding when the parties have the intention to be bound and their intentions are reasonably clear. There is no need to have the contract in writing (Treitel, 2003; Smits, 2014) although in some cases the law requires written contracts. In most jurisdictions, contracts for the sale of land must be in writing, although they do not need to be in the form of a deed (Smits, 2014). Sometimes a contract does not need to be in writing, but the evidence does. When somebody promises to stand guarantee for a debt, the evidence must be in writing although the contract itself does not need to be written down.

The fifth qualification is related to fairness. Although actors are free to form a contract, the contract cannot conflict with other laws, generally accepted morals, or public policy (Smits, 2014).

In sum, the legal definition of contracts assumes that parties act reasonably. Contracts are built around specific terms to which the parties have agreed. The terms of the contract coordinate the desired exchange between the parties, while potential gaps in the contract are filled in by the courts.

An economic approach to studying contracts

The economic approach to studying contracts assumes that actors are utility-maximizing agents (Hesselink, 2004)—either rational agents pursuing their own interests or agents with bounded rationality trying to account for possible contingencies. Negotiating contracts and arranging exchanges is costly. "The essence of the contract is that it should only state the limits to the powers of the entrepreneur. Within these limits, he can therefore direct the other factors of production" (Coase, 1937). Actors weigh their options based on the costs and benefits of each option (Coase, 1960). Here I focus on the transaction costs approach to contracting—one of the most common ways of defining and analyzing contracts (Schepker et al., 2014).

According to transaction cost economics, the contract serves to coordinate business relations in the most efficient way possible—that is, to minimize costs. Actors seek to maximize their self-interest, constrained by their access to information and their ability to process this information. While most actors are socialized to act in a trustworthy manner, some will act opportunistically (Williamson, 1993) Since some actors act opportunistically, all actors should plan for hazards (Williamson, 1993). This is not about the morality of actors but the realization that naïve planning will hurt all those involved. Realism about potential hazards—whether they arise from misunderstanding or outright opportunism—is better than wasting time and resources arguing about how things should proceed (Williamson, 1993). Relying on trust can easily lead to misinterpretation, which can increase transaction costs; being open about opportunism is thus the preferred strategy. When actors plan for hazards, they should distribute credible obligations to mitigate opportunism (Williamson, 1993). Structural safeguards help to enforce cooperation between actors and must materialize in contracts with clear responsibilities and shared risks.

Contracts designed for relatively simple exchanges can be straightforward in their details. When the exchange is more complex, and actors need to consider unforeseen circumstances, the contract is necessarily incomplete. The more customized the contract, the greater the need for coordination (Poppo and Zenger, 2002; Schepker et al., 2014). This implies that expert knowledge is needed to execute the agreement, inflating the transaction costs of the exchange, for example, through the need for specialized training and learning-by-doing. How the exchange is organized rather than the commodity determines how the contract is designed (Williamson, 1981). Who will pay for failed experiments? How will actors deal with investments in specialized training?

When parties need to adapt to new circumstances, they either find a solution through the market or through consent. Contracts need to give clarity on how this consent is reached, which actors must reach a consensus, and on the basis of what information.

In sum, the economic understanding of contracts governs most business relations. Actors seek to maximize self-interest. Complex agreements are incomplete because unforeseen events are bound to happen. The contract is designed in such a way that the transaction will be executed with the assumption that actors will act opportunistically. In order to coordinate the transaction, structural safeguards such as risk-sharing are incorporated into the contract. This also solves potential differences between the efficiency of markets and firms. Flexibility is built into the contract by allowing adaptation to changed circumstances through a price system or consent.

A sociological approach to contracts

The sociological approach to studying contracts focuses on the relations in which the contract is embedded (Granovetter, 1985; Hesselink, 2004). Here I focus on relational contract theory, which goes back to Macaulay's (1963) study of the use of contracts in business relations in the US state of Wisconsin. Macaulay found that contracts are rarely enforced in business relations; when a party is contractually obligated to deliver a good or service but is unable to do so, the parties often work out a solution to the problem. Maintaining good business relationships and reputations are considered more important than enforcing contracts. Lawyers only get involved when the parties cannot find a solution.

According to relational contract theory, even the most straightforward contract—one that does not include much negotiating—is ingrained in relations (Eisenberg, 1995; Macneil, 1980). When two persons meet to exchange a good or service, there is the possibility for future interactions. A truly discrete transaction would require two strangers to agree to exchange and, thereafter, never meet again. Fully discrete transactions are thus rare; strangers moreover cease to be strangers through the exchange. Other factors than merely the transaction will start to play a role, especially those that bear on reputation and trust. In complex, long-term undertakings such as large-scale urban development projects, the relations between actors play an even bigger role as both these relations and agreements about exchanges will evolve over time. For example, if a new technology that allows for the swifter and cheaper delivery of a service is introduced but the contract specifies the use of the old technology, the actors will likely agree to the change, verbally or by rewriting the agreement. But this does not necessarily mean that relations are cooperative; they can indeed also be conflictual or suppressive. Contractual relations should not be over-socialized, as distrust, opportunism, and disorder occur (Granovetter, 1985). Relational contract theory thus holds that contracts are relations among actors who have exchanged, are exchanging, or expect to exchange in the future, and that contracts can only be understood in association with their context (Macneil, 1980). How these relations affect actors is an empirical question.

To write up a contract and choose the right governance structure, actors must consider different possible futures, rank these possible futures, and identify and describe the actions needed to create them (Callon, 1998). All of this assumes that actors are able to process all available information (Granovetter, 1985). But the reality of how contracts are designed is much messier. Actors base their decisions on trust and their relations with others, which can appear highly rational or irrational. A sociological approach does not make sweeping statements about how actors interact or process information; these need to be found out through in-depth studies (Granovetter, 1985).

Through cooperation, parties design contracts to plan for the desired exchange. The planning organizes when and how the exchange takes place and includes provisions for non-performance. For example, contracting parties may agree to build infrastructure at the beginning of the project to service the first residents of a new neighborhood, and on a fine should developers fail to deliver on time. In this process, the parties also think about how they would address potential contingencies. The ability to adapt to new circumstances depends on how far the contract accommodates shared learning and understanding (Veen and Korthals Altes, 2012). For example, will the actors meet throughout the process to reflect on their cooperation? The degree to which the monitoring of project goals enhances cooperation influences the execution of the contract. Contracts are a matter of degree; an agreement can be more or less contractual, depending on the specificity of the agreements and the (legal) sanctions on non-performance (Macaulay, 1963).

According to this sociological definition of contracts, actors are interdependent and use contracts as frameworks to foster trust and maintain good relations. This does not mean that these relations are free of conflict. But because actors generally want to cooperate in the future, they will try to deescalate any conflicts. The monitoring of the project helps to coordinate the exchange. Through learning and sharing knowledge, actors adapt to new circumstances.

Comparing approaches to studying contracts

There are several ways to analyze the contract. The previous sections discussed some prominent legal, economic, and sociological approaches. In a nutshell, legal interpretations assume that contracting parties behave reasonably. Economists assume that actors make decisions based on (bounded) rationality to maximize their own interests, while sociologists argue that actors conduct themselves in light of their embeddedness in social relations. For legal scholars, the purpose of the contract is to enforce promises; for economists, to manage transactions; and for sociologists, to govern social relations. If a party cannot keep a promise, a legal scholar would expect the situation to lead to litigation, an economist that the agreement will be renegotiated, and a sociologist that actors will privilege maintaining good social relations and reputations. If circumstances change, legal scholars

Table 2.3 Different approaches to studying contracts

	Legal	*Economic*	*Sociological*
Actions of actors	Reasonable	Maximizing self-interest	Embeddedness and trust
The goal of the contract	Enforce promises	Govern transactions	Govern relations
What happens in case of non- performance	Litigation	Bargaining	Maintain good relations and reputation
What happens in case of contingencies	Courts interpret the contract	Actors act opportunistically	Actors aim to maintain relations

Source: Author

would expect the contract to be interpreted on the basis of jurisprudence and legislation, economists that actors come to new agreements on the basis of opportunism, and sociologists that actors will work together to reach a joint solution.

While contracts are most often studied as business tools, I approach contracts as a governance tool to achieve public policy goals. Since my research focuses on the forming of contractual relations between residents, commercial parties, and government agencies, I have chosen the sociological approach to pursue my analysis, which considers the broadest range of actors and relations that influence contracts. The sociological approach allows us to study both how contractual relations are formed between diverse actors and how these contractual relations, in turn, (re)configure the social relations in which actors are embedded. In the conclusion of this book, I will reflect on this choice.

Working with a sociological approach to contracting has a further advantage. Amsterdam, Hamburg, and New York City differ in their legal systems. The Netherlands and Germany have a civil law system, and the United States a common law system. Because Hamburg is both a municipality and a state, it has greater latitude to create its own legislation on contracts. In contrast, Amsterdam is more influenced by national legislation, and New York City by state legislation. The sociological approach allows for comparing contracts from different jurisdictions as it studies contractual relations rather than doctrines and jurisprudence (Table 2.3).

References

Baiocchi, Gianpaolo, and Ernesto Ganuza. 2017. *Popular Democracy: The Paradox of Participation*. Stanford: Stanford University Press.

Baxamusa, M.H. 2008. "Empowering Communities through Deliberation the Model of Community Benefits Agreements." *Journal of Planning Education and Research* 27 (3): 261–76. https://doi.org/10.1177/0739456X07308448.

Been, Vicki. 2010. "Community Benefits Agreements: A New Local Government Tool or Another Variation on the Exactions Theme?" *University of Chicago Law Review* 77 (1): 5–35.

Buitelaar, E., E. Grommen, and E. Van der Krabben. 2018. "The Self-Organizing City: An Analysis of the Institutionalization of Organic Urban Development in the Netherlands."

In *Companion to Real Estate Development*, edited by G. Squires, E. Heurkens, and R. Peiser, 169–82. New York: Routledge.
Callon, Michel. 1998. "Introduction: The Embeddedness of Economic Markets in Economics." In *The Laws of the Markets*, edited by Michel Callon, 1–58. Oxford: Blackwell Publishers.
Camacho, Alejandro E. 2013. "Community Benefit Agreements: A Symptom, Not the Antidote, of Bilateral Land Use Regulation." *Brooklyn Law Review* 78 (2): 355–83.
City of New York. 2014. "Housing New York, a Five Borough, Ten-Year Plan."
The City of New York. 2020. "Office of Neighborhood Strategies." https://www1.nyc.gov/site/hpd/about/office-descriptions.page.
Coase, R.H. 1937. "The Nature of the Firm." *Economica* 4 (16): 386–405.
Coase, R.H. 1960. "The Problem of Social Cost." *The Journal of Law and Economics* 56 (4): 837–77.
Ebke, F.W., and B.M. Steinhauer. 1995. "The Doctrine of Good Faith in German Contract Law." In *Good Faith and Fault in Contract Law*, edited by J. Beatson and D. Friedmann, 171–91. Oxford: Clarendon Press.
Eisenberg, M.A. 1995. "Relational Contracts." In *Good Faith and Fault in Contract Law*, edited by J. Beatson and D. Friedmann, 291–305. Oxford: Clarendon Press.
Eisenberg, M.A. 2018. *Foundational Principles of Contract Law*. New York: Oxford University Press.
Flyvbjerg, B. 2001. *Making Social Science Matter*. Cambridge: Cambridge University Press.
Flyvbjerg, B. 2011. "Case Study." In *The Sage Handbook of Qualitative Research*, edited by K. Norman Denzin and S. Yvonna Lincoln, 301–16. Thousand Oaks, CA: Sage.
Franzén, M. 2005. "New Social Movements and Gentrification in Hamburg and Stockholm: A Comparative Study." *Journal of Housing and the Built Environment* 20: 51–77.
Freie und Hansestadt Hamburg. 2010. *Kreative Milieus Und Offenre Räume in Hamburg*. Hamburg: Behörde für Stadtentwicklung und Umwelt.
Freie und Hansestadt Hamburg. 2014. *Perspektiven Der Stadtentwicklung*. Hamburg: Behörde für Stadtentwicklung und Umwelt. https://doi.org/10.1007/3-211-29917-3_4.
Gemeente Amsterdam. 2011. "Structuurvisie Amsterdam 2040 Economisch Sterk En Duurzaam."
Granovetter, Mark. 1985. "Economic Action and Social Structure: The Problem of Embeddedness." *American Journal of Sociology* 91 (3): 481–510.
Hesselink, M.W. 2004. *Contractenrecht in Perspectief*. Den Haag: Boom Juridische uitgevers.
Janssen-Jansen, Leonie B., and Menno van der Veen. 2017. "Contracting Communities: Conceptualizing Community Benefits Agreements to Improve Citizen Involvement in Urban Development Projects." *Environment and Planning A* 49 (1): 205–25. https://doi.org/10.1177/0308518X16664730.
Kimmelman, M. 2019. "Essex Crossing Is Hte Anti-Hudson Yards." *New York Times*.
Kötz, Hein. 2017. *European Contract Law*. Oxford: Oxford University Press.
Macaulay, Stewart. 1963. "Non-Contractual Relations in Business: A Preliminary Study." *American Sociological Review* 28 (1): 55–67. https://doi.org/10.4324/9780429494338.
Macneil, I R. 1980. *The New Social Contract: An Inquiry into Modern Contractual Relations*. New Haven: Yale University Press.
Novy, Johannes, and Claire Colomb. 2013. "Struggling for the Right to the (Creative) City in Berlin and Hamburg: New Urban Social Movements, New 'Spaces of Hope'?" *International Journal of Urban and Regional Research* 37 (5): 1816–38. https://doi.org/10.1111/j.1468-2427.2012.01115.x.
Pickvance, C.G. 2001. "Four Varieties of Comparative Analysis." *Journal of Housing and the Built Environment* 16 (1): 7–28.
Poppo, Laura, and Todd Zenger. 2002. "Do Formal Contracts and Relational Governance Function as Substitutes or Complements?" *Strategic Management Journal* 23 (8): 707–25. https://doi.org/10.1002/smj.249.

Raco, Mike, Emma Street, and Sonia Freire-Trigo. 2016. "The New Localism, Anti-Political Development Machines, and the Role of Planning Consultants: Lessons from London's South Bank." *Territory, Politics, Governance* 4 (2): 216–40. https://doi.org/10.1080/21622671.2015.1036912.

Savini, Federico, Willem R. Boterman, Wouter P.C. van Gent, and Stan Majoor. 2016. "Amsterdam in the 21st Century: Geography, Housing, Spatial Development and Politics." *Cities* 52: 103–13. https://doi.org/10.1016/j.cities.2015.11.017.

Schepker, D.J., W.-Y. Oh, A. Martynov, and L. Poppo. 2014. "The Many Futures of Contracts: Moving Beyond Structure and Safeguarding to Coordination and Adaptation." *Journal of Management* 40 (1): 193–225. https://doi.org/10.1177/0149206313491289.

Schmidt, Stephan. 2009. "Land Use Planning Tools and Institutional Change in Germany: Recent Development in Local and Regional Planning." *European Journal of Social Theory* 17 (12). https://doi.org/10.1080/09654310903322397.

Smits, J.M. 2014. *Contract Law A Comparative Introduction*. Cheltenham: Edward Elgar Publishing Limited.

Stein, S. 2019. *Capital City: Gentrification and the Real Estate State*. London and New York: Verso.

Swyngedouw, Erik, Frank Moulaert, and Arantxa Rodriguez. 2002. "New Geographies of Power, Exclusion and Injustice Neoliberal Urbanization in Europe : Large-Scale Urban Development Projects and the New Urban Policy." *Antipode* 34: 542–77. https://doi.org/10.1111/1467-8330.00254.

Tasan-Kok, T., M. van den Hurk, S. Özogul, and S. Bittencourt. 2019. "Changing Public Accountability Mechanisms in the Governance of Dutch Urban Regeneration." *European Planning Studies* 27 (6): 1107–28.

Tavory, Iddo, and Stefan Timmermans. 2014. *Abductive Analysis: Theorizing Qualitative Research*. Chicago and London: The University of Chicago Press.

Thévenot, Laurent. 2002. "Which Road to Follow? The Moral Complexity of an 'Equipped' Humanity." In *Complexities: Social Studies of Knowledge Practices*, edited by John Law and Annemarie Mol, 53–87. Durham and London: Duke University Press. https://doi.org/10.1215/9780822383550-003.

Treitel, Guenter. 2003. *An Outline of the Law of Contract*. New York: Oxford University Press.

Uitermark, Justus. 2009. "An in Memoriam for the Just City of Amsterdam." *City* 13 (2–3): 347–61.

Veen, Menno van der, and Willem K. Korthals Altes. 2012. "Contracts and Learning in Complex Urban Projects." *International Journal of Urban and Regional Research* 36 (5): 1053–75. https://doi.org/10.1111/j.1468-2427.2011.01053.x.

Vogelpohl, A. 2017. "Consulting Completed: Temporal Aspects of Expertise in Urban Development during Times of Fast Policies." *Geographica Helvetica* 72 (1): 65–76. https://doi.org/0.5194/gh-72-65-2017.

Vogelpohl, Anne, and Tino Buchholz. 2017. "Breaking With Neoliberalization by Restricting The Housing Market: Novel Urban Policies and the Case of Hamburg." *International Journal of Urban and Regional Research* 41 (2): 266–81. https://doi.org/10.1111/1468-2427.12490.

Williamson, Oliver E. 1981. "The Economics of Organization: The Transaction Cost Approach." *American Journal of Sociology* 87 (3): 548–77.

Williamson, Oliver E. 1993. "Opportunism and Its Critics." *Managerial and Decision Economics* 14 (2): 97–107.

3 The shifting of orders

In this chapter, I take a more detailed look at how the different registers were invoked in municipal planning policies in the period around the 2010s. Analyzing municipal planning policies is important to understand the context in which participatory processes are organized, community intermediaries act, and contracts are signed. These municipal policies are materialities that can enhance and limit the abilities of urban actors. Thus, they are active agents in urban politics. However, as we will see in the chapters hereafter, municipal planning policies can shape planning practices, but they do not have the ability to determine planning practices.

However, the importance of city-wide planning policies can be shown by the example of the shift in power from one administration to another in New York. When Bloomberg was mayor of New York, he announced that his most important housing goal was to grow the housing stock. When De Blasio took over from him, he announced that the most important housing goal was to let the most vulnerable, the working class, and the middle class thrive. These priorities are translated into policies, shaping how civil servants, commercial parties, and residents interact. The priorities formulated by the mayors are moral judgments, describing how they see how the housing market of New York ought to be. They are informed by, and are informing, political decision-making processes and legal arrangements. The priorities of the Bloomberg administration will translate into giving a better position to developers in decision-making processes. In contrast, the priorities of the De Blasio administration will give residents more opportunities to decide. In turn, this leads to different legal arrangements. For example, the De Blasio administration has started working with mandatory affordable housing in rezoning projects. Of course, the moral judgments of both administrations are challenged everywhere. Sometimes, they do lead to political and legal processes in line with their values, but more often not. In this chapter, I analyze the municipal policies related to urban development. While the organization of urban development projects varies from project to project, municipal policies often set the parameters. This section outlines the order invoked in municipality-wide policies in Amsterdam, Hamburg, and New York. The descriptions of citywide municipal policies are limited to the administrations in power during the main events of the projects I studied (ca. 2007–2024).

DOI: 10.4324/9781032712840-3

3.1 Planning orders in Amsterdam

In Amsterdam, the spatial vision is a long-term comprehensive planning document that outlines the preferred way Amsterdam should be planned. The Labor party-led Asscher administration advanced a comprehensive spatial vision titled Economically Strong and Sustainable (Gemeente Amsterdam, 2011). The document outlined plans to make Amsterdam economically competitive and invest in high-quality housing and in the city's greening. The city of Amsterdam is portrayed as an emancipatory city. Young people come to the city to develop themselves through education, work, and culture. That Amsterdam is an emancipatory city is seen as a benefit to the economy: "They [young people] make a significant contribution to the knowledge economy and the creative sector in the city" (Gemeente Amsterdam, 2011).

The idea of citizens as eager to have an active role in urban development is highlighted in the spatial vision. The document promoted the idea of incremental urban development, supported by creative entrepreneurs and residents acting as small-scale developers. Thus, participation needs to stimulate an active role of residents in the development process (Gemeente Amsterdam, 2011). In other documents that are produced during the Asscher administration, participation is seen as market research. In the 'woonvisie' (housing vision), it is mentioned that "[t]hey [residents] are thus consumers and producers of regeneration projects" (Gemeente Amsterdam, 2009) and "[t]hey [residents] are the future users, and they produce the quality of the neighborhood" (Gemeente Amsterdam, 2009, p. 63). In the guideline participation, residents were mostly portrayed as end-users of the neighborhood and development projects (Amsterdams Volkshuisvestingsoverleg, 2010). The document advises participation in every phase of a development process but without giving citizens co-decision power. Participation is organized to build support for urban renewal and streamline the development process (Amsterdams Volkshuisvestingsoverleg, 2010, p. 5).

Agreements related to participation are mostly mentioned as part of regeneration projects. Developers need to make individual agreements with residents about the quality and the price of housing, the time the renovation projects will take, and (temporary) residence options for people who need to move with the option to come back to their house (Amsterdams Volkshuisvestingsoverleg, 2010, p. 15).

Participation should be organized to facilitate a conversation between residents and activate them to actively participate in urban development (Gemeente Amsterdam, 2009, p. 65). Innovative ways to organize participation are needed, but these are not specified. The co-decision power of citizens is not present in any of the studied documents. The documents mostly emphasize that consultation with citizens is needed because they are the experts on their environment.

The next administration, Ollongren/Kock, was politically more centrist. Many development projects ground to a halt during the financial crisis, adding to Amsterdam's housing shortage. The policy documents produced during the Ollongren/Kock administration privileged the building of housing and finding new investors for housing projects. The crisis experience inspired an adaptable development strategy "responsive to economic changes" (Gemeente Amsterdam, 2016). According to the document 'Koers 2025' (direction 2025), Amsterdam should benefit from its urban character because everywhere in the world, dense cities are able to foster "innovative, knowledge-intensive and creative economies" (Gemeente Amsterdam, 2016, p. 10). The transformation of underutilized properties in the city center is important because it supports the knowledge and network economy (Gemeente Amsterdam, 2016, p. 4). The document also mentions the risk of growing inequalities and gentrification (Gemeente Amsterdam, 2016, p. 11) but does not formulate concrete ways to prevent this.

The main policy documents written during the Ollongren/Kock administration mention participation mostly as a mandatory part of development projects. The development of housing was considered more important than participation. "In order to flexibly respond to changing market demands, we need to offer a diverse set of development locations" (Gemeente Amsterdam, 2016, p. 23). But the city still created opportunities for residents to act as developers (Gemeente Amsterdam, 2016, p. 23). Before the economic crisis of the 2008s, the city of Amsterdam mostly engaged in large-scale development projects, which came with financial risks. Therefore, incremental urban development, where small-scale developers and residents develop an area step by step, is seen as a valuable alternative to large-scale development projects.

As land is mostly publicly owned and leased for private use, the municipality of Amsterdam has a great deal of control over urban development (Savini et al., 2016). The municipality creates development briefs containing conditions for development on publicly owned land. In an update of the policy concerning development briefs made during the Ollongren/Kock administration, participation needed to be part of the development projects' explorative phase (Gemeente Amsterdam, 2017). The municipality recommended organizing participation to give stakeholders the ability to give advice rather than giving residents co-decision-making power.

After the Ollongren/Kock administration, the Green Party-led Groot Wassink administration took office. The Groot Wassink administration explicitly aimed to give citizens more ownership (Gemeente Amsterdam, 2022). This happened in several policy documents outlining community rights, participation, and participatory budgeting. The use of participation to cover up political decisions or the interests of the municipality was criticized, and it is stated that participation should be "repoliticized" (Gemeente Amsterdam, 2022, p. 3). In a new spatial vision, the follow-up of the spatial vision Economically Strong and Sustainable of 2011, the growing inequalities in the city are highlighted. The neighborhoods in the inner city benefited from economic growth, while other neighborhoods were left behind. Especially the growing prices of housing make it hard for lower- and middle-income households to get access to housing (Gemeente Amsterdam, 2021). The new spatial vision welcomes growth but within limits. There should be attention to rising inequalities and fostering the circular economy (Gemeente Amsterdam, 2021). The vision notes that "collaboration, co-creation, and participation are an inseparable part of the way we work" (Gemeente Amsterdam, 2021, p. 218).

Having decision-making power and influence over urban policies is described as a right for residents. The Groot Wassink administration introduced the 'democratization agenda,' which is multiple policies to strengthen the position of residents. In the guideline, community rights policies are outlined to give residents the right to take over responsibilities of the municipality, buy property for public aims, and to submit plans for public space (Gemeente Amsterdam, 2021, p. 4). Moreover, a broad set of participatory mechanisms is installed in the city: a participatory budgeting program is introduced in every neighborhood, co-creation spaces for public use are financed by the municipality, community benefit agreements are encouraged, and experiments with mini-publics and commons are stimulated. These new participatory mechanisms should give residents a greater say over urban policies. This is justified because

> We want to offer more space for initiatives 'from below'. . . there is a need to build on community well-being and value creation for and by local communities with urban development (Gemeente Amsterdam, 2021, p. 250).

After elections in 2022, the administration changed slightly, with the leadership changing from Groot Wassink to the Labour leader Moorman. However, the Green Party remained part of the coalition. The democratization agenda remained largely intact and was further elaborated in a legal document regulating participation (Gemeente Amsterdam, 2024). In this document, residents of Amsterdam received 'neighborhood rights.' These rights gave residents the possibility to take over the activities of the municipality (Gemeente Amsterdam, 2024). They could come up with a plan and submit this to the municipality. In a centrally planned city as Amsterdam, it is relatively novel that residents themselves can come up with the initiative to plan parts of the city.

During the Asscher and Ollongren/Kock administrations, participation in Amsterdam was mostly framed through the entrepreneurial and market registers. The city promoted active participation, especially small-scale developments by residents and creative entrepreneurs (see Table 3.1). The role of residents in urban development—who were presented as eager to take active roles in new projects (Gemeente Amsterdam, 2021)—was justified through the entrepreneurial and market orders. The use of participation and the value of citizens were also described in terms of the market registers—citizens as producers and consumers—or the entrepreneurial register—citizens as creative beings and entrepreneurs. Residents have a responsibility to improve their neighborhood. Especially during the financial crisis, the city of Amsterdam saw value in residents who were able to take on the role of small-scale developers. After the Groot Wassink administration took office, there was a clear change: the civic order was invoked more often. Citizens had the right to have a say in urban development. Several policies were introduced to improve citizens' ability to use those rights. Although the civic register was activated more often, the entrepreneurial register was also invoked often. There is also an expectation that citizens will act upon their rights and come up with innovative and creative solutions for urban problems. This shows that these orders are often

Table 3.1 Municipal policies concerning participation in urban development in Amsterdam

Amsterdam	*Asscher 2006–2014*	*Ollongren/Kock 2014–2018*	*Groot Wassink 2018–2022*	*Moorman 2022-ongoing*
Main goal of development strategy	Competitive economy Greening the city Emancipation	Competitive economy Building housing	Economic inequality Greening the city Democratization	Economic inequality Greening the city Democratization
How are citizens portrayed	Citizens as experts, citizens as entrepreneurs	Citizens as entrepreneurs	Successful citizens, vulnerable citizens	Successful citizens, vulnerable citizens
Agreements mentioned in relation to participation	Agreements with developers	Development briefs	Community benefit agreements	Neighborhood rights
Justification for participation	Citizens as consumers and producers	Citizens as producers	Citizens having the right to influence policy	Citizens having the right to influence policy
Organization of participation	Involve neighborhood organizations, consult with residents	Consult with citizens	Democratization Introduction of various tools to increase decision-making power	Democratization, introducing right to influence policy

Source: Author based on Gemeente Amsterdam (2009, 2011, 2016, 2021, 2022a, 2022b) and Amsterdams Volkshuisvestingsoverleg (2010)

omnipresent but not omnipotent. These tendencies were continued in the Moorman administration.

3.2 Planning orders in Hamburg

In Hamburg, the Christian Democrats led the executive branch between 2001 and 2011 and were responsible for producing a comprehensive spatial vision for the city. The vision was titled: 'The growing city: metropole at the water.' In the vision, the city promoted development policies that boost economic competitiveness and make Hamburg family-friendly (Freie und Hansestadt Hamburg, 2014). In working toward the latter goal, the administration encouraged investment in quality housing (Freie und Hansestadt Hamburg, 2014, p. 6). "Building high quality, family-friendly housing underlines the goal of developing and upgrading existing residential areas . . . Future new residential construction will be attractive and demand-oriented" (Freie und Hansestadt Hamburg, 2014, p. 36). The vision also states that various policies will be developed to strengthen the competitive position of Hamburg in the global economy. The goal is to attract investment, tourists, knowledge-intensive organizations, sports, and cultural activities to Hamburg (Freie und Hansestadt Hamburg, 2014, p. 18).

The involvement of residents in urban policy during the Von Buest/Ahlthaus administration is mostly related to their entrepreneurial capacities. The administration developed a specific policy to strengthen the creative sector of Hamburg. The policy document is called 'Creative milieus and open spaces in Hamburg' and is inspired by Richard Florida (Freie und Hansestadt Hamburg, 2010, p. 6). The policy document outlines ideas to promote Hamburg as a creative city. Creative people, companies, civil servants, and real estate investors have to work together to develop innovative urban development concepts (Freie und Hansestadt Hamburg, 2010, p. 6). According to the document, residents should be seen as partners in urban development, having an active role in the development process. Residents and creatives organize themselves through 'do-it-yourself' urbanism. They can transform underutilized areas into vibrant spaces. This is valuable for Hamburg because "the users of space become developers of space. Responsibilities over urban development can be shared between the members of the creative class and other key actors" (Freie und Hansestadt Hamburg, 2010, p. 100).

To attract investments into neighborhoods—and share responsibilities over urban development with key actors—the municipality introduced business improvement districts. In these BIDs businesses and property owners plan and execute improvements to the neighborhood. The successful policy was expanded to other residents in 2007 (Freie und Hansestadt Hamburg, 2020a).

After 2011, a left-wing coalition between Social Democrats and the Green Party, takes office. The administration is led by Scholz, who was replaced by Tschentscher in 2018. The administration publishes the policy document 'Green, inclusive, growing city by the water' to specify their policies concerning urban development (Freie und Hansestadt Hamburg, 2014). The title of the document already shows the increased importance of both sustainability and inclusivity for the city's goals. The city's goal will be a just city where "citizens can remain in their neighborhood and enjoy a high quality of live" (Freie und Hansestadt Hamburg, 2014, p. 24). Participation should form the basis of all development projects (Freie und Hansestadt Hamburg, 2014, p. 29). Hamburg should become an open and international "people's city" where diverse people live together as friendly neighbors (Freie und Hansestadt Hamburg, 2014, p. 69). In terms of sustainability the city government of Hamburg will invest in energy efficiency of the housing stock while keeping housing affordable for all citizens and aim to make transport more sustainable (Freie und Hansestadt Hamburg, 2014, p. 37).

The administration made participation more central in their policies and created a new agency, the Stadwerkstatt, to promote consultation, participation, and new means of public dialogue.

> The goal of Stadwerkstatt is to contribute to a new planning culture that is characterized by transparency of interests, the to understand and broadly supported results. Developing a new planning culture must be understood as a learning process that requires time and does not necessarily run in a straight line and without errors. Crucially, all activities taking place under the

> Stadwerkstatt brand are designed to conform to the principles of honesty and fairness in information and participation.
>
> (Senate Hamburg, 2012)

According to the mission of Stadwerkstatt, citizens are partners of the municipality in developing new approaches to face Hamburg's current problems and challenges (Freie und Hansestadt Hamburg, 2020b).

In 2020, Tschentscher is reelected during the COVID-19 pandemic. The administration remains a coalition between the social democrats and the Green Party, continuing their work based on the 'Green, inclusive, growing city by the water' plan. Under the motto of "an attractive inner city for all," the administration announced a redevelopment of the city Centre (Freie und Hansestadt Hamburg, 2024).

To summarize, Hamburg witnessed a clear shift in how it justified participation. During the Von Buest/Ahlhaus administration, participation mainly meant consultation with clients in the housing market or with entrepreneurs willing to invest in the neighborhood. Residents are mostly portrayed as either families that represent the demand side of the housing market or as creatives that are able to take an active role in urban development. Thus, the market and entrepreneurial orders are mostly invoked. During the Scholz/Tschentscher administration, participation became a tool to define priorities in development projects. Residents have not only a responsibility concerning urban development but also the right to participate. The market orders is invoked less, but the entrepreneurial orders is often activated by the Scholz/Tschentscher administration. Participation should be the basis of all urban development, but they also are encouraged to take an active role (see Table 3.2).

Table 3.2 Municipal policies concerning participation in urban development in Hamburg

Hamburg	*Von Buest/Ahlthaus 2006–2014*	*Scholz/Tschentscher 2014-ongoing*
Main goal of development strategy	Competitive economy Greening the city	Greening the city Affordable housing Being a just city
How are citizens portrayed	Citizens as part of families Citizens wanting quality	Citizens as neighbors
Agreements mentioned in relation to participation	BIDs Creative incubators	Development agreements
Justification for participation	Part of the planning process	Citizens are able to improve the quality of neighborhoods Create communities
Organization of participation	Part of urban renewal and development projects Digital discussion	Participation is organized to define priorities in urban development Innovative participatory processes

Source: Author based on Freie und Hansestadt Hamburg (2014, 2020a, 2020b, 2024)

3.3 Planning orders in New York

Unlike Amsterdam and Hamburg, New York lacks a comprehensive approach to city planning. But the Mayor's publish documents that outline their main urban development strategies. In New York City, Bloomberg was mayor between 2001 and 2013. The main urban development goals of the Bloomberg administration, outlined in the New Housing Marketplace Plan, are updated after each election (The City of New York, 2010). According to the document, the most important priority is "ensuring that New York City continues to grow and thrive during these tough economic times, maintaining our role as a world capital and strengthening our position as a global leader in affordable housing" (The City of New York, 2010, p. 4). Bloomberg's administration aimed to create more affordable housing and new housing for moderate and middle-income households (The City of New York, 2010, p. 2).

The involvement of residents in urban development was mainly as participants in the housing markets, waiting to be served.

> Over the next four years, HPD will continue working to keep our City's housing stock growing, . . . But we won't stop there—we will keep growing beyond the targeted units to ensure every New Yorker has the safe, quality affordable housing they deserve.
>
> (The City of New York, 2010, p. 3)

Next, residents who are hit hard by the financial crisis of 2008 are also mentioned. The administration strives to prevent foreclosures and will work with "with our governmental and not-for-profit partners to focus on comprehensive neighborhood strategies and solutions" (The City of New York, 2010, p. 9).

Financial incentives and rezoning were the main instruments to achieve these goals. Through rezoning, an area receives a new designation. While rezoning proposals are subject to review by community boards (Angotti, 2008), they can be sidelined by agreements such as Memoranda of Understanding or Community Benefit Agreements (Angotti, 2010). The financial incentives include tax exemptions, bond market financing, and short-term loans (City of New York, 2010, p. 2).

The Bloomberg administration was followed by the De Blasio administration, who took office for eight years. De Blasio set out a set of progressive development policies at the beginning of his term. He introduced a mandatory inclusionary housing program, to enlarge the affordable housing stock of New York. Moreover, he proposed policies to protect the housing rights of tenants and introduced policies to invest in affordable housing. These goals had to be achieved in close cooperation with residents and neighborhood organizations.

> This is a five-borough, ten-year plan. It will marshal people and resources from every corner of this city behind a singular purpose: to make this city again a place where our most vulnerable, our working people, and our middle class can all thrive. Together, let's make that vision a reality.
>
> (The City of New York, 2014)

Participation became more important in urban planning after De Blasio's election as mayor of New York City in 2013. According to the administration's plan Housing New York, residents were to be involved in identifying areas well-suited to affordable housing development (City of New York, 2014, p. 8). Moreover, residents should be involved from the early stages onward in development projects.

> When City-sponsored housing developments are initiated, the City will identify opportunities to incorporate facilities and services into the projects that directly address local needs. This process will begin with agencies reaching out to community stakeholders during the planning stage and will continue through construction and occupancy.

Like Stadwerkstatt in Hamburg, the administration created an agency—the Office for Neighborhood Strategies—to promote participation (The City of New York, 2020). The Office for Neighborhood Strategies organized vision workshops for areas identified for rezoning. The workshops created community visions on how the neighborhood should develop in the coming years, outlining development priorities. The community visions were used to find "quick wins" in collaboration with residents and other stakeholders (City of New York, 2020).

De Blasio was term-limited, and in 2022, Eric Adams became the new mayor of New York. In the document 'Rebuild, renew, reinvent: A blueprint for New York City's economic recovery', his administration outlined how they wanted to restart New York's economy after the COVID-19 pandemic. Although the focus is on the economy, one of the five main strategies is targeted at planning and building 'inclusive growth now and in the future.' The document announced to "advance neighborhood planning with different approaches to engagement and investment based on local needs" (City of New York, 2022, p. 50). The goal was to work with residents to create new jobs and improve transit connections. Moreover, the document noted the importance of working with community intermediaries such as neighborhood organizations. They could help stimulate economic growth in areas with large percentages of Black, Indigenous, and People of Color. Investments were to be made along the principle that "all New Yorkers should have access to housing options and good jobs along with essential services and infrastructure" (City of New York, 2022, p. 53). This is also supported by creating a long-term strategy to foster the creation of BIDs. Moreover, in order to create more space for (affordable) housing, the document stipulates that strategies will be employed to allow a wider range of unit sizes, broadening existing density allowances for affordable housing, easing alteration or the addition of accessory units, and reevaluating parking requirements (City of New York, 2022, p. 55). Lastly, the document describes the need to achieve carbon neutrality in 2050 (City of New York, 2022, p. 56). This should partially be achieved through changes in zoning regulations. No mention is made related to the involvement of residents, although neighborhood planning practices will be implemented to make New York's waterfront resilient to climate change. The principles that are outlined in 'Rebuild, renew and reinvent: A blueprint for New York City's economic recovery' are further elaborated in the 'City of Yes' plans (City of New York, 2024b, 2024c, 2024d). The focus on involving residents in development plans of the De Blasio administration was largely gone. According to the City of Yes plans, less regulation and more possibilities within zoning plans would lead to more affordable housing and more economic opportunities (City of New York, 2024b, 2024c, 2024d).

Like in Amsterdam and Hamburg, there was a shift in planning orders in New York. The Bloomberg administration mainly saw residents as passive actors in the housing market. They form the demand side of the housing market, and developers and investors—with help from the government—should take care of the supply side. Thus, the Bloomberg administration mostly invoked the market order to justify their policies. The De Blasio administration made participation more central to their policies. The participatory policies were mostly aimed at neighborhood organizations. Those neighborhood organizations had to be involved in the various phases of the development processes and help with designing plans for urban renewal and redevelopment projects. They were expected to play an active role and come up with creative solutions, showing the importance of the entrepreneurial order to justify participatory policies for the De Blasio administration. During the Adams administration, this reverted back to an embrace of the market register and the entrepreneurial register. There was attention to fostering economic growth and local entrepreneurship. The main goal to increase the housing stock in the city was materialized by allowing for higher densities and creating less regulation.

Table 3.3 Municipal policies concerning participation in urban development in New York

New York	*Bloomberg 2001–2013*	*De Blasio 2013–2022*	*Adams 2022-ongoing*
Main goal of development strategy	Competitive economy	Affordable housing	More housing, more economic activity
How are citizens portrayed	Citizens customers of the housing market, citizens that are vulnerable	Citizens as partners in development	Citizens as entrepreneurs
Agreements mentioned in relation to participation	Memorandum of Agreements Community Benefit Agreements	Community visioning reports	BIDs
Justification for participation	-	Citizens are able to improve neighborhoods	Neighborhood planning to create more economic activity and housing
Organization of participation	Working with non-for-profits and neighborhood organizations	Mostly through neighborhood organizations	Mostly through neighborhood organizations

Source: Author based on City of New York (2010, 2014, 2020, 2022, 2024a, 2024b, 2024c)

3.4 Comparing municipal orders

Municipal policies in Amsterdam, Hamburg, and New York reveal that the entrepreneurial register is increasingly invoked. Moreover, they show how pragmatic registers create bonds between specific ideas about citizenship, legal arrangements, and political decision-making processes. This helps us to understand the growing use of contracts, participation, and community intermediaries in urban development. Public meetings, now considered outdated, were increasingly being replaced by co-creation workshops, while planning instruments were based on negotiation, and residents were encouraged to take over responsibilities from the welfare state. The entrepreneurial order was often invoked in combination with the market order in municipal policies before the financial crisis. The market register valued efficiency and competition, whereas the entrepreneurial register valued innovation and collaboration. Participation as a right was being eclipsed by participation as a responsibility. After the financial crisis there was a further embrace of the entrepreneurial register, but often in combination with the civic register. Participation should encourage empowerment and enhance democratic practices. This happened especially in Amsterdam after 2018. Still, residents in all the three cities were expected to play an active role in urban development. This shows that the idea of participation as a responsibility rather than a right remained strongly embedded in planning policies in Amsterdam, Hamburg, and New York.

Although broadly similar tendencies can be observed in invoking the market and entrepreneurial registers to justify and organize participation in Amsterdam, Hamburg, and New York, they played out differently in the three cities. In Amsterdam and Hamburg, municipal governments had greater leverage over developers and were able to enforce policies such as mandatory social housing. While the city of New York also aimed to enforce affordable housing, this includes both middle-class and social housing units. Amsterdam and Hamburg both had comprehensive visions for spatial planning; without such a planning instrument, New York's spatial policy was more fragmented, making enforcing residents' principles in each project harder.

3.5 Resistance from below

It is important to note that the influence of the executive branch has its limits. The registers embraced in city-wide municipal policy documents do not necessarily translate into activating that register in specific projects. As material objects, they can enhance or limit the ability of actors to undertake action, but they can also be actively resisted. For example, the municipality of Amsterdam mainly used the entrepreneurial register to press for a flexible, incremental approach to planning based on negotiating. Enhancing the ability of actors that know how to set up projects require funds and are considered entrepreneurial. However, residents can mobilize support from the media, politicians, and the courts to alter the direction of development projects. As we will see in other chapters, they do this mainly by activating the civic register to justify their actions and criticize the plans. For example, residents at the K-Buurt in Amsterdam were able to achieve their goals by strategically using their access to media and politicians so they could bend the project towards their goals. They were able to position themselves as decision-makers over several policy processes in the neighborhood. The success of residents in invoking the civic register differs from project to project. In the same city, the residents of Oostenburg-Noord had to compromise more with developers' goals but were able to reach agreements on the size of the apartments and the amount of social housing. These agreements cut into developers' profit margins. These local compromises were not a consensus; some actors were disappointed by the final results. However, the compromise was stable enough to coordinate the actions of the actors toward a common goal—realizing the project. Residents mostly failed to invoke the civic register in another part of Amsterdam. For the Havenstraatterein, the city of Amsterdam invoked the entrepreneurial and market registers to justify quick action in the area and undercut participatory processes. The goal was to realize housing as soon as possible because of Amsterdam's pressing lack of affordable housing. Only after a long judicial process could residents prevent the total demolition of a beloved museum, although they had to give up some land. The judicial process cost the municipality around one million euros (Kempen 2021b, 2021a).

While I selected the cases I studied in this book because residents were able to meaningfully influence agreements, I also noted the mobilizing power of residents in other projects in Amsterdam: Zeeburgerpad and Landtong Nieuwe Meer. To a greater or lesser extent, the same held for the projects I explored in New York: Essex Crossing, Columbia University, Sendero Verde, Kingsbridge Armory, and The Peninsula and Hamburg: Paloma Viertel, Neue Mitte Altona, and the Gängeviertel.

Residents in New York are also organized at the borough or city-wide level. Under the banner of Housing Justice for All, neighborhood organizations were able to pressure politicians to reform housing laws in 2019 (Ferré-Sadurní et al., 2019; Michener, 2020). In these battles over legal reform, neighborhood organizations mostly invoked the civic register, arguing that housing should be affordable to all New Yorkers. They also criticized how the City of New York defined affordability: it cost as much as $6.661 per month for a three-bedroom apartment (City of New York, 2024a). It should be noted that those rents are related to your income, and if you earn 100% of the average income, you pay $4.037, and 30% of the average income, the rent is $1.211 for a three-bedroom apartment (City of New York, 2024a). Developers and their allies used the market register to argue that greater government control over the housing market would lead to their bankruptcy and further housing problems in the city. In Hamburg, the Recht auf Stadt—or right to the city—movement mobilized thousands to demonstrate against pro-market housing policies by invoking the civic order. While this movement grew powerful and led to changes in municipal housing policies, this did not mean the civic register became predominant. Since registers are not omnipotent and are often compromised with other registers, some of the voiced critiques were displaced. For example, the Recht auf Stadt movement demanded more transparency and resident involvement in decision-making. The municipality responded by publicly making all agreements and documents available in its transparency portal. However, it excluded financial obligations, which remained secret to protect the privacy of commercial parties. Although the municipality created a new agency to improve participation, the Stadwerkstatt, it did not guarantee residents decision-making power; the agency mainly justifies its projects through the entrepreneurial order. Nevertheless, these compromises between activists and the municipality coordinated the conflicting aims of contentious actors towards a common goal, both providing public legitimacy and creating opportunities for commercial parties. The compromises were thus able to administer the capitalist-democracy contradiction and set actors on a specific course.

As stated, compromises also displace part of the critique. While the portal increased transparency, one must possess expert knowledge to understand the agreements and documents (more than 1,200 documents about Neue Mitte Altona have been published online). And while Stadwerkstatt stimulates participation, it does not guarantee residents' decision-making power. The more often these compromises are reproduced, the more ingrained they become, potentially generating new registers. It also remains possible that these compromises will one day fall apart. The point is that although these orders may appear to be omnipresent, they are not omnipotent. Through political action, compromises between different orders are assembled to direct actors toward common goals. The compromises only include parts of the social critique while displacing its other parts.

Community intermediaries, especially consultants, are often responsible for assembling compromises. Consultants are hired because they appear to be "neutral" actors focused on the process rather than the outcome. Their position as outsiders is often used to gain the trust of different actors in the project. For instance, contentious relations in the Lower East Side had prevented the development of Essex Crossing for decades. A planning consultant was hired to act as an intermediary between the different parties and to broker a deal. Because the planning consultant could gain the trust of the actors, he succeeded in bringing the parties together. Consultants are increasingly hired to perform public responsibilities: formulating policy, executing plans, and organizing participation. Neighborhood organizations are involved in making compromises as negotiating parties that represent residents.

In the next chapters, I will explore in more detail how resistance from below challenges and transforms city-wide municipal policies on urban development.

References

Amsterdams Volkshuisvestingsoverleg. 2010. "Leidraad Participatie." *Amsterdamse Volkshuisvestingsoverleg*, 1–25.

Angotti, T. 2008. *New York for Sale: Community Planning Confronts Global Real Estate*. Cambridge and London: The MIT Press. https://doi.org/10.1080/14649351003759797.

Angotti, Tom. 2010. *Land Use and the New York City Charter*. New York: Hunter College Center for Community Planning & Development.

The City of New York. 2010. *New Housing Marketplace Plan: Creating a More Affordable, Vialbe, and Sustainable City for All New Yorkers*. New York: Department of Housing Preservation and Development.

The City of New York. 2014. "Housing New York: A Five-Borough, Ten-Year Plan."

The City of New York. 2020. "Office of Neighborhood Strategies." https://www1.nyc.gov/site/hpd/about/office-descriptions.page.
City of New York. 2022. "Rebuild, Renew, Reinvent: A Blueprint for New York City's Economic Recovery." *City of New York*. https://www.nyc.gov/assets/home/downloads/pdf/office-of-the-mayor/2022/Mayor-Adams-Economic-Recovery-Blueprint.pdf.
City of New York. 2024a. "Average Median Income." https://www.nyc.gov/site/hpd/services-and-information/area-median-income.page.
City of New York. 2024b. "City of Yes; Carbon Neutrality." https://www.nyc.gov/site/planning/plans/city-of-yes/city-of-yes-carbon-neutrality.page.
City of New York. 2024c. "City of Yes: Economic Opportunity." https://www.nyc.gov/site/planning/plans/city-of-yes/city-of-yes-economic-opportunity.page.
City of New York. 2024d. "City of Yes; Housing Opportunity." https://www.nyc.gov/site/planning/plans/city-of-yes/city-of-yes-housing-opportunity.page.
Ferré-Sadurní, Luis, Jesse McKinley, and Vivian Wang. 2019. "Landmark Deal Reached on Rent Protections for Tenants in N.Y." *New York Times*.
Freie und Hansestadt Hamburg. 2010. *Kreative Milieus Und Offenre Räume in Hamburg*. Hamburg: Behörde für Stadtentwicklung und Umwelt.
Freie und Hansestadt Hamburg. 2014. *Grüne, Gerechte, Wachsende Stadt Am Wasser: Perspektiven Der Stadtentwikclung Für Hamburg*. Hamburg: Behörde für Stadtentwicklung und Umwelt.
Freie und Hansestadt Hamburg. 2020a. "Private Initiativen Zur Stadtteilentwicklung." https://www.hamburg.de/bid/4350374/business-improvement-districts/.
Freie und Hansestadt Hamburg. 2020b. "Was Will Die Stadwerkstatt." https://www.hamburg.de/politik-und-verwaltung/behoerden/behoerde-fuer-stadtentwicklung-und-wohnen/themen/stadtentwicklung/stadtwerkstatt/aufgaben-und-ziele/was-will-stadtwerkstatt-187102.
Freie und Hansestadt Hamburg. 2024. "Aufwertung Der Hamburger Innenstadt." https://www.hamburg.de/politik-und-verwaltung/behoerden/behoerde-fuer-stadtentwicklung-und-wohnen/themen/stadtentwicklung/konzepte-und-strategien/innenstadtkonzept-start−184556.
Gemeente Amsterdam. 2009. *Wonen in de Metropool: Woonvisie Amsterdam Tot 2020*. Amsterdam: Dienst Wonen.
Gemeente Amsterdam. 2011. "Structuurvisie Amsterdam 2040 Economisch Sterk En Duurzaam."
Gemeente Amsterdam. 2016. "Koers 2025: Ruimte Voor de Stad."
Gemeente Amsterdam. 2017. "Plaberum 2017." *Amsterdam*.
Gemeente Amsterdam. 2021. "Omgevingsvisie Amsterdam 2050." *Gemeente Amsterdam*.
Gemeente Amsterdam. 2022. "Samen Werken Aan Een Democratische Stad: Programma Democratisering." https://www.amsterdam.nl/bestuur-organisatie/invloed/democratisering/.
Gemeente Amsterdam. 2024. "Participatieverordening." *Gemeente Amsterdam*.
Kempen, Jop van. 2021a, December 3. "Akkoord over Havenstratterrein: Nieuwe Woningen, Maar de Museumtram Blijft." *Het Parool*.
Kempen, Jop van. 2021b. "Terrein Museumtram Moet Inkrimpen Voor Huizen: 'We Vechten Voor Ons Levenswerk.'" *Het Parool*.
Michener, Jamila. 2020. "Power from the Margins: Grassroots Mobilization and Urban Expansions of Civil Legal Rights." *Urban Affairs Review* 56 (5): 1390–422. https://doi.org/10.1177/1078087419855677.
Savini, Federico, Willem R. Boterman, Wouter P.C. van Gent, and Stan Majoor. 2016. "Amsterdam in the 21st Century: Geography, Housing, Spatial Development and Politics." *Cities* 52: 103–13. https://doi.org/10.1016/j.cities.2015.11.017.
Senate Hamburg. 2012. "Mitteilung Des Senats an Die Bürgerschaft - Einrichtung Einer Hamburger Stadtwerkstatt." *Hamburg*.

4 Institutional contradictions and change in urban politics

St. Pauli is an infamous neighborhood in St. Pauli, Hamburg. The neighborhood is renowned for its left-wing activism, with squatted buildings and recurring demonstrations. One of the main streets of St. Pauli, the Reeperbahn, is even more notorious. During the day, the streets seem to be a bit desolate and faded. But when the night starts, neon lights shine bright, and clubs and cafes open their doors. The area turns into one of the most vibrant parts of Hamburg. The nickname of the street is Die sündigste Meile der Welt (the most sinful mile in the world). The oldest S&M club in Europe is located at the Reeperbahn, Club de Sade. Famously, the Beatles played in clubs around St. Pauli before their big breakthrough. Today, St. Pauli is popular with middle- and high-income groups, and the area faces gentrification. The street was also home to the Esso-Häuser. Built during the years after the second world war housing complex included social housing, a hotel, a club, a garage, and a gas station (hence the name Esso-Häuser). As a real meeting point for the neighborhood, the gas station sold groceries and was open 24/7. This building complex would be turned into one of the focal points of urban politics in Hamburg.

This chapter will follow the events that play out around the Esso-Häuser. The goal of the chapter is to understand how actors invoke registers in uncertain situations. Moreover, this chapter shows how those registers are not outside forces but embedded and embodied between urban actors. I define registers as entangled constellations of morals, politics, and laws that coordinate actors' actions. They are threads that bind actors and objects together to realize collective action in a justified way. Morals are used to give direction toward actors' actions; they provide a vision of how society ought to be. Politics concerns decision-making processes; it arranges which actors can make decisions. Laws are the rules that bind actors together; they stabilize the relations between actors. Pragmatic registers are the arrangements in which those actors and objects are brought together. They are invoked to provide clarity in uncertain situations where collective action is needed. Although there are infinite ways to combine morals, politics, and laws, there are only a few pragmatic registers in society. The reason for this is in uncertain situation, actors must move from a particular individual judgment to general, collective understandings in order to mobilize collective action (Thévenot, 2002). As mentioned in Chapter 1, the civic, market, and entrepreneurial registers are prevalent

DOI: 10.4324/9781032712840-4

in contemporary North American and European urban politics, while the green register is on the rise.

Registers are invoked to provide clarity in uncertain situations; they are coordination mechanisms. In order to pull actors in a particular direction, those registers have a degree of generality. Different registers are often combined, creating local variations. The combination of different registers could potentially mobilize more support from different actors. Thus, they are not a coherent mechanism in which everything fits friction-free together. They require work to be invoked (Mol, 2010). Importantly, they are not a representation of ideal types. They are deeply embedded and entangled in materialities. When registers are invoked, objects are drawn in for support (Boltanski and Thévenot, 1991). Registers are thus not only linguistic. Moreover, certain actors strongly embody certain registers (Thévenot, 2002). For example, a developer is strongly associated with the market register, while a community organizer is deeply associated with the civic register. This will be explained further in this chapter.

The point of this chapter is to show that although actors are embedded in structural positions, their capacity to critique makes urban politics a highly contingent process. Government agencies, commercial parties, and residents deal with those contingencies through the activation of registers. First, I will explain how hermeneutic institutional contradictions lead to constant change within society. Thereafter I will show how actors use moral artifacts to deal with those contradictions. Next, I will set out how political decisions are made and how legal orders stabilize relations. I rely mainly on the tools provided by pragmatic theory and the sociology of critique (Boltanski and Thévenot, 1991; Dewey, 1927; Lamont, 1992; Thévenot, 2002).

4.1 Institutional contradictions

In 2009 the owners of the Esso-Häuser sold the building the investor Bayerische Hausbau. The old owners did not invest much in the maintenance of the building, and the building was in dire need of renovation. However, the new owners preferred to demolish the building and develop a new complex. In anticipation of this, they asked their tenants to sign new contracts. Claiming the original contracts were out of date, the replacement contracts proposed by Bayerische Hausbau significantly reduced tenants' rights. As a community activist explained:

> The people had good contracts, but they didn't know that they had good contracts because in the contract there was a section that it will end in 2010, but as the reason for this was not right, they had actually contracts were they could live all their lives longs there. But they didn't knew it. And one of the first things that the Bayerische Hausbau did was give them new contracts and say you have to sign this now because you have to leave the flat.
>
> (Resident 25, Hamburg, 2018)

The new contracts no longer guaranteed tenants could keep living in the housing complex, making the path to demolition easier for Bayerische Hausbau.

Bayerische Hausbau attempted to change the legal relationship between them and their tenants. Law is one of the threads that binds actors and objects together. Law is diverse and can take many forms (Durkheim, 1984). They can result in rights for actors, which is the increased probability that a certain expectation will occur (Weber, 1978). Law provides a textuality to promises made. Textuality manages expectations and can, therefore, stabilize relations between actors and objects (McGee, 2015). The tenants had the right to remain in their houses indefinitely. Thus, they gave the tenants a source of power over Bayerische Hausbau. The neighborhood organization GWA heard of the new contracts at their regular tenants' meeting. Warned, they decided to go door to door in the Esso-Häuser to inform tenants of their rights and warn them not to sign the new contract. In the light of these events, tenants, neighborhood residents, and business owners decided to establish the Esso-Häuser Initiative (Kaiser, 2010). The goal of the Esso-Häuser Initiative was to prevent to demolition of the Esso-Häuser and protect the rights of the tenants. Soon, their actions caught the attention of the media, making the proposed demolition of the Esso-Häuser a widely debated topic in Hamburg (Kaiser and Von Appen, 2010).

The contention between the Esso-Häuser Initiative and Bayerische Hausbau lays bare the classic fault lines of urban politics. Developers versus residents. The power of the establishment versus the power of movements. The vicious versus the virtuous. Although these fault lines can be distinguished everywhere in the world, they are always in motion, creating new fractures and junctures (see: Lamont, 1992, p. 47). This implies that there are endless variations in the conflicts and compromises between actors in urban politics. The junctures and fractures are created because human conduct tilts toward the reproduction of interactions. The reproduction of interactions leads toward more or less stable partners of activity called practices. When the practices serve collective purposes, they become institutionalized. Institutions are thus recurring patterns of interactions. Institutions function as reference points for collective action, especially related to objects that are highly valued and must be stabilized by definitions (Boltanski, 2011). Institutions prescribe rules to human activities and give meaning to the position of actors and objects within the world.

Institutions can be transformed by weaving together objects and actors through morals, politics, and laws. The moral thread prescribes how society ought to be, what is being valued, and what is being devalued. Morals help actors to make sense of uncertain situations and provide paths forward. For example, they make it obvious for the community activists to help the tenants vis-à-vis the developers. The political thread arranges how decisions are being made. Politics empowers actors to choose between various paths forward. To illustrate, Bayerische Hausbau choosing demolition instead of renovation is a political decision, not to involve the tenants. The legal thread increases the likelihood that certain actions will be undertaken. Law stabilizes relationships and provides textuality to promises made. This is shown by Bayerische Hausbau's attempt to change the contracts.

To change recurring patterns of actions on a large scale, moral, political, and legal threads have to be woven together. They form registers, the mechanisms that order institutions, crystalizing in a particular social fabric. When these registers are reproduced on a societal scale, they gain a degree of generality. In their more general form, they are able to be activated in more and more situations of uncertainty. The industrial, civic, market, entrepreneurial, and green registers described in the introduction are examples of morals, politics, and laws woven together in a particular pattern reproduced on a societal scale. Those registers are deeply ingrained in how North America and Europe urban actors deal with uncertainties. They are recognizable patterns that can mobilize actors to engage in collective action.

Their generality makes it possible to mobilize support from various actors in various situations. To illustrate, Bayerische Hausbau can activate the market register to argue that they are the property owners and have the right to change the contracts with the tenants. They use a moral thread to justify their plans to demolish the property; renovation would be too costly and would not use the area's full potential. Next, they use a political thread to justify that the property owners can make the decisions concerning the future of the building. Finally, they attempt to use a legal thread to change the textuality of the promises made to the tenants. The combination of these threads can be seen anywhere in the world and can be recognized as the market register. Although the arrangements can be recognized everywhere in the world, the objects and actors that are woven together through the arrangement are always local and specific. GWA is a very specific organization active in St. Pauli, Hamburg. The Esso-Häuser has a specific meaning for St. Pauli that is very local.

Although institutions appear to be coherent, they are not consistent with the lived experiences or viewpoints of all members of society (Boltanski, 2011). These hermeneutic contradictions open institutions up for critique. When enough critique builds up and uncertainty grows, registers are invoked to provide clarity. The activation of registers can lead to changes in practices, and institutional change is possible. The fault lines in urban politics are institutionalized everywhere in the world, but there are always local variations. In order to understand these variations, I distinguish between two major institutional contradictions in urban politics: the property-planning contradiction and the capitalist-democracy contradiction (Boltanski, 2011; Foglesong, 1986; Stein, 2019; Young, 1990).

The property-planning contradiction is the dependence of commercial parties on government intervention for their business activities, while they remain hostile toward anything that restricts their activity (Stein, 2019). Whereas the logic of property values possession, the logic of planning values the common good. Although government interventions such as safeguarding credits and investments in infrastructure make development projects possible (Logan and Molotch, 1987), the constraints they place on commercial parties are routinely met with opposition. There is a clash between property institutions that prescribe that owners can make decisions about their real estate without interference, whereas the planning institution privileges decisions from government officials. Land use plans are useful to protect property rights but should not restrict landowners in any way. Investments in infrastructure are necessary, but taxes that raise money for these investments are opposed. I argue that contracts and agreements are used to deflect the property-planning contradiction. Property owners can compromise with government actors by negotiating deals on a case-to-case basis.

The discrepancies in the planning-property contradiction result in tensions between actors. As we will see, the Bayerische Hausbau will clash and cooperate with the planning departments of Hamburg. They need changes to the land use plan to achieve their goals. But the municipality also wants to work with the Esso-Häuser Initiative. Moreover, different commercial parties have different needs for intervention, resulting in tensions and alliances between commercial parties and between commercial parties and other actors (Foglesong, 1986).

The capitalist-democracy contradiction is the incompatibility between the benefits of democracy for commercial parties and the threat of democracy to their profits (Boltanski, 2011; Stein, 2019; Young, 1990). Whereas the logic of democracy attributes worth to majority decisions, the logic of capitalism attributes worth to profits. Democracy provides legitimacy and the public resources needed to invest in infrastructure. Urban development projects need to maintain their legitimacy as residents mobilizing against the project can disrupt the development process. Although organizing public consultations and realizing benefits for residents bolsters the legitimacy of projects (Young, 1990), the influence of residents can threaten profit margins for commercial parties. During public consultations, some criticisms are incorporated into the project while others are displaced (Boltanski, 2011). Although processes of public participation can lead to greater citizen influence, residents rarely share actual decision-making power (Levine, 2017; Stein, 2019). Legislation is useful to enforce promises, but commercial parties prefer the flexibility of agreements.

Citizens' participation and the use of mediators such as consultants, I argue, help to circumvent the capitalist-democracy contradiction. Planning consultants are hired because they can mediate between developers and residents. Participation is organized to legitimize development projects. In most cases, participatory processes are often organized after contracts between developers and the municipality are signed. This means that the opportunities for residents to shape decisions are limited. This does not imply that participation is mere window dressing. Residents can use participatory processes and public debates to bend development projects towards their goals, but they have to organize politically to achieve this. In the case of the Esso-Häuser, we will see that there is a dispute about the potential profits of the commercial parties. Residents' needs will eventually be incorporated into the project, but sometimes subsidized by the government to protect the profits of the commercial parties.

Both contradictions materialize differently on various geographical scales. While the disparities between planning, democracy, and profitability help us to understand the politics of urban planning, it always remains an empirical question of how the related tensions between actors manifest locally. Studying the nuances and particularities of these processes provides insight into how actors' reflexive engagement with structural features transforms these very features and lead to new political and social imaginaries (Emirbayer, 1997).

4.2 Moral categories and artifacts

In order to decrease tensions in the area, the Bayerische Hausbau started roundtable talks with the Esso-Häuser Initiative in 2011. However, the talks went nowhere, and Bayerische Hausbau ended the dialogue in 2012. The district alderman, Andy Grote, warned Bayerische Hausbau that they wouldn't get approval for their plans without input from the Esso-Häuser Initiative (Lena Kaiser, 2012). This shows the tension that flows from the planning-property contradiction; the property owner needs support from the municipality but does not want any interference in their plans. In response, the Esso-Häuser Initiative published a manifesto supported by some of Hamburg's most prominent public figures (Gassdorf and Fischer, 2013). The manifesto demanded that the Esso-Häuser complex would not be demolished. Moreover, the manifesto outlined a vision of politics that prioritized the needs of the residents of St. Pauli. Meanwhile, the Bayerische Hausbau warned that the building was at risk of collapse. They felt forced to place structural supports around the buildings.

Here, we see a set of sequences where actors invoke different conceptions of the common good to overcome hermeneutic contradictions. In public disputes, actors cannot act in an atomized way. They depend on each other for collective action. Therefore, actors must move from a particular individual judgment to general, collective understandings (Thévenot, 2002). The common good is a moral institution that orders and attributes value to actors, objects, and practices and is widely—geographically and historically—reproduced. The common good prescribes a pathway to overcome public disputes by specifying what ought to be. It spins a moral thread between actors and objects that establishes relations of worth.

In this situation, the Esso-Häuser Initiative would invoke a common good based on their position as representatives from the neighborhood (Gassdorf and Fischer, 2013). Meanwhile, Bayerische Hausbau appeals to a common good based on technical expertise and market logic. The Esso-Häuser Initiative pointed out that they consist of residents and tenants and have, therefore, the right to make decisions over development projects in their area (Gassdorf and Fischer, 2013). They used the manifesto, neighborhood meetings, and the local media to draw support from other actors. The Bayerische Hausbau invoked the condition of the building—and, to a lesser extent, the fact that they were the owners—to justify the demolition of the building. They asked technical experts to investigate the state of the building, which was on the brink of collapse. This process is not linear or straightforward. Some of these objects will start to play a more important role in mobilizing support than others.

These objects are not randomly chosen but are locally invented. Through decades of repeated reproduction, some objects become strongly associated with particular notions of the common good. They become moral artifacts. Many commonwealth nations use wigs—the type that is out of fashion for centuries—as part of their court dress. These wigs are unpractical but embody authority (and colonialism). The same goes for public meetings; they notify actors that democracy is practiced through debate and open discussion. Of course, there are local and time-specific variations. It is a process of valuing rather than a static value (Heuts and Mol, 2013). Some objects are important moral artifacts locally but do not transcend time and space around the world. Other objects are widely associated with a particular moral quality across the world. For example, in demonstrations related to the Esso-Häuser conflict, a toilet brush becomes an object with moral qualities. Those days there are many demonstrations against the housing and planning policies of the municipality in Hamburg. The demonstrations were condemned by national politicians and media outlets. The police state that the St. Pauli area is a danger zone: gefahrengebiet. This has legal consequences, and the police are allowed to search people in the danger zone (Zand-Vakili, 2014). During one of the searches, a toilet brush from a demonstrator is confiscated and filmed. The confiscation of the toilet brush is ridiculed by the protest movements, and the toilet brush is embraced as a symbol. A local politician explained: "You had to show your ID and open your bags, and then they confiscated, for instance, in Kloburste, which was the craziest thing to do because it was such a laugh, and everybody was running around with Kloburste" (Politician 9, Hamburg, 2018). Hundreds of memes are created where figures like Yoda, Harry Potter, and art from Banksy are mixed with a toilet brush. A bond is created between a local particularity and widely renowned symbols of resistance. Although important in Hamburg for a particular time, it is unlikely that the toilet brush will be embraced by social movements around the world.

Those actors and objects that are deeply associated with particular moral orders can help actors to navigate uncertain situations. The bond is omnidirectional. The actor depends on valued actors and objects in order to co-ordinate actions. But the valued actor or object also depends on the actor for its own position. We can see this in the way the Esso-Häuser Initiative navigates the tension with Bayerische Hausbau. They reach out to local media to influence the public debate and mobilize support from other actors. But the local media also depends on them for creating news stories. This can also be seen concerning the manifesto of the Esso-Häuser Initiative. The manifesto receives meaning because other actors—such as journalists—value its ability to present the position of neighborhood residents in a coherent, unifying way.

This does not imply that actors only take actions based on moral artifacts. The boundary between moral evaluations and evaluations based on a person's position within society is extremely fuzzy (Sayer, 2010). The morphology of these bonds can be changed through critically reflecting on their value. When valued actors or objects fail to confirm the lived experience of actors or fail to mobilize support from other actors, they are bound to be disregarded (Boltanski, 2011). This opens possibilities for new valued actors or objects, which eventually can lead to institutional change. Actors might have a deeply rooted preference for particular valued actors or objects, but they are flexible to respond to variations in circumstances (Sayer, 2010). For example, the tenants lost their trust in Bayerische Hausbau because the property owner tried to let them sign new contracts with fewer rights. This opened the possibility for organizations such as the GWA to become spokespersons of the tenants. The relation between the tenants and Bayerische Hausbau became devalued, whereas the relation between GWA and the tenants gained value.

In response to these events, the Bayerische Hausbau asked technical experts to underline their claim that the Esso-Häuser should be demolished. Technical experts were seen as worthy actors who can independently judge whether buildings should be demolished. In this way, Bayerische Hausbau tried to pull actors entangled in the Esso-Häuser conflict toward their preferred direction. Through the technical experts, Bayerische Hausbau tried to mobilize support from other actors. Also, in this instance, the common good, the moral thread, functioned as a coordination mechanism that created linkages of commonality with other actors (Thévenot, 2002). The Bayerische Hausbau intended to mobilize support with actors who share a preference for their notion of the common good. Politicians, media outlets, and residents of Hamburg thought it was important to prevent the concentration of poverty in neighborhoods, value technical expertise above politics, and that property owners should be protected from the pressure of activists. The outcome of the investigation by the technical experts was predictable, but the response to their reports wasn't. When the reports were published, activists claimed that the results were not objective because the experts were paid by Bayerische Hausbau. The technical experts failed to mobilize support through their apparent neutrality. Instead, they were objectified as part of the market register. This shows how strongly certain actors embody a particular register. A civil servant explained the situation:

> And then we had technical expert reports, which were paid by the Bayerisch Hausbau, that told the construction was in bad condition and that we have to lay them down because we can't refurbish them. It was doubted because it was the wrong people that paid for the reports. So there was no trust.
>
> (Civil servant 13, Hamburg, 2018)

Politicians were also skeptical of the results. Hence, the report fails to mobilize support from politicians, and the stand-off continues.

As the examples show, actors and objects do not function in an atomized way but depend on each other. Valued actors and objects specify the range of possible actions an actor can undertake (Yaneva, 2009). When an actor invokes a notion of the common good, it creates linkages of commonality that can widen (or narrow) the range of possibilities an actor has to undertake action. The common good then becomes a tool to assess situations, enabling associated actors and objects to be valued as worthy or unworthy (Boltanski and Thévenot, 1991). This is an open-ended process; the situation depends on whether moral actors and artifacts can be invoked as coordination mechanisms. The Bayerische Hausbau hoped that the report would diminish the possible actions that the actors would undertake. However, the report was seen as unworthy by activists and some politicians because it was strongly associated with Bayerische Hausbau. While the actors remained in a gridlock vis-à-vis each other, the Esso-Häuser became an object in action. The walls started shaking, and the building covered cars in dust. The risk of a sudden collapse of the building increased daily.

Thus, the building narrowed the range of possible actions the municipality could undertake. In December 2013, the Esso-Häuser was evacuated by the police.

The municipality decided it was not safe anymore to live in the building. The Esso-Häuser was thus demolished, and the goal of neighborhood activists to maintain the building failed. A politician told me that she taught the actions of Bayerische Hausbau and the municipality "smelled" (Politician 8, Hamburg, 2018). The evacuation was just before the Christmas holidays. This was convenient because many students had left to their families for Christmas. Moreover, many argued that it was the negligence of the owners that had let to the deteriorating state of the building. An employee of the municipality told me that those acquisitions were "a very mean thing because we wouldn't throw out people from their houses before Christmas. It was a real danger. And we couldn't take the responsibility, and the people who are experts in engineering and the city of Hamburg and so on they looked into it and said that nobody could stay in there" (Civil servant 13, Hamburg, 2018), and that he had decided with a heavy heart to evacuate the people from their homes just before Christmas.

This was a clear turning point in the story of the Esso-Häuser. Although the building was razed, the people of St. Pauli still wanted to decide about what happened next. During a meeting organized by the Esso-Häuser Initiative, a group of citizens decided to form a group, PlanBude, with the intention of taking ownership of the participatory process (Schäfer, 2014). Because the demolition of the Esso-Häuser was very unpopular, there was a lot of pressure on Bayerische Hausbau and the municipality to agree to PlanBude's proposal. There was still no clear way of dealing with the planning-property contradiction; the property owners needed public legitimacy in order to change the land use plans. Therefore, the municipality arranged funding and commissioned PlanBude to organize the participatory process. Thus, an organization that was from the neighborhood found itself in charge of the participatory process of the Esso-Häuser. PlanBude stated very clearly that they did not represent the neighborhood. They aimed to organize the process in such a way that as many residents of St. Pauli would be involved, but they could not speak for the neighborhood. However, increasingly, PlanBude function as the spokespersons of the neighborhood since elected politicians were distrusted by residents (Welt Online, 2014).

Representation is a slippery slope, with the risk of putting the infinite diversity of social positions, lived experiences, and identities in fixed categories (Hall, 1996). Therefore, I use Young's (2000) definition of representation to understand how actors can represent constituents without seeing the groups they represent as homogenous social groups. Representation is a process of mediation between constituents and the representative (Young, 2000). Representatives can speak for their constituents but cannot speak as them (Young, 2000). In the next years, elected politicians would speak for the needs of residents in general. They would advocate more social housing but wouldn't strongly advocate for neighborhood facilities. PlanBude would speak for the needs of the St. Pauli residents, putting emphasis on neighborhood facilities and the preservation of the St. Pauli culture.

4.3 Somewhere in between the private and the public

The Esso-Häuser became a focal point of urban politics and debate in Hamburg for several years. If we follow Dewey's relational conceptualization of the public and private sphere, it becomes understandable why the Esso-Häuser became a public issue. Moreover, it becomes understandable why the actions of Bayerische Hausbau are deemed controversial enough to become a public issue in Hamburg but that comparable practices are not deemed controversial in New York. Dewey argued that a public—a space in which decisions are made about collective action—appears when the consequences of transactions between actors extend beyond those directly concerned, affect the welfare of many others, and require public action (Dewey, 1927). Transactions are dynamic, unfolding processes in which actors and objects receive meaning, significance, and identity without final attributions (Dewey and Bentley, 1949; Emirbayer, 1997). Public action is undertaken by officials who represent the state. Those officials are persons who bring together those actors who are affected and create an arrangement to deal with the consequences of the transaction (Dewey, 1927). Thus, when officials consider transactions to go beyond those directly involved, they pull the transaction into the public sphere. This is a political choice. Politics is raising issues and deciding how institutional relations should be organized (Young, 1990). Politics either includes or excludes actors and objects. In New York, there are large-scale practices of developers that evict tenants without interference from officials. But in the case of the Esso-Häuser—and on a broader scale in Hamburg—officials interfere with negotiating between developers and residents in order to come to a settlement: "And we also take part in the negotiations between the Bayerische Hausbau, PlanBude and the politicians" (Civil servant 13, Hamburg, 2018). The planning-property and capitalist-democracy contradiction helps to understand how the public and private spheres are differently drawn in Hamburg and New York. The public and private spheres are a set of relations created through the actions of actors. It makes less sense in New York to intervene in property than in Hamburg. Because the planning-property contradiction tilts towards protecting property against planning interventions. Moreover, the capitalist-democracy contradictions tilt toward prioritizing processes of capital accumulation over democratic practices. Hence, the institutional contradictions in New York create less potential for public spheres to emerge than in Hamburg. Social movements, court cases, and media discourses affect those relations and are able to redraw the boundaries between public and private spheres. Hence, what is considered public or private and its underlying logic are open for critique and change.

The goal of PlanBude was to plan the new Esso-Häuser in a creative, bottom-up way so that all residents of St. Pauli could get involved. Therefore, they organized a six-month participatory process incorporating many creative planning methods and concepts. Its epicenter was a container that was put next to the building site, where people could visit, talk through their proposals, or give input on the plans. On its rooftop was a platform overlooking the site, and inside, a small library encouraged local citizens to read about urban design. Visitors were also invited to use Lego or plasticine to express their ideas or draw them. Because the area around the Reeperbahn is infamous for its nightlife, PlanBude asked residents as well as passing tourists to think about how they wanted their neighborhood to feel after dark, organized sound walks and held a photo workshop. In addition to a survey to help quantify residents' input, there were seminars, readings, and even an urban education program for the local school. Residents were also asked to make designs with plasticine. They also had "PlanBuddies," speaking in six different languages, who helped residents to be involved in participatory activities. The residents used various forms to represent their needs, ideas, and wishes for the neighborhood. Now, PlanBude was tasked to organize a coherent arrangement of all their input. It is a process of ordering in which PlanBude includes, excludes, and transforms the contributions of the residents. Delving through the material, it became apparent that the majority of people wanted a playful design: an indented façade, public space on rooftops, and building blocks with different heights. While coding the survey there were a lot of references to Park Fiction, a nearby park. At first, the people from PlanBude were placed in the parks and green space category. However, through the abundance of references to Park Fiction, they understood that residents not only wanted green space:

> [I]t showed that people were mentioning Park Fiction as often as they would name the Harbor and the Elbe River together, and that was something like really wow, okay what is important, and then you could see like what do people actually like about Park Fiction, and it was very helpful for us too.
> (Community intermediary 26, Hamburg, 2018)

For this, the PlanBude group figured that the residents wanted the space to be designed to stimulate social interactions and various uses.

4.4 From rules to enforcements

The results of the participatory process were summarized and present in two neighborhood meetings. The meetings resulted in the 'St. Pauli code' a set of seven rules that formulated requirements for development projects in the area:

1. Difference and diversity before homogeneity
2. Small-scale structures
3. Low-budget before luxury (cheap before expensive)
4. Originality and tolerance
5. Appropriation and vibrancy
6. Experiment and sub-culture
7. Open space without consumerism.

The rules codify the outcomes of the participatory process. The textuality of the code provides a framework in which actors can be held accountable for the promises they make; it stabilizes the relations between actors. The rules call for the embrace of subcultures and non-conformity. Moreover, in the presentation of the rules, there is an explicit call for schmuddeliger Glamour (trashy glamour); the particular culture of St. Pauli should be reflected in the new development plans. PlanBude engaged in a process of moral valuing that encompasses three different aspects. First, they made an evaluation of what is valuable and what is not valuable

(Heuts and Mol, 2013; Thévenot, 2002).This happened by comparing the input of residents and selecting recurring perspectives. Second, they engaged in a process of valorizing, the activity of making things more valuable (Heuts and Mol, 2013). The use of rooftops as public space is a striking example of this. Third, they turned all pieces of evidence into general principles, as seen in the St. Pauli Code (Boltanski and Thévenot, 1991). Through this process of valuing, drawings, models of plasticine, outcomes of seminars, sounds, and surveys were turned into unifying principles on text. Texts are key devices in transforming people's ideas, wishes, and needs in particular local settings and times into transcending generalities that are needed for political decision-making (Smith, 2001).

Interestingly, PlanBude used images to explain the meaning attached to the principles. Whereas a principle such as 'appropriation and vibrancy' can mean many things, the image shows that it should be allowed to appropriate space through graffiti, stickers, etc. Space might be privately owned but is created in a communal process. This should be allowed and stimulated in the building block according to PlanBude.

It is important to note that PlanBude was only able to complete this valuing process because they were trusted by the neighborhood residents. Attributing value to something is a process that needs to be accepted by a large group of people; otherwise, it fails to have meaning in social processes. Since there was not much resistance from neighborhood residents toward the St. Pauli Code, the St. Pauli Code could become a coordination mechanism. This does not mean that everybody was fond of the methods of PlanBude: "there are also some people who don't trust the PlanBude people, that they feel that they are too radical, too crazy, and too artistic, the more middle-class people, the more conservative people" (Politician 9, Hamburg, 2018). However, the disapproval was not strong enough that it gathered support to obstruct the position of PlanBude. Therefore, the St. Pauli Code could be presented and accepted as an unifying set of principles which could function as the starting point for the development process of the Esso-Häuser.

For the design process, several architects were invited to visit the area. The idea was to first introduce the architects to the (night)life of St. Pauli, before they would start designing. They were also extensively briefed on the results of the participatory process. Moreover, the architects had to present their preliminary plans to the neighborhood in order to receive feedback from residents. The jury who picked the final design included residents and ended up picking a plan by the Dutch architect Kamiel Klaasse. The design included rooftops with a basketball court and a climbing wall, shops that embraced counter-culture (including a queer-feminist sex shop), baugemeinschafts or housing cooperatives (where ownership of the buildings are collectively owned), social housing and market-rate housing, and a hotel. The market-rate housing and the hotel were a compromise with the Bayerische Hausbau.

All negotiating parties were happy with the design, and it seemed that the actors had overcome the planning-property contradiction by giving PlanBude ownership over the participatory process. Although PlanBude was a private entity, they were accepted as worthy actors who could organize the public process of organizing participation. Whereas PlanBude had already turned the many ideas, needs, and wishes of residents into a unifying set of principles, the transformation of the outcomes of the participatory process was not yet done. In order to start the development of a new building complex, one more hurdle needed to be overcome. The textuality of the St. Pauli code needed to be turned into enforceable commitments. The municipality and Bayerische Hausbau needed to sign a development agreement to stipulate what was going to be built. Without a development agreement, the municipality wouldn't change the land use plan. There was a sense of agreement around the main propositions of the development. None of the main actors had expressed the intention to be legally bound. A legal framework was needed to give confirmation to all actors that the complex would be built. Law gives an actor a higher degree of certainty that a promise will be kept. The durability of relationships in which the actor engages becomes stronger through legal guarantees (Weber, 1978). Thus, law stabilizes relationships in precise forms (Durkheim, 1984). Public and private law are commonly distinguished as different legal registers. In the sense that public law regulates the relationship between private citizens and the state and private law regulates relations between private citizens. However, as we see in the case of Esso-Häuser, there is a strong entanglement of public law and private law. A more useful distinction is to analyze the enforceability of legal orders (Stapper, 2021, 2022). Agreements can be used to give assurances to actors that a transaction will take place. When actors break promises that are given as an assurance, their reputation and relationships will be hurt, but the promise is not enforceable (Macaulay, 2003). When actors clearly state that they have the intention to be legally bound, an agreement becomes a commitment that is enforceable. Most legal orders—contracts, public laws—are a mix of assurances and commitments. Thus, a final transformation needs to take place, from individual ideas, needs, and wishes to general principles toward a legal order. This proved to be a contentious process. The open and transparent participatory process was suddenly pulled into the private sphere. Public debate was replaced by back-door negotiations that would take more than three years before they were completed.

Whereas the Bayerische Hausbau had allowed PlanBude to organize the participatory process, they still wanted to make a profit. It was clear that the capitalist-democracy contradiction was not dealt with yet. Especially the housing cooperatives brought the negotiating parties almost to a breaking point: "both the investor and PlanBude, are really, you can say that, they are really fighting for their interests" (Politician 9, Hamburg, 2018). Bayerische Hausbau wanted market rate prices for the land, whereas PlanBude wanted affordable prices. Bayerische Hausbau threatened to walk away from negotiations, postponed meetings, and gave the impression that they were not in a hurry to come to an agreement. During the negotiations, the actors invoked notions of the common good. PlanBude invoked a civic notion of the common good—residents should decide—while Bayerische Hausbau invoked a market notion of the common good—the property owner should decide. PlanBude had agreed to include a hotel and market-rate housing, which was against the St. Pauli Code, but was a compromise they were willing to take. They were not willing to compromise on the prices for the housing cooperatives.

Although Bayerisch Hausbau had the benefit during the private sphere, the issue of Esso-Häuser had become too public. So, in the end, Bayerische Hausbau and Plan-Bude agreed to compromise on the housing cooperatives. One-third would become market rate, and two-thirds would become affordable. After this compromise, the parties agreed to sign the development agreement.

4.5 The mechanics of urban politics

To sum up, institutional fault lines of cities constitute the property-planning and the capitalism-democracy contradiction. Junctures in these fault lines are created by weaving morals, politics, and laws together. Those registers turn local particularities into generalities that are able to mobilize support from actors. Morals enable actors to evaluate and navigate in uncertain circumstances. By drawing in the support of moral artifacts, actors can coordinate with each other and undertake collective action. Politics pulls actors and objects into the public or the private sphere. Actors and objects in the public sphere are subjected to democratic practices and steering processes through officials, whereas actors and objects in the private sphere are ordered through market mechanisms. Disputes in the private sphere are mainly settled through mediators. Laws increase the probability that the expectations of actors will come out. By establishing sanctions and through the enforcement of those sanctions, the law stabilizes the way actors coordinate their actions.

Although urban actors are deeply embedded in structural positions, the property-planning and capitalism-democracy contradictions create situations in which there is a lot of uncertainty. The critical capacity of urban actors results in the activation of pragmatic registers to create junctures in those contradictions. The critiques of the residents of St. Pauli helped to introduce a novel way of combining moral, political, and legal arrangements in the Esso-Häuser project. Time will tell whether this will be reproduced across Hamburg and thus lead to a new institutional order.

References

Boltanski, Luc. 2011. *On Critique: A Sociology of Emancipation*. Cambridge: Polity Press.

Boltanski, Luc, and Laurent Thévenot. 1991. *On Justification: Economies of Worth*. Princeton: Princeton University Press.

Dewey, John. 1927. *The Public and Its Problems*. Ohio University Press.

Dewey, John, and Arthur Bentley. 1949. *Knowing and the Known*. Boston: Beacon Press.

Durkheim, E. 1984. *The Division of Labour in Society*. London: The MacMillan Press.

Emirbayer, Mustafa. 1997. "Manifesto for a Relational Sociology." *American Journal of Sociology* 103 (2): 281–317.

Foglesong, R.E. 1986. *Planning the Capitalist City: The Colonial Era to the 1920s*. Princeton: Princeton University Press.

Gassdorf, Ulrich, and Marlies Fischer. 2013. "Prominente Abrissgegner." *Die Welt*.

Hall, Stuart. 1996. "New Ethnicities." In *Critical Dialogues in Cultural Studies*, edited by David Morly and Kuan-Hsing Chen, 441–49. New York: Routledge.

Heuts, Frank, and Annemarie Mol. 2013. "What Is a Good Tomato? A Case of Valuing in Practice." *Valuation Studies* 1 (2): 125–46. https://doi.org/10.3384/vs.2001-5992.1312125.

Kaiser, L. 2010, September 22. "Gentrifizierung Auf Dem Areal Der 'Esso Häuser' Am Spielbudenplatz Könnte Die Politik Eine Der Letzten Chancen Nutzen, Der Yuppisierung von St. Pauli Etwas Entgegenzusetzen." *Taz*.
Kaiser, Lena. 2012. "Kein Abriss Ohne Kompromiss." *Die Tageszeitung*.
Kaiser, Lena, and Kai Von Appen. 2010. "Büroturm Im Sperrgebiet." *Die Tageszeitung*.
Lamont, M. 1992. *Money, Morals, and Manners*. Chicago and London: The University of Chicago Press.
Levine, Jeremy R. 2017. "The Paradox of Community Power: Cultural Processes and Elite Authority in Participatory Governance" 95 (3): 1155–79. https://doi.org/10.1093/sf/sow098.
Logan, R.J., and H.L. Molotch. 1987. *Urban Futures: The Political Economy of Place*. Berkeley, Los Angeles and London: University of California Press.
Macaulay, Stewart. 2003. "The Real and the Paper Deal: Empirical Pictures of Relationships, Complexity and the Urge for Transparent Simple Rules." *The Modern Law Review Limited* 311 (1): 44–79.
McGee, Kyle. 2015. "Introduction." In *Latour and the Passage of Law*, edited by Kyle McGee. Edinburgh University Press.
Mol, Annemarie. 2010. "Actor-Network Theory: Sensitive Terms and Enduring Tensions." *Soziologische Theorie Kontrovers* 50: 253–70.
Sayer, Andrew. 2010. "Class and Morality." In *Handbook of the Sociology of Morality*, edited by S. Hitlin and S. Vaisey, 163–78. New York.
Schäfer, D. 2014, April 25. "Anwohner Wollen Selbst Ideen Für Neubau Auf Esso-Areal Entwickeln." *Die Welt*.
Smith, Dorothy E. 2001. "Texts and the Ontology of Organizations and Institutions." *Culture and Organization* 7 (2): 159–98.
Stapper, E.W. 2021. September. "Contracting with Citizens: How Residents in Hamburg and New York Negotiated Development Agreements." *Land Use Policy* 111: 105743. https://doi.org/10.1016/j.landusepol.2021.105743.
Stapper, E.W. 2022. "Private Ordering of Public Processes: How Contracts Structure Participatory Processes in Urban Development in Amsterdam and Hamburg." *Urban Studies* 59 (9): 1872–88. https://doi.org/10.1177/00420980211024144.
Stein, S. 2019. *Capital City: Gentrification and the Real Estate State*. London and New York: Verso.
Thévenot, Laurent. 2002. "Which Road to Follow? The Moral Complexity of an 'Equipped' Humanity." In *Complexities: Social Studies of Knowledge Practices*, edited by John Law and Annemarie Mol, 53–87. Durham and London: Duke University Press. https://doi.org/10.1215/9780822383550-003.
Weber, Max. 1978. *Economy and Society: An Outline of Interpretive Sociology*. Los Angeles and London: University of California Press.
Welt Online. 2014, April 24. "Bürgerbeteiligung; Esso-Häuser-Initiative Pocht Auf Mitspracherecht." *Welt Online*.
Yaneva, Albena. 2009. "Making the Social Hold: Towards an Actor-Network Theory of Design." *Design and Culture* 1 (3): 273–88. https://doi.org/10.2752/174967809x12556950208826.
Young, Iris Marion. 1990. *Justice and the Politics of Difference*. New York: Princeton University Press.
Young, Iris Marion. 2000. *Inclusion and Democracy*. New York: Oxford University Press.
Zand-Vakili, A. 2014, August 4. "Geheimpapier: Staatsschutz Warnt Vor Weiteren Linksradikalen Anschlägen." *Die Welt*.

5 Morals in the city

True spokespersons and principles

Modernist towers in honeycomb patterns once dominated the south-east of Amsterdam. Architects and city planners inspired by CIAM—Congrès Internationaux d'Architecture Moderne—built a vertical city in the grasslands neighboring Amsterdam. With the intention to create a modern utopia, they separated traffic flows and built high-rises surrounded by parks. Parking lots were built to give inhabitants a place to park their cars, while a metro line was built to connect the neighborhood with the city center of Amsterdam. The new neighborhood was called Bijlmer. Imagined as a utopia, separating traffic flows should have led to less hassle, less chaos, and fewer traffic accidents. But it turned out that urban chaos also provided safety to city dwellers. Without the protection of buzzing crowds, crime crept into the neighborhood. It also became a heavily segregated neighborhood; the white middle class left the area, and the residents were predominately from Suriname, the Caribbean, and Ghana. The failures of modernist planning have been extensively analyzed and criticized by urban scholars such as Jane Jacobs and James C. Scott (Jacobs, 1961; Scott, 1998).

This chapter will follow the events that play out around the K-Buurt in the Bijlmer. The chapter aims to explain how actors claim the mantle of being the true spokesperson of the neighborhood and create guiding principles for collective action. This is a moral process, a process of valuing. The process of valuing has three steps: setting apart what is valuable and what is not valuable, making actors and objects more valuable, and generating generalized principles. The point of this chapter is to show how the process of valuing is firmly embedded in materialities and the position of actors within society. Qualifications need to be tested; it is not a merely linguistic exercise. Plans can promise utopia on paper but can mobilize resistance in society.

Next, the process of valuing distinguishes between who is worthy of making political decisions or drawing up and enforcing legal arrangements. Therefore, it is entangled with political and legal processes, creating hierarchies regarding who and what can engage in them.

Claiming the mantle of being the true spokesperson of the neighborhood is an important moral and political process. In this process, the question of who is worthy of speaking for the neighborhood is being addressed. This is not merely a political process in which designated persons are positioned as neighborhood representatives,

DOI: 10.4324/9781032712840-5

such as politicians or civil servants. However, this is a highly moral process in which the spokesperson must earn the worth of speaking for the neighborhood. This gives them a moral aura that makes them highly trusted by the communities they represent. For example, politicians can lose their worthiness of being the true spokesperson of the neighborhood when they make decisions that go against the interests of most neighborhood residents. Often, local activists then take over the mantle of being the true spokesperson from the politicians. In that instance, the local activists become more valuable, whereas the politicians are being devalued.

Next, the process of valuing is also entangled with legal processes. The complexities of public disputes are being turned into general principles. These principles help distinguish between who and what is valuable and are the starting point for legal arrangements. Principles can be turned into legal arrangements when they become enforceable. But often, those principles are not yet legally enforceable. They can be the summaries of a participatory meeting, a special code designed by residents, or criteria used in a request for proposal. Closely connected to legal institutions, however, they are often not binding.

5.1 The city planners plan

The imagined utopia of the Bijlmer soon became known in the Netherlands as one of the most notorious neighborhoods (Pinkster et al., 2020). Faced with growing problems in the area, city planners and politicians drew up plans to improve the neighborhood. This also happened in the K-Buurt, in the south-east of Amsterdam south-east. City planners and politicians engaged in a process of valuing the K-Buurt. The city planners evaluated what is valuable and what is not (Heuts and Mol, 2013; Thévenot, 2002).

The city planners devalued the once-hailed principles of CIAM. The area's separated traffic flows were being integrated. The high-rise was replaced by single-family housing, which was deemed to be worthy housing for the area. The choice to replace modernist high-rise with single-family housing also had implications for its inhabitants. The inhabitants of the modernist high-rise were being devalued, while future inhabitants of single-family housing were being valued as being worthy of living in the K-Buurt.

Next, the city planners wanted to demolish the shopping mall Kraaiennest. The shopping mall was built according to the principles of CIAM. The entrances to the mall were small, and there were not many windows. The mall became known as a place that could be dangerous. Pressured to go ahead with the urban renewal plans for the Bijlmer, a new shopping area was developed a few metro stops from Kraaiennest. This led to vacancies in the shopping mall. Kraaiennest became stuck in a downward spiral, and thus, the municipality decided to demolish the building. The walls were broken down, and the field was cleared entirely so that only a green field remained where once the residents of the area had a meeting place. It should be noted that the problems of the neighborhood weren't solved; they were displaced. The closing of the shopping mall didn't solve problems with crime in the neighborhood. Moreover, the neighborhood lost a meeting place.

The second step of the valuing process is the activity of making things more valuable (Heuts and Mol, 2013). The green field was more valuable to the municipality than the shopping mall. The green field could attract investors, while the shopping mall could not. The same goes for the future inhabitants of single-family housing. They are deemed to be more prosperous and able to give a boost to local shops and businesses. This is in line with the strategy of 'social mixing' that many Dutch municipalities pursued in disadvantaged neighborhoods since the 1980s. The idea behind social mixing is to mix low-income families with middle-class families to prevent 'poverty pockets'. This would boost social mobility and revitalize neighborhoods. Through social mixing, municipalities could better manage those neighborhoods (Uitermark and Bosker, 2014). Notably, wealthy neighborhoods were never the target of 'social mixing' strategies. Moreover, this process is heavily racialized; low-income families in disadvantaged neighborhoods are often migrants or people from former Dutch colonies (Smets and Den Uyl, 2008).

The third step is turning all the complexities of reality into general principles (Boltanski and Thévenot, 1991). The municipality attempted to do that by developing a new land use plan that designated a significant area for housing. There was a strong feeling that the city should act quickly because the economy was improving but that could change again. Moreover, the demolition of the shopping mall and the renovation of infrastructure in the area were development costs; the rest of the development should result in a profit. "Then the crisis hit, and the vacant plots never got developed. . . . They stand there like a kind of profit yet to be made" (Civil servant 3, Amsterdam 1, 2017). The land use plan aimed to attract investors so development agreements could be signed.

Moreover, the city wanted to build quickly more housing to deal with the growing housing crisis. The complexities the city planner regarded were mostly the complexities of the bureaucracy of the municipality. Costs regarding the neighborhood's infrastructure were made in the past, and those costs needed to be covered. Moreover, there was a city-wide need for more housing. This resulted in a land use plan primarily geared toward the needs of the municipality, not the neighborhood's residents.

Thus, the city planners mostly valued the K-Buurt through the market register. Their goals were to make a profit, attract investors, and respond to the demand for more housing.

But this time, many residents were fed up with the plans from the municipality. Since the 1970s, the municipality had responded to problems in the area by demolishing buildings and attempting to attract new residents. The residents of the K-Buurt felt they should represent the neighborhood's interests, not the planners and politicians. They gathered on the square—next to the demolished shopping mall—and stood in the shape of a heart, holding hands. The picture showed a diverse group of people claiming the right to have a say over development plans in the area. What we see here is an object—the picture—is drawn in to support the political claims of actors. With the picture, the residents claimed to be the true neighborhood representatives. The photo shows the diversity in terms of class, race, and gender of the neighborhood and is a sharp contrast with the city planners who are predominately higher educated and white. Through this process, the residents distinguished between who is valuable and who is less valuable in the neighborhood. Moreover, they made a strong appeal to the municipality to open a public debate about the future of the K-Buurt. They asked policy makers to open up a public, because they wanted to be included in decision-making processes (Dewey, 1927; Young, 1990).

The actions of the residents show their critical capacity and ability to mobilize against a dominant register. The neighborhood residents activated the civic register to resist the market register invoked by the city planners. The city planners invoked the market register to justify their plans; the reasoning was that the economy was good, and the municipality had to act quickly. The residents were activating the civic register to defend their claim as the true spokesperson of the neighborhood. It is a clash with three layers: a legal clash between giving priority to development agreements versus public input on land use plans; a moral clash between what is valued more—the potential profitability of a project and the needs of residents; and a political clash whether there should be governed through supply and demand or through democratic processes.

The fault lines between residents and planners also have a distinctive material layer. The residents mobilized their bodies to claim they represented a very diverse neighborhood. The sign of the heart symbolizes both their centrality to the neighborhood and their need for a new heart for the neighborhood after the loss of the shopping mall. The group also became known as the heart of the K-Buurt (HoftKB). The pictures that landed in newspapers pressured politicians to have a second look at the plans.

5.2 Educating the residents

The actions of the residents had an effect and were promptly supported by politicians from various parties. The idea that residents wanted an active role in urban development fitted with most municipal policies. Thus, the municipality changed course, and the city commissioner of spatial planning promised the neighborhood they could organize the participatory process themselves. Thus, they opened up a public about the future of the K-Buurt (Dewey, 1927; Young, 1990). But this led to a problem for the municipality, because HoftKB was an unknown entity that suddenly claimed to represent the neighborhood. They did not have legal documents arranging them as an association, they did not have a long history in the neighborhood, nor was there a clear leadership. This shows the importance of the materiality of law in the process of claiming the mantle of being the spokesperson of the neighborhood. The legal documents would show that the group has the potential to become a stable partner of other actors. It would reduce the unpredictability of the group.

Another problematic point for the municipality was that various other organizations represented the neighborhood. There was even an umbrella organization that officially represented a broad coalition of neighborhood organizations in the area. Some of the neighborhood organizations voiced their opposition to this new group.

Thus, it was decided that a consultancy firm would organize the participatory process and aim to bring the neighborhood together as much as possible. However, the municipality also had listened to HoftKB's critique. It gave the consultancy firm the mission to provide residents an active role and decision-making power over the result. This shows that simply activating a pragmatic register does not automatically mobilize support from other actors. The register needs to be tested. When there is enough resistance to the register, the register will either need to adapt to local circumstances or become less relevant. Moreover, this shows that the municipality changed the way they justified their plans; the market registers failed to mobilize support. Thus, they started to invoke other registers: the civic register to justify the involvement of citizens, but also the entrepreneurial register to justify collaboration between actors. Although HoftKB wanted to organize the participatory processes, and were instrumental in opening the public, they could not decide on how public debate would be organized.

The consultancy firm organized a participatory process that included six co-creation workshops, an advisory board of residents that would support the design of the plans, and the opportunity to vote on three alternative plans for all residents. The co-creation workshops allowed everybody to participate in the planning process. The planners aimed to mobilize support through the workshops by promoting collaboration and creativity through the entrepreneurial register. Next, they tried mobilizing support through the civic register by involving residents in decision-making. The advisory board consisted of residents from each part of the K-Buurt. This showcased that the board was (at least geographically) representative of the neighborhood. The voting on the plans displayed that the process was democratic. Thus, what was being valued and what was not being valued changed. Instead of a process without public discussion, co-creation and involving residents became more valued. Instead of valuing the goals of municipal actors and investors, the needs of residents were commended.

When the participatory process started, HoftKB protested that they could not design it. They felt that the commissioner of spatial planning had promised them to organize the participatory processes themselves. However, they decided to participate in the process cautiously. During the advisory board's first meeting, this led to a conflict between Mike Brantjes and the consultants. Mike Brantjes proposed seven rules for the participatory processes. An attempt was made by HoftKB to create general principles to ensure that residents would have the final say in decision-making processes and cement the position of HoftKB as the lead spokesperson for the neighborhood. However, the seven rules were 'taken into account' by the consultancy firm and the city planners and HoftKB was deemed "just one of the organizations representing residents" (email from civil servant, 2017).

In response, HoftKB threatened to pull back from the participatory process. However, a local politician intervened and convinced the people from HoftKB to stay involved. During the conversation between the local politician and HoftKB, the local politician explained: "We know that you can mobilize people and create energy in the neighborhood. It would be a waste not to do something with that energy. But you cannot be the only partner we work with" (Politician 5, Amsterdam,

2017). The attempt of HoftKB to claim the mantle of being the spokespersons of the neighborhood failed. The municipality's response toward HoftKB's claim showcases the way participatory processes can fragment the influence residents have. Residents have to prove that they are not speaking for themselves but articulating widely shared perspectives. Civil servants and consultants can dismiss residents by arguing that they speak for themselves. Thus, the efforts to change the process of valuing from the market register to the civic register in the participatory process largely succeeded, but the civic register was not omnipotent.

Meanwhile, tensions between the different actors rose again. Neighborhood residents enthusiastically visited the first co-creation workshop. However, over time, the number of visitors has become less diverse. People of color predominately live in the neighborhood, but they showed up less and less at the workshops. Some of the consultants and civil servants also responded to the residents' statements in a very technocratic way. In the discussion, two spatial issues came up again and again. Residents wanted to realize a lively square in the middle of the new development.

Moreover, they tried to move the entrance to the subway station. The subway station split the neighborhood into two, creating a physical barrier. However, the subway station was recently renovated. Whereas the municipality was willing to listen to the arguments about the square, they were dismissive about the subway station.

The municipality had already renovated the subway station and demolished the old modernist infrastructure and shopping mall; the area was simply "millions in the minus" (Civil servant 3, Amsterdam 2017). New developments should make even for those earlier investments: "everything that was paid by the government is realized, and all the housing that should have been developed by the market is not there" (Civil servant 4, Amsterdam 2017). This demonstrates that while the municipality used the civic and entrepreneurial registers to justify its actions toward the broader public, it still fell back on the market register to distinguish between worthy and unworthy proposals in the participatory process. The processes needed to be justified for the residents in the K-Buurt and internally in the municipality. Within the municipality, the market register seemed to be the only register able to mobilize support. The civil servants active in the participatory process had to balance dealing with the dynamics of the participatory process and the internal structure of the municipality. The Excel sheets used by the civil servants required them to make up for costs made years ago. However, the civil servants were also instructed to adhere to residents' wishes.

The city planners of Amsterdam are deeply ingrained with particular practices. As discussed in Chapter 3, the city of Amsterdam has a strong tradition of comprehensive planning. Layers of plans pull a preferred future into being. The spatial vision of Amsterdam coordinates these plans over long periods: 10–15 years. Elections do have an effect, and new policy documents can trigger changes in planning practices.

Moreover, the city of Amsterdam is divided into seven boroughs, and those can make different choices. However, there is a strong tendency to follow the direction set out in the major planning documents of Amsterdam. City planners of Amsterdam are commonly educated at the University of Amsterdam, especially at the Department of Geography, Planning, and International Development Studies. They often feel strongly responsible for the city and have strong opinions about how the city should develop. They are career officials who work mainly on a project basis. They develop plans and negotiate with developers and investors when they work on a project.

In most cases, the city planners take the initiative. Since most land is leased, the city has a lot of leverage over development policies. Moreover, the municipality also invests in development projects (Needham, 2007). All the plans start with an extensive overview of how the plan relates to other municipal plans—from environmental plans to cultural-historical heritage plans to regional and national plans. This constrains how civil servants can consider the ideas and needs of residents. The idea that K-Buurt has already received considerable investments and has to make even with new developments should also be seen in this light. The civil servants review the municipal plans and the Excel sheets with financial models. They are trained to follow these directives as far as possible, although they can also develop creative solutions. Thus, the municipality apparatus privileges its practices above the practices of residents.

The dominance of the market register within the municipality limited how civil servants could act in the case of the K-Buurt. However, they were committed to justifying the participatory processes through the entrepreneurial and civic registers. A compromise emerged because they had to justify their actions in two distinct arenas. The civic and entrepreneurial registers were activated in the actions toward the residents, but the residents had to justify their actions to the municipality through the market register.

For example, the municipality organized training sessions about how the municipality operated. Residents received training in architectural principles and how the municipality makes public value capture models. These training sessions were one-directional; the residents needed to be educated on how the municipality operated, while there were no training sessions about how the neighborhood worked for the civil servants. In those sessions, it was constantly mentioned that everything had a cost. To illustrate, during the workshop on public value capturing, a civil servant explained that "the length of the participatory process costs money because of the delays in decision-making. This project is very costly" (Civil servant 3, Amsterdam, 2017). Residents' wishes could only be realized if enough investors and developers could be attracted. This forced residents to think along with the municipality during the participatory process rather than a municipality that aimed to incorporate the needs of residents in their plans. The ideas and needs of residents had to be translated into a set of goals that are compatible with the city's plans. The discussions and designs in co-creation workshops had to be translated into texts that can be integrated into other texts: texts used for communication purposes, texts used for new policy documents, and texts for contracts.

However, this doesn't mean that the market register can be forced upon the residents in totality. The residents would protest if they felt they were not taken seriously. The participatory process aimed to mobilize support from the residents for future development plans in the neighborhood. Complete citizen control over the participatory process had proved to be difficult partly because it was hard for government actors to decide who would be the spokespersons for the neighborhood and partly because they wanted to earn money through the development process. Therefore, the civic register was activated to make political decisions; the residents would decide which plan for the neighborhood would be the best alternative. However, the plans would be created through co-creation and collaboration in workshops. In these workshops, residents could collectively develop designs. Each workshop would have different themes, ranging from general needs to the design of the neighborhood square. These workshops were organized mainly through the entrepreneurial register. Post-its, flip-overs, and Legos were used to create a new vision for the neighborhood playfully.

This is different from a participatory process organized by activating the civic register. The civic register would value a centralized discussion and making decisions through voting. An entrepreneurial approach to participation lacks a centralized discussion and values creativity and collaboration. A stark contrast between the civic and the entrepreneurial register is that the civic register sees participation as a right, whereas the entrepreneurial register sees participation as a responsibility. The entrepreneurial register values those who enthusiastically participate, whereas the civic register would put the burden on reaching out to neighborhood residents civil servants, and politicians.

The Post-its signal that everybody can voice which issues they think are important. One of the attendants said: "Last time they wrote a nice report with all the points written [on post-its]. If you don't write something down, it's not there. So, I thought, I will write something' (Csome, 2017). This shows the importance of filling in the Post-its for reporting and that it is an individualized exercise. Lacking a central discussion with questions and answers, the civil servants will contextualize and analyze the issues from the Post-its. The Lego stimulates playfulness and gives the possibility to create a design together. The focus is on creativity and design, not on who is attending the meeting or who is making decisions. "We have received a lot of input, see how many ideas we received [noting at a map with pins with ideas], we take all those ideas into consideration" (Csome, 2017). A resident noted, "I just hope that we also include the people who are not here now, also the people that are now at home and do not know about this meeting."

Thus, residents were trained to work with the municipality to achieve municipal goals. Moreover, the words they speak in a participatory setting were translated into policy language. Civil servants mostly coordinated this translation process. They made the minutes of meetings and selected which ideas to be highlighted and how problems should be described. In this translation process, there is a tendency to skew contradictory views or conflict. This results in a set of unequivocal and unified goals considered the residents' principles for development projects. An important step in the process of valuing is generating generalized principles. These residents' principles include goals formulated by residents but aligned with municipal plans and filtered through civil servants. Contrarian opinions, conflicting perspectives, and contestations are displaced.

Using co-creation workshops to give moral and political significance to a participatory process makes it harder to use legal instruments only shaped by civil servants or politicians. The legal tools that are used should be flexible to align with the set-up of the co-creation workshops. Residents might be hesitant to sign a contract with many pages and clauses in legal language but willing to support a set of principles. Moreover, a set of principles leaves more space for interpretation and is thus more flexible than a detailed contract. This is linked to the civic and entrepreneurial registers. Whereas the market register would justify seeing residents as equal parties that can negotiate about shared risks and responsibilities, the civic register sets residents apart as citizens with rights that must be protected. The entrepreneurial register sees residents as creative agents. Thus, whereas the market register could justify a contract signed by residents, the entrepreneurial and civic registers would justify a set of principles in a neighborhood code. The difference between the entrepreneurial register and the civic register is that the entrepreneurial register values shared responsibilities. In contrast, the civic register nudges towards the protection of rights.

This shows that civic, market, and entrepreneurial registers are used to transcend local particularities and mobilize support. However, they are often activated in entangled forms. The more general justifications allow mobilization in sites further away. They help gain support from city councils and boardrooms. But closer to the area itself, the justifications become more specific and often compromise different elements of the registers.

However, a compromise between different registers needs to hold or mobilize more support from actors. This can be seen the moment the alternative plans were presented. Instead of three, the municipality presented only two alternative plans. The first plan was called 'social and open,' and the second was called 'intimate and closed.' The guiding principles of the 'social and open' design were:

- The buildings are separated from each other through courtyards and small streets.
- The space in between building blocks is semi-public. All residents are welcome, but at night, fences will close in the area.
- There will be space for apartments.

The guiding principles of the 'intimate and closed' design were:

- There is no separation between buildings and there is a clear distinction between public and private space.
- The courtyards are private.
- There is space for family housing with gardens and apartments.

There were no mentions of the neighborhood square or the metro station, which residents prioritized. Although the 'social and open' alternative has public space, it does not address residents' questions about facilitating meeting spaces for the diverse social groups in the neighborhood. The principles are mostly filtered through the municipality's need to adhere to internal financial and regulatory procedures. Both alternatives fit quite well with standard planning practices throughout Amsterdam.

This is an example of how the capitalist-democracy contradiction is administered in a way that favors the accumulation of capital over democratic processes. The project needs to break even financially, and therefore negotiations with investors and developers are given more weight than negotiations with residents. Thus, the capitalism-democracy contradiction is dealt with by prioritizing processes of capital accumulation. Moreover, the capitalism-democracy contradiction strongly pressures the municipality to work through the market register, even educating residents to work within the register.

Also, in the case of the K-Buurt, the city formulated the residents' principles for the residents—although there was supervision from the advisory board, they needed to be aligned with municipal goals. The residents' principles were thus filtered through the municipal apparatus. This had another—unintended—consequence. The civil servants and consultants organizing the participatory process were higher educated. They expressed themselves in a professional language that was familiar to the higher-educated residents of the K-Buurt, but not for the residents without a college degree. Moreover, you need time to participate. For working people, especially those with families, it might be hard to have an active role in a participatory process. This leads to the reproduction of social inequalities through the participatory process. This leads to the formulation of citizens' principles that are skewed toward the needs of the already privileged residents of the K-Buurt.

5.3 The residents take charge

When two alternative plans were presented instead of three, and the two plans looked very similar, HoftKB had enough. They boycotted the voting process, and during the presentation of the plans, they called for a participatory strike. They walked toward the microphone with banners and claimed that the neighborhood did not support the plans. This action effectively discredited the way public debate had been organized in the K-Buurt; it did not reflect the diversity of the neighborhood. This had a considerable impact on the neighborhood. People actively participating in the participatory process felt disappointed that all their time and energy seemed wasted. Civil servants and consultants felt like they had done something wrong. The people who called for the participation strike felt like they had crossed a line, although they felt forced to do it. Through their participation strike and their appropriation of the presentation of the plans, HoftKB claimed the mantle of being the true spokespersons of the neighborhood. Their claim has a strong material aspect; they used banners, claimed the microphone, and appropriated the space in which the municipality's plans were presented. These material objects are strongly associated with social movements that go against vested interests. Moreover, HoftKB used a picture of one of the participatory meetings in the media to show that the public processes needed to be more representative of the neighborhood. The photo showed mostly white people, while the neighborhood is predominately Black.

HoftKB invoked the civic register to become spokespersons for the neighborhood. Most importantly, their claim was not resisted. People responded with disappointment, but there was no strong rejection of their claim. This shows how the activation of registers and the claim of being representative must always be tested. If other groups in the neighborhood had publicly supported the municipal plans or discredited the HoftKB, the municipality could have continued with its plans. However, this did not happen, and the municipality felt they had to freeze their plans. Their compromise of the civic and entrepreneurial register had failed to mobilize support in the neighborhood. Moreover, the HoftKB was unwilling to compromise and clashed with the municipality. The HoftKB received attention from the media, in which they could explain their side of the story, while the municipality did not receive such a platform. The moral and political significance of the participatory process was too weak to result in enforceable agreements.

After the participation strike, there were local elections, and new politicians took office. As described in Chapter 3, the new Groot Wassink administration invoked the civic register to justify a new democratization agenda. The democratization agenda aimed to give the people of Amsterdam more ownership and decision-making power over their neighborhoods. This created a new political current in Amsterdam. Moreover, HoftKB organized election debates and filmed politicians while they were taking positions. This kind of material strategy had two functions: to hold future politicians accountable and to spread the work of HoftKB through various WhatsApp groups. The Green Party had won the local elections and was sympathetic to HoftKB. These created a strong political position for HoftKB.

Their political standing affected the way the city planners treated the HoftKB. Civil servants were tasked with making amends with HoftKB and creating a plan for the neighborhood together. HoftKB would be recognized as the representatives of the neighborhood. They did not have to compete with other groups anymore. During the participation strike, HoftKB also criticized consultants for being paid to do their work, while residents had to give advice, come up with solutions, and participate for free. Therefore, three members of HoftKB got financial compensation to negotiate directly with the municipality.

This led to a change in the relationship between HoftKB and the municipality. During meetings, civil servants tried to understand the viewpoints of residents. When residents wanted the municipality to acknowledge that the K-Buurt was an evening neighborhood, the civil servants initially did not know what to do. Thus, they talked about what the acknowledgment meant for the residents. The residents explained that, for example, in the Caribbean culture, much of the social life is in the evening and on the streets. But there are no good spaces available to meet in the evening in the K-Buurt. There is also no evening shop in the whole of Amsterdam South East. The same goes for coffee shops (the first coffee shop in Amsterdam South East opened in the center in 2017 (Witte et al., 2016). This meant that residents made use of street dealers. The municipality of Amsterdam had actively prevented the creation of meeting places in the evening, evening shops, and coffee shops in order to fight crime in the area. However, this also limited the ability of residents to socialize with each other and arguably led to more crime. Therefore, the civil servants recognized that the K-Buurt was an evening neighborhood and made this one of the pillars of the new design. Thus, the HoftKB used the civic register to mobilize support from politicians and their neighborhood residents. Their mobilization of support was durable enough that they could position themselves as the true spokespersons of the neighborhood. Their position was even strong enough to affect the attitudes and practices of the city planners. The interests of developers and investors were no longer prioritized but the interests of HoftKB. Their activism tilted the democracy-capitalism contradiction towards more democratic practices instead of capital accumulation.

HoftKB was now a recognized negotiation partner and co-organizer of the participatory process in the K-Buurt. They could decide, together with the municipality, about how the organize public debate. HoftKB started to receive funding from the municipality and was invited to meetings at the municipality. Instead of residents who needed to think along the municipality, the residents from the HoftKB educated the municipality on several issues. This made the negotiation process between HoftKB and the municipality two-directional; both groups of actors needed to learn from each other. The municipality also started to change some of its practices. For example, giving financial compensation to residents is rare in Amsterdam. The justification for deviating from standard practices was often that it was an experiment; in this way, the entrepreneurial register was activated. Activating the entrepreneurial register was important for finding support within the municipality. Deviating from common practices is difficult, but framing it as an experiment mobilized support from actors within the municipality. The new way of cooperating between HoftKB and the municipality led to several small and big initiatives, from a new participatory process to design a land use plan to create a team of volunteer handymen that helped residents to isolate their homes better. HoftKB also started to receive funding for its activities from the municipality. This also meant that HoftKB needed to become a legal association and professionalize its practices. The volunteers from HoftKB were to become proficient in making budgets with Excel, writing reports, and knowing how the different layers of government worked. They also needed to change their practices.

The residents of the K-Buurt also recognized the relative success of HoftKB. The leader of HoftKB—Mike Brantjes—was often approached when something needed to be fixed or changed. HoftKB organized weekly meet-ups where residents could chat and socialize. The HoftKB sign was seen all across the neighborhood. This made HoftKB the authority in the K-Buurt, which mediated the relationship between the municipality and the neighborhood. When residents had a problem, they went to HoftKB, not to politicians or civil servants. The proximity of the members of HoftKB played a crucial role in this. They could be approached through WhatsApp, calling, or simply dropping by. The members of the HoftKB could also speak the language of the neighborhood and the language of the municipality. They strengthened their position as the mediators of the neighborhood.

This does not imply that their role was not criticized within the neighborhood or that the municipality accepted their role as representatives in every instance. From time to time other groups voiced their opposition to HoftKB, which the members of HoftKB needed to address. They often did this by joining meetings of different organizations, going on local radio shows, and convincing people to cooperate. They needed to be very diplomatic in order to cement their position within the neighborhood. HoftKB also required to prove their claim of being the neighborhood's representatives towards the municipality occasionally. The municipality started implementing participatory budgeting as part of its new democratization agenda. HoftKB was asked to mobilize the neighborhood, but they weren't given influence over how the process was organized. This annoyed HoftKB, mainly because the participatory budgets gave residents a say about small initiatives in the neighborhood but not about structural processes. HoftKB argued that neighborhoods should not be forced to use the participatory budgeting technique and that other ways of working with communities were also possible. But in this case, HoftKB lost the argument, and the municipality went ahead with their plans.

5.4 The moral thread in urban politics

This chapter describes the moral thread in urban politics. The moral thread is woven together with the political and legal threads to deal with conflicts and uncertainty. The moral thread plays an important role in prescribing how society ought to be, what is being valued, and what is being devalued. This provides actors with a notion of how to deal with uncertain situations. It provides a path forward. The moral thread makes actors and objects more valuable or less valuable. This is an important process because it gives actors the opportunity to claim the mantle of being the true spokesperson of the neighborhood and create generalized principles in the form of residents' principles. This allows them to coordinate actions from various actors.

The story of the K-Buurt shows that the process of claiming the mantle of being the true spokesperson of the neighborhood and creating residents' principles is precarious. HoftKB smartly used their connection with politicians and the media to claim their position; they were not willing to compromise on essential issues and gained the support of the neighborhood. But their position is contested from time to time. The role of being the true spokesperson of the neighborhood is both a mediating and a translating role. In the mediating role, the representatives have to resolve differences between the practices of the municipality and residents. In the translating role, the spokesperson plays an important role in translating moral and political significance into enforceable agreements.

References

Boltanski, Luc, and Laurent Thévenot. 1991. *On Justification: Economies of Worth*. Princeton: Princeton University Press.

Csome. 2017. "K Buurt D2." https://www.youtube.com/watch?v=O7OW2uvsSKc.

Dewey, John. 1927. *The Public and Its Problems*. Ohio University Press.
Heuts, Frank, and Annemarie Mol. 2013. "What Is a Good Tomato? A Case of Valuing in Practice." *Valuation Studies* 1 (2): 125–46. https://doi.org/10.3384/vs.2001–5992.1312125.
Jacobs, Jane. 1961. *The Death and Life of Great American Cities*. Random House.
Needham, Barrie. 2007. *Dutch Land Use Planning: Planning and Managing Land Use in the Netherlands, the Principles and the Practice*. The Hague: Sdu Uitgevers.
Pinkster, Fenne M., Marijn S. Ferier, and Myrte S. Hoekstra. 2020. "On the Stickiness of Territorial Stigma: Diverging Experiences in Amsterdam's Most Notorious Neighbourhood." *Antipode* 52 (2): 522–41. https://doi.org/10.1111/anti.12608.
Scott, James C. 1998. *Seeing Like a State - James C. Scott(1).Pdf*. New Haven and London: Yale University Press.
Smets, Peer, and Marion Den Uyl. 2008. "The Complex Role of Ethnicity in Urban Mixing: A Study of Two Deprived Neighbourhoods in Amsterdam." *Urban Studies* 45 (7): 1439–60. https://doi.org/10.1177/0042098008090683.
Thévenot, Laurent. 2002. "Which Road to Follow? The Moral Complexity of an 'Equipped' Humanity." In *Complexities: Social Studies of Knowledge Practices*, edited by John Law and Annemarie Mol, 53–87. Durham and London: Duke University Press. https://doi.org/10.1215/9780822383550–003.
Uitermark, Justus, and Tjerk Bosker. 2014. "Wither the 'Undivided City'? An Assessment of State-Sponsored Gentrification in Amsterdam." *Tijdschrift Voor Economische En Sociale Geografie* 105 (2): 221–30. https://doi.org/10.1111/tesg.12072.
Witte, Anki, Henk Ruigrok van der Werven, Renate Guitink, and Charlot Verlouw. 2016, November 16. "Zuidoost Krijgt Eindelijk Een Coffeeshop: Hoe Kon Het Zo Lang Duren?" *Het Parool*.
Young, Iris Marion. 1990. *Justice and the Politics of Difference*. New York: Princeton University Press.

6 Politics in the city

The forming of publics

Manhattan is undoubtedly one of the priciest pieces of land in the world. Yet, in the Lower East Side, a 175,000 m^2 area remained undeveloped for nearly five decades. Often referred to as SPURA, or 'Seward Park Urban Renewal Area,' the vacant lot was created when a public housing complex was demolished in 1967. The mostly Puerto Rican, Black, and Asian families have a long history of community struggles. The story of SPURA will help us understand politics' role in participation, community intermediaries, and contracts.

In this chapter, I explore how politics is organized. I understand politics as the process through which decisions are made about how to work together; it is the space where the ordering of society is criticized, justified, or transformed. Whereas actors mostly follow institutional practices, those institutional practices can be opened for critique. When that happens, a political space opens—a public—and institutional change is possible. Although change is possible, more often these critiques are displaced, co-opted, or compromised.

My understanding of politics is inspired by critical pragmatism and the work of John Dewey (1927) and Iris Marion Young (1990, 2000). I see politics as a relational process embedded in specific contexts and embodied in actors such as politicians, activists, and judges. Publics are the spaces in which there is a discussion about how to organize collective action (Dewey, 1927). Moreover, there is a discussion—an inquiry—about what topics and objects are of concern to the public debate (Dewey, 1938). This is a fluid process: the topics and objects that are of concern can change over time. Moreover, it can be a contentious process in which different actors try to define the problems at hand in a way that favors their goals. For example, there is an area available for redevelopment, but it is not yet clear whether there should be social housing or market-rate housing. Different actors will aim to shape the discussion as a problem that is aligned with their experiences. For instance, activist groups will argue for social housing based on the length of waiting lists of social housing. While developers will show Excel sheets with the demand for housing and argue that the size of housing should be reduced. This is a deeply material process; waiting lists, Excel sheets, and newspaper articles all play an important role. They shape how arguments are presented in public discussions and shape what is considered the main problem. After a period of discussion about what is of concern, a plan develops about how to organize collective action.

DOI: 10.4324/9781032712840-6

Thus, publics are not only the spaces in which there is a discussion about topics and objects but also spaces in which decisions are made (Dewey, 1927).

It is important to note that the political process is not static and that publics can open and close without decisions being made. However, within the public, actors are positioned to discuss and debate issues requiring collective action. But they are not positioned equally. Dewey already noted in 1935 that the power of government agencies was "pale in contrast with that exercised by concentrated and organized property interests" (Dewey, 1935, p. 64). Moreover, access to publics is shaped by social privileges based on gender, race, and class (Young, 1990). The relative privilege of some actors allows them to influence publics more forcefully. For example, investors can call politicians to discuss their plans, while everyday residents only have the opportunity to talk to politicians during public meetings.

The political process is strongly entangled with moral and legal processes. However, whereas moral processes value who is worthy of being a spokesperson, the political process deals with who will make decisions—whether they are worthy or not. The legal and political processes are also deeply entangled. But whereas the legal process aims to stabilize relations through the appearance of objectivity and impartiality, the political process holds the potential to alter relations and give actors the authority to make decisions.

6.1 Co-option and displacement

The story of SPURA started in 1957 when Robert Moses announced that two Lower East Side impoverished areas would be 'relocated'. These areas contain public housing complexes where low-income families of mostly Puerto Rican, Black, and Asian descent lived. This plan is a clear example of displacement: low-income families are forced out of their homes to make a new development project possible. As described in the introduction, this was a period in which activists were increasingly invoking the civic register to claim decision-making power for residents. However, most of the legally required participatory processes still needed to be implemented. After the demolition of public housing, the area was intended to be bought by the municipality to be sold to developers at a reduced price (The New York Times, 1957b). The plan to sell the area to a developer soon created a heated discussion, which resulted in the forming of a public that discussed the future of the area. The *New York Times* noted that 500 people flooded a public hearing about plans to build a 1.728-unit cooperative building (The New York Times, 1957a). This shows how public hearings are spaces in which political and legal decisions can be challenged, and the vested interests of developers can be challenged. Although both the municipality and developers have the power to make decisions on their own, the neighborhood residents could criticize their decisions and stall the process. During the public hearing, one speaker—Harris Present, chairman of the New York City Council on Housing Relocation Practices—activated the civic register to criticize the municipality's plans. He noted that the demolition of the houses of underprivileged people aggravated the lack of housing in New York (The New York Times, 1957a).

The conflict around the redevelopment continued into 1965. The New York City's board of estimate approved plans for redevelopment without specifying when construction would start. During another public hearing, Wilbert Tatum of the Cooper Square Committee voiced opposition to the plan by invoking the civic register. He presented an argument that would limit the amount of displacement in the neighborhood. He argued "that this plan be replaced by one that will provide principally for the people who live there now at rentals they can afford. By doing this, you would be joining the war on poverty rather than making war on the poor" (Bennett, 1965). In contrast, a democratic state senator argued that the plan would cause the "rebirth of the Lower East Side," and the chairman of the Housing and Redevelopment Board noted that "this plan is an appealing concept for an attractive community graced by tree-shaded sitting and recreation areas, pleasant shops, off-street parking, and community facilities" (Bennett, 1965). This shows how the public is used to define what is of concern, creating housing for low-income families or creating an attractive neighborhood. This also shows the moral character of political discussions; low-income families seem to be able to devalue an area and prevent it from becoming attractive.

Finally, in 1967, 1852 families in the Lower East Side of New York were displaced through 'slum clearance' (Bendiner, 2012). Most of the tenants were low-income families and families of color (Bendiner, 2012). The critique that the relocation would lead to a war on the poor was displaced because the first apartments that were built in the area were cooperative housing mostly occupied by middle-class Jewish families (Buettner, 2014). However, partially due to continued resistance from residents, the majority of the land remained undeveloped.

As the first public clashes around SPURA show, tensions between planning, democracy, and profitability are administered through a political process. For an urban development project to be realized, the political decision-making surrounding it must generate legitimacy, framing the project in such a way that it appeals to conceptions of the common good. Residents of neighborhoods do not simply accept new development projects because they are profitable; they need a form of justification not to obstruct the development project. Their engagement with processes of capital accumulation needs to be justified (Boltanski and Chiapello, 2005). This does not imply that residents will be successful in their attempt to halt a development project, but some form of public acceptance is needed. This acceptance is reached through compromise, cooptation, or displacement (see: Boltanski and Chiapello, 2005). A compromise is reached when actors reach an agreement that is more or less satisfying for all parties. In the case of SPURA that could have been reached through the realization of public housing combined with some market-rate housing. Criticisms can be displaced, for example, when social movements in one neighborhood pressure the city government to invest in public spaces, but at the cost of investing in neighborhoods with less organized activist groups. Criticism can also be co-opted, leading to cosmetic changes for certain policies, for instance, when new housing was developed around the SPURA sites, but only for middle-class people. Finally, force can be used to thwart political processes and subdue critique, for example, when the police arrest protestors during a public meeting. The use of force leads to depoliticization and domination.

The practice of slum clearance in New York is also an example of how the planning-property contradiction can result in a deadlock. Commercial parties depended on government intervention to get access to the Seward Park area. Without the support of local and federal government agencies, the area could not have been appropriated. Moreover, commercial parties only seemed interested in realizing new buildings with government subsidies and with a good outlook on profit. However, due to a shrinking city budget and ongoing activism against slum clearance, the original plan for redevelopment was never completed (Bendiner, 2012). This also shows that the contradiction is not always dealt with in favor of planning or property; an impasse is also possible.

In the 1970s, tensions around the redevelopment of the area continued. The Jewish community was well organized and partly represented through the United Jewish Council of the East Side (Buettner, 2014). They aimed to claim the mantle of being the true spokesperson of the neighborhood and co-opt the decision-making processes instead of Puerto Rican, Black, and Asian representatives. Central figures with close ties to the United Jewish Council were Sheldon Silver, who became an assemblyman, and William Rapfogel, who held different positions at city agencies, developers, and NGOs. The two men effectively lobbied the city administration to prevent low-income housing in the area and keep the Jewish identity of the community (Buettner, 2014). They used their position to shape how the problem within the public was defined; they argued that there was already too much social housing in the area. This illustrates how the market register is invoked to avoid realizing social housing, which covered the discriminatory goals of Sheldon Silver and William Rapfogel. While social housing embodies the civic register by framing housing as a right, middle-class housing embodies the market register by portraying housing as the result of supply and demand. The buildings that were built in the area had a 97% Jewish occupancy (Johnston, 1971). When a new 360-unit housing project was constructed in the area, again, most of the occupants were from the Jewish community (Buettner, 2014). This shows that the United Jewish Council could co-opt the decision-making processes to a certain degree. Moreover, the housing built in the area also signaled how some residents were seen as more than others. Because it seemed impossible to realize public housing for the displaced Puerto Rican, Black, and Asian communities, whereas the Jewish community could realize cooperative housing. The struggle of Puerto Rican, Black, and Asian communities to bend the discussion in the public toward their experiences led them to take legal action. They filed litigation cases against the municipality, blaming the city for discriminatory practices (Weisman, 1973). Although the court ruled that the rights of Black and Puerto Rican people were not violated, the redevelopment project was once more stalled.

As Dewey argued in his most known book, *The public and its problems* (1927), public officials play an important role in deciding when the actions of non-state actors should be regulated. Public officials can be civil servants, but also politicians or judges. Dewey argued that the public sphere appears when the consequences of transactions between actors extend beyond those directly concerned, affect the welfare of many others, and require public action (Dewey, 1927, p. 13). In the case of SPURA, the transactions of the municipality clearly affected Puerto Rican, Black, and Asian families. Public action is coordinated by officials who represent the state. Those officials bring together those affected actors and create an arrangement to deal with the consequences of the transaction (Dewey, 1927, p. 16). Although the City of New York decided to demolish the area, they were also forced to bring together those who were affected by that decision. This creates a political space, a public, in the form of a public hearing. Thus, when officials consider transactions to go beyond those directly involved, they pull the transaction into the public sphere (Dewey, 1927).

Publics function as the space where the contradiction between capitalism and democracy is negotiated by forging justifications for public action. Capitalism must furnish acceptable reasons in order for actors to engage in capitalism; thus developers need to justify why a development project would benefit the neighborhood (Boltanski and Chiapello, 2005). Potentially, the public can be regarded as the space in which there is a potential for institutional change. Actors can mobilize support for altering the direction of institutional practices or even transform institutions. This does not imply that all actors are in the same way positioned to criticize institutions; the capacity to do so is strongly related to social privileges such as gender, race, and class. I see politics as the processes and spaces where decisions are made about acting and living together. In that light, the decision to pull activities into the public sphere can be considered to be a meta-political decision. Officials decide when a political space opens up to decide on specific topics. This also means that officials can try to prevent public action, which happened in the case of Seward Park. Sheldon Silver obstructed any attempt for public action on Seward Park, effectively displacing any critique that did not serve his core group of voters: the Jewish community. Through this process, he could co-opt the decision-making process at the cost of Puerto Rican, Black, and Asian groups.

In 1988, the municipality announced that LeFrak Organization would finally develop SPURA. Through the market register, it was justified that LeFrak paid a symbolic $1 per year for a 99-year lease (Smith, 1996). This was justified, according to the municipality, because LeFrak would take a risk in developing the area. Advocacy groups invoked the civic register and criticized the plan's goal to develop only units for the middle class (Buettner, 2014). They reasoned that the plan included 1,200 apartments for middle-income households but no units for low-income people. Moreover, after 20 years, the rental units could be turned into luxury co-opens for the open market. However, the economic crisis of the 1980s made Lefrak withdraw from the proposal (Smith, 1996). Later Richard Lefrak noted in the *New York Times* that "it was an exercise in frustration. You had the collision between the Jewish community in the Grant Houses and the Latino and Asian communities" (Bagli, 2013). This is an example of how the planning-property contradiction can lead to a stalemate. LeFrak Organization needs government support to develop the area; this is arranged by paying a symbolic amount for the lease. LeFrak Organization doesn't aim to build public housing but opts for middle-class and market-rate units.

They want to maximize profit on their (future) property. This is an example of a government siding with property developers. However, since the plans need to be supported in the city council, they also need public support. None of the groups in the area can claim the mantle of being the true spokesperson of the neighborhood and the public debate remains fragmented. Decision-makers face no pressure to act, leading to the plan's abandonment.

However, neighborhood organizations representing Puerto Rican, Black, and Asian families did not give up their fight. They again used legal action to mobilize support for their cause through the course. This time, the city of New York had to admit that they discriminated against Black and Hispanic people applying for public housing projects—including projects around Seward Park (Pear, 1992). An example is a public official—a judge—who pulled an issue into the public sphere. Whereas the city had argued through activating the market register that they had made decisions in order to attract investors, residents had invoked the civic register by arguing that they were discriminated against. The judge ordered the city to reserve 1991 apartments for Black and Hispanic families who can prove the municipal housing selection policies discriminated against them (Pear, 1992). Although the direction of institutional practices was temporarily changed in favor of these families, this did not have a real effect on the development of SPURA or the city's broad development practices.

In 1994, Sheldon Silver became speaker of the Assembly of the state of New York. This provided an opening to launch another proposal for the site. This restarted a new inquiry into what was at stake in the area. This time, the idea was to develop no housing but create space for a large retailer. The developer was South Manhattan Development Corporation, which was chaired by William Rapfogel (Buettner, 2014). The idea to develop large supermarkets was supported by the United Jewish Council. Again, they argued that the area was statured with public housing (Buettner, 2014). They invoked the market register to argue that more public housing would lower the value of the area. In contrast, the Chinatown Planning Council proposed developing public housing in the same area. They invoked the civic register to argue that the harm done in the past needed remedy; they were promised more public housing. The public hearing about the proposal was contentious. Supporters of low-income housing chanted "racists, racists" while representatives of the United Jewish Council stated that "the people living there now need the security of the knowledge that the economic level of the community will be maintained" (Purnick, 1980). However, this proposal also failed to gain enough support. Local shop owners protested plans to develop large supermarkets in the area (Greenberg, 1973). The only organization that supported the plan was the United Jewish Council, and through political connections, they forced the municipality to come up with a compromise. A small affordable housing project was combined with a senior housing project that the United Jewish Council and a synagogue were initiated (Buettner, 2014).

The conflict between the United Jewish Council and the Chinatown Planning Council is an example of how the position of actors within society can help influence public officials' decisions to open up a public. Publics form when there is a need for collective action. Those publics are organized by public officials who act in the name of the neighborhood and the public interest. Public officials can be civil servants, planning consultants, or community workers who act in the neighborhood's name. This is not a static process: both who is being excluded and included and who is considered to act in the name of the neighborhood are relational, fluid processes full of contention. The public meetings allowed both the United Jewish Council and the Chinatown Planning Council to voice their critiques and argue for their goals.

In Chapter 5, I described how the position of claiming the mantle of being the true spokesperson is a moral process. This means that acting in the name of the neighborhood cannot be done by everybody; those actors need to be morally valued to claim the position. Although the United Jewish Council attempted to claim the mantle of being the true spokespersons, they received strong opposition from the Chinatown Planning Council. Because both groups failed to claim the position, there was no clear way forward for the discussions around SPURA. Neither group could frame the problem that was being discussed in the public in their favor.

In potential, the organization of publics can be democratic. However, the conflict between the United Jewish Council and the Chinatown Planning Council shows that access to publics is closely related to the social position of actors in society. While actors are all differentially positioned within society, those positioned in comparable ways will experience similar barriers (Young, 1990, p. 9). Access to publics is highly racialized, gendered, and ordered through other oppressive structures. The relative privilege of certain actors gives them an advantage in structuring political processes in such a way that their wishes, needs, and ideas are prioritized. The United Jewish Council could harness its class position to pull the debate around SPURA out of the public sphere into back door rooms. Public officials are instrumental in deciding who is being included and who is being excluded in the public. This can be seen in the position that the Puerto Rican, Black, and Asian communities have vis-à-vis the Jewish communities. Because of the political connections of the Jewish community, they could prevent low-incoming housing from being realized in the area. The Jewish representatives could not claim the mantle of being the true spokespersons of the neighborhood. Time and time again, they were being discredited in public meetings and discussions. However, because they had access to the spaces in which decisions were made, they could hold outsized power over Seward Park. This shows how entangled political, legal, and moral processes are. The clash between the Puerto Rican, Black, and Asian representatives and the United Jewish Council is moral, who is worthy enough to receive housing; political, who has the right to make decisions; and legal, who can design development agreements.

The cooperative housing units built in the 1960s, also known as 'co-op village,' remained affordable because owners had to sell the housing back to the cooperative for the original price when they moved out (Kelley, 2000). However, in 2000, this policy was stopped, and owners could sell their houses for market-rate prices (Kelley, 2000). While the neighborhood was changing, the Bloomberg administration made a new attempt to develop SPURA in 2003. The plan was to develop 300 low-income units and 100 middle-income units coupled with market-rate units (Kurutz, 2003). During the hearing on the community board, racial slurs were ousted, and the debate became again very heated (Kaysen, 2013). The proposal failed to mobilize support in the area, as the leader of the advocacy group Seward Park Area Redevelopment Coalition (SPARC) told the *New York Times*: "We've always said mixed-income, but there should be an emphasis on low because that's the housing that we've lost." However, SPARC started to organize support for developing the area. The old fault lines were still there; advocacy groups with roots in Puerto Rican, Asian, and Black communities vowed 100% for low- or moderate-income families, whereas the mostly Jewish owners of cooperative housing complexes wanted to prevent more low-income housing in the area (Gonzalez, 2007). However, the attempts of SPARC were not supported by Sheldon Silver, who refused to work with them (Gonzalez, 2007).

6.2 A time for compromise

Finally, in the 2010s, development plans gained momentum. As the story of SPURA shows, there were stark fault lines in the public discussing the future of Seward Park. On one side, there was a collection of advocacy groups—such as Good Old Lower East Sides (GOLES), Chinatown Planning Council, and SPARC—representing the interests of Puerto Rican, Black, and Asian communities. They were mostly arguing for housing for lower-income people. They justified their claims by arguing that the area used to be public housing and that the displaced people were promised that they could return. Thus, they invoked the civic register. Conversely, the co-op owners—mainly represented by the United Jewish Council—argued against affordable housing. They mostly justified their claims by stating that the area already had a high concentration of low-income housing. They activated the market register to prevent the development of public housing. Moreover, they wanted to protect the Jewish character of the neighborhood. ". . . that, you know, was deemed a threat to the Jewish culture, you know, people were afraid, so, you know, it was definitely race related, I would say race related it became classist as well. Which is ironic because all these building that are build are for middle-income housing and these people get tax benefits for around a thousand dollars, so they benefitted from the government that made it possible that these people would be homeowners" (Resident 31, New York, 2018). However, the fault lines in the public were changing. Due to the possibility of selling the co-op houses against market rate prices, the neighborhood was already changing. This also meant that the voting base of Sheldon Silver was changing. The alliance of the United Jewish Council with Sheldon Silver remained strong, but other middle-class residents started to intervene in the discussions around SPURA. This shows how political processes are deeply embedded in materialities. The changing occupants of the co-op houses opened up the possibility for compromise.

In the early 2010s, the community board had achieved success by successfully going through a rezoning process. The rezoning process brought together a wide variety of actors who were able to reach a consensus on the rezoning. Those factors led the New York City Economic Development Corporation (NYCEDC) to approach the community board about Seward Park and ask them to set up a task force. The task force was in charge of creating guidelines for the development of SPURA. Those guidelines summarized the residents' principles around Seward Park. After the guidelines were adopted by the community board, the city sent a request for proposal and the area was developed.

The policy process looked clear and straightforward on paper. However, the whole process turned out to be an intricate battle between different actors, groups, and interests. Moreover, notwithstanding the participatory process, in the end, Sheldon Silver needed to vote in the assembly on the plan. A planning consultant involved in the processes discovered later:

> [A]nd then it hit me. Shelby didn't want anything to happen. He was inscrutable and created an environment where everyone was afraid to go to him. Because if any housing was built on the site, they won't pay for him. So supposedly the rule was that he doesn't want affordable housing because they won't pay for him and he may lose votes among the conservative Jews and the co-ops.
>
> (Community intermediary 28, New York, 2018)

This reveals again that the market register was invoked to cover up discriminatory goals by Sheldon Silver. His goal was to protect the Jewish identity of the neighborhood and prevent the influx from Puerto Rican, Black, and Asian communities. However, in order to create public support, he needed to activate the market register. It also shows that certain actors are better positioned to close and open up public; because of his own political position and connections, Sheldon Silver could do this for decades.

However, the process of creating residents' principles in the form of guidelines was put in motion. In order to create the guidelines, a participatory process was organized. Since the city supported the effort to develop housing at Seward Park, they agreed to hire a facilitator. The facilitator that was selected was someone who was respected by the advocacy groups and had a good reputation. "it was helpful to have someone outside the board, it was helpful to have someone who could dedicate time to it, and really talk to all the different stakeholders, and try to show people this is how you can go to a compromise" (Resident 31, New York, 2018). The facilitator talked to all the actors who had a stake in the Seward Park development process. He described his role as follows:

> Being an advocate for each of the advocates for each of the parties means that you know what their bottom line. . . . I met with all of the stakeholders, with particular attention to those who had veto power. So let's say out of 15 participants. . . . So I would do New York type of things. You know, I would call. Like, what do you care?
>
> (Community intermediary 28, New York, 2018)

The community intermediary was needed to navigate a complex actor landscape. Moreover, the community intermediary was needed to create a clear understanding of what was of concern to the public and what kind of solutions were viable. There were different representatives of Puerto Rican, Asian, and Jewish communities. Those representatives needed to ensure that their constituents' needs were met and were satisfied with the deal. However, the community intermediary also needed to deal with the New York Economic Development Corporation and different politicians. "In the process, they would come to trust me because they would see that I was an attentive listener" (Community intermediary 28, New York, 2018). Knowing their bottom line, he moved the parties together. Next to knowing their bottom line, he ensured that all the parties were satisfied with the plan.

> They can't actually go back to their constituency and said I got 51%. Where can they feel good about the plan with only 51%? So you have to make sure that no one's going to walk away from the table, but they'll stick it out until the end.
>
> (Community intermediary 28, New York, 2018)

This shows how the process of creating a common definition of what is of concern and formulating solutions for those problems is an intricate process of negotiations and justifications.

As the case of SPURA shows, increasingly, political decisions on neighborhood issues are made or strongly influenced by community intermediaries rather than civil servants or democratically elected officials. The reason for this change is a growing distrust toward civil servants and democratically elected officials and a belief that residents themselves are better positioned to make their own decisions (Levine, 2016). This is also the case with SPURA. Rather than politicians openly proposing solutions or civil servants presenting plans, community organizations are asked to devise a plan together. Moreover, a facilitator is hired to bring those organizations and people together and prepare a suitable compromise for all the parties involved. Community intermediaries fall grossly into two categories: private sector consultants, like the facilitator, and community workers aligned with neighborhood organizations, such as representatives from the United Jewish Council, GOLES, SPARC, and the Chinatown Planning Council. With the growing complexity of urban planning involving diverse actors, private sector consultants are increasingly hired for their reputed ability to address cooperation and coordination issues (Grijzen, 2010). These consultants act as mediators by understanding the interests of different stakeholders and the organizational contexts in which they operate (Caloffi and Gambarotto, 2017). Often, consultancy firms adapt standardized solutions to fit local contexts, a practice known as "fast policies" (Prince, 2012; Vogelpohl, 2017). Neighborhood organizations provide various services to residents, such as cultural activities, healthcare, and social care. Leaders of these organizations often act as neighborhood representatives, speaking on behalf of the residents. Over recent decades, these leaders have gained legitimacy as neighborhood representatives, often at the expense of elected officials

(Levine, 2016). Additionally, neighborhood organizations play a crucial role in urban redevelopment projects by partnering with governmental agencies and developers to design and implement plans (Kort and Klijn, 2011; Swyngedouw, 2005; Tasan-Kok, 2010).

After the negotiations between community representatives, a participatory process was organized.

> As a planner, I interpret that everyone speaks their own language and you are going to speak the language of making money. Now the community is going to speak the language of quality of life and you now the activists are going to speak the language of justice.
>
> (Community intermediary 28, New York, 2018)

In urban development processes, publics are often organized through participatory processes. Participation is often assumed to be a democratic practice and enhance democracy (Walker et al., 2015). Participation facilitates discussions about public issues with those who are affected. Everybody with a direct or indirect interest in the issue can join participatory processes and voice their opinion. Participation is deemed to enhance democratic practices because it involves residents in decision-making processes. But, as I have shown in Chapter 5, participatory processes can reproduce social inequalities. Residents need time to partake in participatory meetings, which is more difficult for those with jobs and families to take care of or have health issues.

Moreover, language plays an important role in participatory meetings. The goal of those meetings is the production of public policies. Those are written in a policy language that is very different from the language of different social groups. In order to prevent those problems, the facilitator and the community board designed a process that would be sensitive to the neighborhood's diversity. Moreover, it was clear that some groups distrusted the motives of the city of New York. Therefore, public meetings were organized in different parts of the neighborhood. During the meetings, notes were taken live so that everybody could see what would end up in the meeting minutes. "There was a trust issue, having it typed in black and white in front of everybody, everybody saw it [the notes]" (Community intermediary 28, New York, 2018).

The public note taking also helped to improve clarity and understanding among participants: "Can you change that word? Is that what you really meant? I didn't mean that [I did not support] it at all. I thought you were saying this because [you] said this and that." (Community intermediary 28, New York, 2018). Additionally, there were Spanish, Mandarin, and Cantonese translators. Next, tenant- and community leaders were asked to put on signs about the meeting and the process in buildings. In this way, the guidelines for development in Seward Park could be developed. Next to public meetings, people could also email comments because not everybody could participate in public meetings. Again, this shows that publics can be potentially organized along democratic principles, but that it requires work to achieve this.

The main issues that ended up in the guidelines were mixed development, so commercial and residential. The residential development should be at least 50% affordable housing, including units for low-income families. No 'big box' development, such as a Walmart, but a large grocery store was needed. The Essex Market, a beloved and historic vendor market, should preferably be kept in the same place, but it can be relocated if it remains public, and the moving processes will be reimbursed. In addition, there should be space for cultural organizations and offices for nonprofits.

The minutes of the community board meeting showed that the guidelines were not approved without controversy. Some residents felt that 50% affordable housing was unfair and that residents were being co-opted by participating and accepting watered-down proposals. Wendy Cheung said: "Public land is being sold away from the people who built this community. 50/50 isn't democratic for the majority of low-income people who make up this community" (Community Board no. 3, 2011). Moreover, Yolanda Donato criticized the participatory process: "The great majority of the community didn't participate in the meetings and are always asked why they weren't when the answer is that they are working" (Community Board no. 3, 2011).

However, there were also people in support of the compromise. Lisa Kaplan argued that only a few residents who had moved out were able to stay in the area. "It wasn't an easy decision to support this resolution. She can't tolerate the idea of looking at parking lots anymore. Various past proposals have been stopped; this can't be allowed to go on. A fair compromise was reached" (Community Board no. 3, 2011). The community board chairman Dominic Berg replied to the critique:

> The SPURA vote was 19 to 1, with one abstention. There were open meetings every month. There were translators and facilitators at every meeting. Comments were taken online from the public and given the same weight as those of committee members. The City didn't drive this process. Many partners, including Senator Squadron, Council Member Chin, HDC, and the Economic Development Corporation. The City saw the community was serious about finally doing something about this 43-year-old problem. The City offered additional lots, meaning more units and more affordable units. There was a timeline. This was a once-in-a-generation shot. We need to pass these guidelines or the lots will stay vacant for another generation. Every elected official came out to support this today because they saw it was an open process. Everyone on the committee was well past their comfort zone. We must prove to the City that we can control our destiny and have influence from the community board level.
>
> (Community Board no. 3, 2011)

The tensions within the public between community activists, the community board, and politicians can be understood through the lens of Young's (2000) writings on democratic practices. She argues that participation is an important tool to understand the needs of specific groups. However, democratic decision-making does not require citizens to be present when decisions are made. Nor does it mean that representatives replace the groups they represent, implying that the diversity of citizens, groups, and interests can be reduced to a single entity; there is no single will of the people that can be represented (Young, 2000). Instead, formulating and executing policies through fair representation means acknowledging the differences between people and between representatives and the represented (Young, 2000). While representatives should engage with their constituencies through public debate and speak for them, they do not speak as them (Young, 2000). Representation is a cycle of authorization and accountability: authority is given to representatives to make political decisions, and they need to be held accountable for their actions (Young, 2000). The increased importance of community intermediaries in planning processes has made the cycle of authorization and accountability murky. Often, it is presumed that community intermediaries can speak as the community.

Moreover, in the end, elected officials can be voted out of office; community representatives can often not be voted out. Therefore, it is important in democratic practices to balance community representatives' goals and elected officials' decisions. Elected officials need to listen to community representatives, but community representatives need to understand that elected officials are responsible for taking care of all their constituents. The decisions of elected officials will always be a compromise between the needs of different communities. If residents disagree with the compromise that the elected officials present, they can vote the officials out. By presenting participatory processes as places where citizens can decide what happens, these processes become murky, and residents are bound to be disappointed, which runs the risk of undermining trust in democracy. This does not imply that elected officials always come up with fair compromises and listen to all the voices in their community. The example of Sheldon Silver shows that the decisions of elected officials can also lead to displacement and co-option.

After the guidelines were approved, the land use review process started. The community board needed to vote on approving the land use review. This again divided the neighborhood. During a heated community board meeting in May 2012, residents mainly debated whether enough affordable housing was included in the plans. Joel Feingold led the chant, "Fight! Fight! Fight! Housing is a human right!" (Community Board no. 3, 2012). Joel Feingold spoke of the right of evicted tenants to return and the demand for as much low-income housing as possible: "We need 100% low-income housing"(Community Board no. 3, 2012). Wah Lee argued that CB3 must use its power to fight for low-income families in the district. "Low-income people's rights in the community are being taken" (Community Board no. 3, 2012). But there were also proponents of the deal. Val Orcelli said:

> [V]ote unanimously for this agreement, knowing that we have to keep working on some issues. We'll speak up at every step of the ULURP process. . . . Who is protesting for 100% low-income housing and has developed any housing units? 50% of something is 100% better than nothing.
>
> (Community Board no. 3, 2012)

Partly due to the unrest within communities, nine SPURA task force members threatened to vote against ULURP. The compromise that was painstakingly brought together by the community intermediary and community board members was to fall apart.

Moreover, Sheldon Silver was also not yet convinced of the plan. This was a problem because Sheldon Silver had the power to stop the deal at the state level. The community intermediary tried to persuade him, but he refused to support the deal. "It hit me. It was worse than that. It wasn't that he was holding out for a better deal. He didn't want any deal" (Community intermediary 28, New York, 2018). Therefore, the community intermediary said: "we have to make the cost of no deal higher than the cost of a bad deal." So, the community intermediary started to talk to everybody that Sheldon Silver was the problem, which was picked up by the *New York Times*. This shows how he could use his connections to mobilize support from the media. The negative article in the *New York Times* created political pressure on Sheldon Silver: "Just enough political pressure for him to approve to deal" (Community intermediary 28, New York, 2018). Through political pressure, the resistance of Sheldon Silver was diverted, and the city promised permanent affordability to deal with the critique from the community board. This meant that the land use review process could be finalized with the support of the community board. State Senator Daniel Squadron noted in the *New York Times*: 'a unanimous vote on the Lower East Side may be a first' (Buckley, 2011).

Moreover, Sheldon Silver wrote in a statement, "The final guidelines that were approved by the committee tonight strike an appropriate balance between the needs and concerns of all stakeholders" (Buckley, 2011). In the end, the city sent out a request for proposal—including the guidelines developed by the community board—with a regulation that 50% of the housing needed to be affordable. This led to some critique from commercial parties. Joshua Schuster from DHA Capital noted in the *New York Times*: "I think at that ratio, we would have pause to throw our hat in the ring." For advocacy groups, the deal was bittersweet. Damaris Reyes noted in the *New York Times*:

> I don't think it's possible ever to make them whole. Being displaced from your home is traumatic, no matter how you paint it. You are uprooted from your home, your routine, and even your grocery store. You can never get back what you lost. A community disappeared. We'll never learn the stories of the great things people did after they had to leave. Or the bad things that happened because they were displaced. What we know is that it was too easy for that to happen and to stay vacant for so long.
>
> (Gonzalez, 2014)

The design guidelines were also important to the ULUPR process so the developer would know the community's expectations. This was important because the community board played a part in selecting the developer. This was a novelty in New York City, but it gave the community a role beyond the community board's traditional advisory role. There was a strong sense among community board members that a developer close to Sheldon Silver would be selected.

> There is a developer that we kind of all that, we knew, we did not which bid was theirs, but we knew that they were close to Shelly Silver. And we so kind of felt that we, that it was probably was going to be the developer.
>
> (Resident 31, New York, 2018)

However, during those days, William Rapfogel was arrested for fraud. Sheldon Silver denied a close relationship with William Rapfogel. However, their close relationship was well-known. For example, William Rapfogel's wife was also the chief of staff of Sheldon Silver's office. Thus, William Rapfogel's arrest also hurt Sheldon Silver's position.

> He was hiding money in the walls of his apartments and this all came out at a time when we were making the selections, and that cost a shift in kind of the influence, in any kind of spell of influence he may have had in the selection.
>
> (Resident 31, New York, 2018)

This allowed the community board to have a decisive say in the developer selection. The task force of the community board got a rubric, each with the residents' principles. In a conference room, they met different developers, filled in their rubric, and evaluated the proposals. "Individually, each of the task force members with our own rubric, we're able to go around and kind of rank each of the proposals where we got to see the major cut" (Resident 32, New York, 2018). After the development deal was announced, there were criticisms, however: "we felt like there wasn't enough on the lower end, but in the end we supported it because we said 50% of something is better than 0% of nothing" (Resident 34, New York, 2018). It is important to highlight that the fall of William Rapfogel created space within the public to give the community board a say in selecting the developer. This is a unique situation in New York, rather than a common practice. Publics open up space to discuss how to organize collective action. However, they are often dominated by actors with social and political privileges, tilting discussions within publics to their favor.

After the developer was selected, the collaboration between the developer and the task force continued. The way decisions were made had largely stabilized after decades of conflict. The task force and the developer had regular meetings during the development phase to discuss the timeline of the project and discuss problems that arose during construction work. "[I]t's become a very collaborative group, right? Because I would say 75% of the membership has stayed the same over time five or six years, right" (Resident 32, New York, 2018). This doesn't mean that delivering the promises to the residents was easy. The deal with the developers also included agreements for local hiring for jobs and giving the people that were displaced in the 1960s priority to getting housing. "it's very complicated because there's different city, state and federal guidelines about how [to monitor], you know, some people count it how many hours they work. Some people count how many days, how many quarters, right?" (Resident 32, New York, 2018).

Moreover, helping people get access to housing was also difficult.

> We were in touch with people, they were in touch with us or, you know, people moved away. So, when this happened, you know, when finally it happened, you know, we jumped up and down and said awesome. But, you know, there had to be a lot of outreach.
>
> (Resident 34, New York, 2018)

A list of displaced people was created, and a group of volunteers working for the community intermediary SPARC tried to locate them and reached out to them. Moreover, via a website, people could also fill in a form to show they were displaced in the 1960s. SPARC needed to go through all those forms to evaluate who had actual proof they were displaced and had the right to housing in Essex Crossing. Those who had a right to housing were helped by SPARC and the community board in the application process. It could also be difficult: "a couple of constituents who said that it was really burdensome when they got selected in the lottery to go all the way up to 125th St. to do their interview, right, because a lot of them are . . . senior" (Resident 32, New York, 2018).

6.3 The political thread in urban politics

This chapter highlighted the political thread in urban politics. The political thread works with the moral and legal threads to deal with public disputes. The political thread plays a part in organizing decision-making processes. Institutional practices can be opened for critique, creating publics where there is a potential for institutional change. Public officials are crucial in pulling specific issues into the public sphere. Those public officials—such as politicians, judges, or civil servants—are thus instrumental in deciding when and how public disputes are being discussed. Public officials can be pressured to open a public. However, the ability to pressure public officials is unequally distributed. Established actors such as developers, investors, and certain advocacy groups can pressure public officials better than loosely organized residents.

Moreover, when a public is opened, access to the public is related, not determined, by class and race. Community intermediaries often shape discussions within publics; these are either consultants that are hired to represent residents or neighborhood organizations. Consultants are often hired to be neutral. However, they often organize participatory processes or advise on making decisions. This means that they do not make decisions per se but strongly shape the context in which decisions are made. Neighborhood organizations are often involved in publics because they are seen as residents' representatives. However, whether neighborhood organizations speak as the residents or for the residents is often unclear. This lack of clarity can undermine the position of elected officials, who are elected to represent their entire constituency and can be voted out, which is often not possible with the leaders of neighborhood organizations. Thus, access to decision-making processes is often unequal and shaped by vested interests.

References

Bagli, Charles V. 2013, September 17. "City Plans Redevelopment for Vacant Area in Lower Manhattan." *The New York Times*. https://www.nytimes.com/2013/09/18/nyregion/city-plans- redevelopment-for-vacant-area-in-lower-manhattan.html.

Bendiner, Gabrielle. 2012. "Layered SPURA: Spurring Conversations through Visual Urbanism." *Radical History Review* 114, 206–16.

Bennett, Charles G. 1965, July 23. "Renewal Is Voted in East Side Area." *The New York Times*.

Boltanski, Luc, and Eve Chiapello. 2005. *The New Spirit of Capitalism*. London, UK: Verso.

Buckley, Cara. 2011, January 25. "Board Backs Development of Site on Lower East Side with Housing." *The New York Times*. https://www.nytimes.com/2011/01/26/nyregion/26seward.html.

Buettner, Russ. 2014, March 21. "They Kept a Lower East Side Lot Vacant for Decades." *The New York Times*. https://www.nytimes.com/2014/03/23/nyregion/they-kept-a-lower-east-side-lot-vacant-for-decades.html?searchResultPosition=996.

Caloffi, Annalisa, and Francesca Gambarotto. 2017. "Cognitive Distance in Public Procurement and Public—Private Partnerships : An Analysis of the Construction Sector." *Environment and Planning C Government and Policy* 35 (5): 765–83. https://doi.org/10.1177/0263774X16680108.

Community Board no. 3. 2011. *January 2011 Full Board Minutes*. Manhattan Community Board no. 3.

Community Board no. 3. 2012. *May 2012 Full Board Minutes*. Community Board no. 3.

Dewey, John. 1927. *The Public and Its Problems*. Ohio University Press.

Dewey, John. 1935. *Liberalism and Social Action*. New York: G.P.Putnam's Sons.

Dewey, John. 1938. *Logic: The Theory of Inquiry*. New York: Henry Holt and Company.

Gonzalez, David. 2007, August 27. "Forty Years of Growth, Except Where It Was Expected." *The New York Times*. https://www.nytimes.com/2007/08/27/nyregion/27citywide.html.

Gonzalez, David. 2014, November 5. "Rebuilding a Neighborhood, But Not a Community." *The New York Times*, sec. A.

Greenberg, Paul. 1973, November 3. "Letters to the Editor." *The New York Times*.

Grijzen, Jantine. 2010. *Outsourcing Planning: What Do Consultants Do in Regional Spatial*. Amsterdam University Press.

Johnston, Laurie. 1971, August 31. "Housing Complex Slated for Seward Park in '73." *The New York Times*.

Kaysen, Ronda. 2013, February 26. "After Years of Delay, a Lower East Side Gap Is Ready to Be Filled." *The New York Times*, sec. B.

Kelley, Tina. 2000, June 15. "Free Market Comes to Lower East Side; As Co-Op Price Caps Are Lifted, Some Residents Are Wary of Change." *The New York Times*, sec. B.

Kort, Michiel, and Erik-Hans Klijn. 2011. "Public-Private Partnerships in Urban Regeneration Projects: Organizational Form or Managerial Capacity?" *Public Administration Review*, 618–26.

Kurutz, Steve. 2003, November 30. "Neighborhood Report: Lower East Side; A Plan for Five Vacant Lots Gets Plenty of Vacant Stares." *The New York Times*. https://www.nytimes.com/2003/11/30/nyregion/neighborhood-report- lower-east-side-plan-for-five-vacant-lots-gets-plenty-vacant.html.

Levine, Jeremy R. 2016. "The Privatization of Political Representation: Community-Based Organizations as Nonelected Neighborhood Representatives." *American Sociological Review* 81 (6): 1251–75.

The New York Times. 1957a, July 18. "City Planners Aid 3 Slum Projects." *The New York Times*.

The New York Times. 1957b, January 27. "Two Slum Areas Will Be Vacated." *The New York Times*.

Pear, Robert. 1992, January 6. "Bias Is Admitted by New York City in Public Housing." *New York Times*.

Prince, R. 2012. "Policy Transfer, Consultants and the Geographies of Governance." *Progress in Human Geography* 36 (2): 188–203.
Purnick, Joyce. 1980, May 25. "Low-Rent Units on Delancy St. Are Voted Down." *The New York Times*.
Smith, Neil. 1996. *The New Urban Frontier: Gentrification and the Revanchist City*. London and New York: Routledge.
Swyngedouw, Erik. 2005. "Governance Innovation and the Citizen: The Janus Face of Governance-Beyond-the-State." *Urban Studies* 42 (11): 1991–2006.
Tasan-Kok, Tuna. 2010. "Entrepreneurial Governance: Challenges of Large-Scale Property-Led Urban Regeneration Projects." *Tijdschrift Voor Economische En Sociale Geografie* 101 (2): 126–49. https://doi.org/10.1111/j.1467–9663.2009.00521.x.
Vogelpohl, A. 2017. "Consulting Completed: Temporal Aspects of Expertise in Urban Development during Times of Fast Policies." *Geographica Helvetica* 72 (1): 65–76. https://doi.org/0.5194/gh-72-65-2017.
Walker, E.T., M. McQuarrie, and C.W. Lee. 2015. "Rising Participation and Declining Democracy." In *Democratizing Inequalities: Dilemmas of the New Public Participation*, edited by C.W. Lee, M. McQuarrie, and E.T. Walker, 3–23. New York: NYU Press.
Weisman, Steven R. 1973, September 13. "Housing for Jews Upheld by Court." *The New York Times*.
Young, Iris Marion. 1990. *Justice and the Politics of Difference*. New York: Princeton University Press.
Young, Iris Marion. 2000. *Inclusion and Democracy*. New York: Oxford University Press.

7 Law in the city

The many faces of contracts

Parts of this chapter have been published in Urban Studies and Land Use Planning under a creative commons license that allows for commercial re-use (Stapper, 2022, 2021).

Law seems to be an invisible force in urban politics. Law does manifest itself materially, but this often happens in the background of other actions. During participatory meetings, lively debates are structured according to what is legally allowed; however, this is not usually made explicit. As described in the introduction, the results of community discussions are summarized in the residents' principles, presented as a set of unequivocal and unified goals but often obscuring conflicting needs. These residents' principles need to be translated into contractual terms in order to be realized. However, those contractual terms are rarely discussed in public meetings. Even more striking is that the development agreements between developers and municipalities are secret or difficult to access. Public law arrangements like land use plans are publicly available; however, the general public often does not know how they work. However, sometimes law manifests itself very clearly. Signing contracts—often secret (!)—is a photo moment to present a new deal to the broader public. Changes in land use plans show that new developments will take place.

In this chapter, we explore how law shapes cities. I understand law as the thread that binds actors and objects together. Law is diverse and multifaceted; it can grant rights to actors, enforce promises, and define commitments (Durkheim, 1984; Macaulay, 1985; Weber, 1978). The textuality of law creates a structure that increases the probability that specific actions take place. Formalizing promises stabilizes relations between actors and objects. This is done by articulating obligations and rights in clear, documented terms. These processes give assurances to actors that specific interactions will occur. As stated, laws are diverse and come in various forms. Public law and private law are commonly distinguished as different legal spheres. Public law governs the interactions between individuals and the state, while private law deals with the relationships among private citizens. However, this book has shown that public and private law are often deeply interconnected. A more practical approach is to assess the enforceability of legal tools (Stapper, 2021, 2022). Some parts of legal tools bind actors toward specific goals. For example, there is a necessity to have some form of

DOI: 10.4324/9781032712840-7

public outreach in most planning laws or a clause in a contract that dictates how many social houses will be developed. Some parts of legal tools are more related to conduct or references, such as a particular vision of architecture in a development agreement or guiding principles on sustainability in German planning laws. Next, legal tools that are more or less enforceable are often supported by other legal tools that are more or less enforceable. For example, public laws dictate how contracts between developers and municipalities should be designed, and those contracts are influenced by non-enforceable agreements with resident groups. Thus, next to studying the enforceability of legal tools, I describe how the tools relate to each other.

Since this book focuses on contracts, it is useful to make a conceptual distinction between an agreement and a contract, although in practice, the distinction is often far from clear-cut. A contract is always an agreement, but an agreement is not always a contract. The American Law Institute and the Principles of European Contract Law define contracts as legally binding agreements. The American Law Institute defines a contract as "a promise or a set of promises for the breach of which the law gives a remedy, or the performance of which the law in some way recognizes as a duty" ((The American Law Institute, 1981a) Restatement (Second) of Contracts §1 (The American Law Institute, 1981a)). The Principles of European Contract Law states: "A contract is concluded if: the parties intend to be legally bound, and they reach a sufficient agreement without any further requirement" (Principles of European Contract Law art. 2:101: (1), (Commission on European Contract Law, 2002)). The Restatement (Second) of Contracts uses the word 'promise', which is "a manifestation of intention to act or refrain from acting in a specified way, so made as to justify a promise in understanding that a commitment has been made" (Restatement (Second) of Contracts §2 (The American Law Institute, 1981b)). A contract is thus an agreement with the intention to be legally bound to act or refrain from acting. Legal here means that the parties assume their agreement does not interfere with law, public policy, or good morals (Smits, 2014). The terms of a contract are thus enforceable.

Agreements without an intention to be legally binding have another function. Those agreements do not entail explicit commitments; they "are designed to give a promisor assurance that an exchange will occur" (Eisenberg, 2018). Agreements are thus less enforceable than contracts. According to Macaulay, an agreement can be more or less contractual: "transactions can be described relatively as involving a more contractual or a less contractual manner (a) of creating an exchange relationship or (b) of solving problems arising during the course of such a relationship" (Macaulay, 1963). Agreements are thus assurances that a deal has been made; contracts bind the parties to the deal.

Note that neither contracts nor agreements need to be in writing. But there needs to be clarity for both parties about what the goals are and how they will be achieved; the parties cannot hold contradictory assumptions (Macaulay, 1963). As described in the introduction and this chapter, developers and the resident group called the Koordinierungsgremium held contradictory assumptions in Hamburg.

They thus did not reach an agreement. In contrast, the recommendations made by the resident group Q8 were referenced in policy documents and the development agreement; there was an understanding that all recommendations would be implemented, which paved the way for Q8 to enter contractual relations with the developers. To recap, agreements exist on a continuum, from more enforceable agreements to less enforceable ones. There must be clarity for all parties that a deal has been reached and a plan for how their goals will be realized.

In this chapter, I explore the legal shift that has been taking place in cities in the last decades. Increasingly, development projects are steered through development agreements rather than public law arrangements. Development agreements are contracts between commercial parties and government agencies. Often those development agreements are signed before a participatory process is organized, severely limiting residents' options to influence development projects. Contracts and agreements are thus important objects that enable or constrain the actions of actors. The interests of residents are incorporated in less enforceable agreements. Most empirical evidence suggests that less enforceable agreements are complementary to (contractual) agreements. However, in participatory processes, less enforceable agreements are substitutes for contracts. Neighborhood codes, community agreements, and manifestos are not intended to be legally binding but act as documents that portray the interests of residents as unequivocal and coherent. They are the principles that summarize the needs and wishes of neighborhood residents. As described in previous chapters, I refer to them as residents' principles.

In the next section, we discuss the development projects Neue Mitte Altona in Hamburg, Oostenburg-Noord in Amsterdam, and Kingsbridge Armory in New York. Each development project shows that there are layers of legal tools used to steer the actions of actors. Moreover, contracts are not set in stone but change over time. They also show the diversity in which residents' principles are codified through manifestos, community criteria, community benefit agreements, or guidelines. The cases of Neue Mitte Altona, Oostenburg-Noord and Kingsbridge Armory show how these residents' principles, over time, are displaced or integrated into enforceable agreements.

7.1 Neue Mitte Altona

Neue Mitte Altona is situated in Altona, a rapidly gentrifying district of Hamburg with a rich working-class legacy and a strong activist tradition (Franzén, 2005). Altona, historically an independent city, was incorporated into Hamburg in 1937. The southwestern part of Altona, where Neue Mitte Altona is located, has been gentrifying over the last decades. The project's launch was triggered by Deutsche Bahn's decision to relocate the Altona train station to Diebsteich, thus opening up the area for residential development. Ownership of the land was split between Deutsche Bahn, two major landowners, and several smaller landholders.

The planning process incorporated various legal tools to facilitate development. As a first step, the municipality utilized Section 165 of the German building code, a provision allowing local authorities to initiate what is known as an "urban development measure." This rarely employed mechanism permits municipalities to compel landowners to engage in negotiations or allows the municipality to acquire the land if necessary. However, this approach is subject to strict conditions, requiring a clear public need beyond general housing shortages, with detailed probability studies regarding housing demand in the (metropolitan) area (Beck Online, 2019). Additionally, the municipality must rigorously calculate the project costs (Beck Online, 2019). As one civil servant noted, " So it is a very strict law, so we cannot do it all the time and everywhere, of course; only if you have special interests in the city, and if you have an area that will be transformed in its land usage in the next years" (Civil servant 10, Hamburg, 2018). The landowners agreed to enter negotiations with the municipality since the development of the area would be highly profitable. Key stakeholders in the land and development negotiations included Holsten Brewery/Carlsberg Germany, aurelis Real Estate, KG Panta, Deutsche Bahn (covering the Altona shopping center), Metro AG, Deutsche Post, and Hamburger Hochbahn.

The initial move toward a development agreement was taken in 2007 when Hamburg's Senate approved the "Vorbereitende Untersuchungen" (preliminary survey), a prerequisite for the urban development measure. By 2010, negotiations had led to an agreement defining the municipality's and landowners' financial responsibilities. These discussions, however, excluded residents. Following the preliminary financial arrangements, further investigations supported the assertion of public necessity for the project, leading to clear agreements on the program, funding, and design. Key negotiation themes included housing, green spaces, and the financial contributions of each party.

The way the municipality justified the use of the development measure is to highlight the need to increase the supply of housing in Hamburg. "This can make a significant contribution to expanding the urgently needed housing stock in Hamburg, which also supports the city's senate's goal of building 6,000 new apartments in Hamburg every year" (Steg et al., 2012, p. 10). Thus, the municipality invokes the market register to emphasize the goal of increasing the housing stock. In addition, the municipality explains how the development measure would increase the negotiation position of the city vis-à-vis the landowners. This is important to make the project financially viable. This type of argumentation includes an activation of the market register.

> This measure also allows it to have an early and comprehensive influence on the direction and design of the development of this part of the city, which gives it significantly greater scope for action in planning and a stronger negotiating position with the owners than would be possible at this time if general urban development law were applied. The City of Hamburg can also use this method to get the owners to share in the costs incurred by the city as part of this measure, which gives it a further advantage over other urban

> development processes. It can benefit from these advantages when concluding urban development contracts and formally defining a development area.
> (Steg et al., 2012, p. 202)

Interestingly, this shows how a public law prioritizes a specific type of register: the market register. By emphasizing specific calculations about the costs of the development project, it forces actors to put the worth of the plan into terms related to the market register. Rather than arguing that housing is a right for everyone, which would be connected to the civic register, the actors need to calculate the market value of the land. In addition, it shows how intertwined public law and private law are. A public law made it possible to negotiate a private law agreement.

As described, residents did not participate directly in the negotiations. The municipality could only use section 165 of the German building code and use the development measure if the landowners agreed to negotiate a deal with the municipality. This led to a negotiated agreement between landowners and the municipality before participatory processes were organized. Although the municipality made sure that there were specific areas in which citizens could have significant influence, such as the public park, the development project parameters were decided in the agreement between the municipality and landowners. This shows how the development measure's legal process constrains the influence citizens can have on the project. Notwithstanding the negotiations with the landowners, the municipality opened up a public and conducted an extensive participatory process to capture residents' priorities. Workshops, seminars, and guided walks gathered feedback from the community, resulting in over 600 resident recommendations (Freie und Hansestadt Hamburg, 2013). The master plan for Neue Mitte Altona incorporated input from residents who were part of the tender jury (without voting rights) and attended workshops (Freie und Hansestadt Hamburg, 2013). This participatory process highlighted residents' principles, including preserving historic buildings, ensuring 20% of housing units for self-build cooperatives, creating a public park, promoting cycling over car usage, maintaining accessibility for people with disabilities, limiting commercial spaces to small-scale businesses, and providing ample opportunities for resident involvement (Freie und Hansestadt Hamburg, 2013). The municipality aimed to integrate these outcomes; there was no formal commitment to doing so.

Interestingly, two registers were invoked during the participatory process by two citizen groups: the civic register and the entrepreneurial register. The municipality installed the first citizen group, the Koordinierungsgremium (KG), as an independent group of residents advising the municipality. In this, the public was shaped by residents themselves, rather than public officials. KG organized itself around the principles of the Recht auf Stadt (Right to the City) movement. They invoked the civic register to justify their actions, organizing the participatory process in such a way that it would reflect the needs and priorities of residents of Altona. Moreover, they activated the civic register to position themselves. KG argued that because they had organized themselves according to the rights of the city principles and represented the residents, they had decision-making power. During its assemblies,

KG crafted statements on the project, which were then deliberated and voted upon. Key topics included citizens' role in decision-making, housing cooperatives, space for small entrepreneurs, noise control, green initiatives, and a preference for cycling over car transport. KG also emphasized the Altonaer Mischung, a mixed-use model of housing, small shops, and workspaces, for the new neighborhood. All meetings were transcribed live for transparency, with 12 meetings held and 389 statements voted on (Birzer et al., 2011). However, the municipality and KG had differing expectations about the follow-up on KG's recommendations; while the municipality viewed them as advisory, KG had anticipated that these citizen-defined interests would be fully integrated into the development agreements. This shows how invoking a register is also a test of strength. Registers can be invoked but can also be resisted.

The second group, Eine Mitte für Alle (EMfA), focused on making Neue Mitte Altona fully accessible for people with disabilities. This group activated the entrepreneurial register in their participatory process. The process was designed according to the ideas of co-creation and aimed at negotiating with the municipality. Supported by the non-profit Q8, the group held several meetings, which were well-attended and led to a list of formal recommendations. "They initiated a forum, Eine Mitte für Alle. Around 30 people came together to continuously work on the topic of inclusion and urban development especially for Mitte Altona" (Community intermediary 24, Hamburg, 2018). Their recommendations included creating accessible housing, offering job counseling for people with disabilities, establishing professional neighborhood management sensitive to disability issues, ambitious green initiatives, and ensuring places of worship. Invoking the entrepreneurial register, these recommendations were crafted in contractual language for easier integration into official agreements. EMfA engaged in lobbying efforts with politicians and developers to secure the adoption of their proposals.

Between April and September 2012, the municipality published the preliminary survey outcomes and the master plan for Neue Mitte Altona, which KG criticized. "From my point of view, it was camouflage" (Resident 20, Hamburg, 2018). In a pamphlet titled "A moratorium for Neue Mitte Altona," KG declared the initiative—and its own involvement—as window dressing, questioning the transparency of the participatory process. Activating the civic register, they withdrew their support for the development plans of Neue Mitte Altona. They reasoned that residents did not influence the plans in a substantial way. KG also argued that the planned allocation of 33% social housing and 33% rent-controlled housing was insufficient, that prior occupants could not return, and that plans to preserve historical buildings were vague. Additionally, KG contended the design lacked the Altonaer Mischung, the mobility plan was insufficiently green, and developers gained excessive profits (Koordinierungsgremium Mitte Altona, 2012, 2015). Some of KG's proposals ultimately made it into the urban development agreement signed in May 2014, such as rent controls for shops, preservation of historical buildings, self-build cooperatives, support for small businesses, and a cycling-centered mobility strategy. However, KG felt these measures were diluted, particularly as they had sought more than 33% social housing. The agreement underscored the importance of accessibility for people with disabilities, though it lacked clear guidance on achieving this goal. The Hamburg Senate approved a strategy to implement EMfA's recommendations, though the landowners of Neue Mitte Altona were not directly bound by it. Nonetheless, the involved actors had an informal understanding to ensure accessibility for individuals with disabilities in the new development.

The development agreement informed changes in the land use plans. The municipality prepared the changes in the land use plan, and according to German law, private actors can comment on proposed changes in the land use plan. After private actors have commented on the plan, the city council takes a decision to approve the new land use plan; which happened in 2014.

This led to the situation where one citizen group had influenced the development agreement to a certain degree and was able to make their demands enforceable but denounced the deal. Achievements such as the rent control for shops could be used to litigate if shop owners were faced with rent hikes. In contrast, the other citizen group could not come to an enforceable agreement but strongly supported the deal. However, the group believed that the commitments made in public were strong enough that their ideas would be implemented. Moreover, enthusiasm for their approach led to the application of their ideas in city-wide policies. This shows that the degree of enforceability does not always align with how citizen groups evaluate their success. Furthermore, it shows that there is often a layering of different legal tools to stabilize relations between actors (see Savini, 2016). The national building code, the development agreement, and land use plan were used to ensure that the commitments of all involved actors were enforceable. The contradiction between the rights of the property owners and the objective of the planners of Hamburg was resolved through the signing of a development agreement. A development agreement is often more flexible and context-specific than public laws.

7.2 Oostenburg-Noord

Oostenburg-Noord is an area close to the harbor of Amsterdam, which was deindustrialized in the 1970s and is known for its working-class history. The neighborhood has a network of well-organized, active citizens. Municipal strategies of liberalizing the housing market and countering segregation by mixing low-income and middle-income households led to a decrease in the number of lower-income inhabitants and a rise in house values in the area (Uitermark and Bosker, 2014). The area of Oostenburg-Noord is owned by two landowners: a housing association called Stadgenoot and the development agency of the national government called Rijksvastgoedbedrijf.

Since it was the height of the financial crisis, Stadgenoot needed to find new ways to develop the area and attract investors. Therefore, Stadgenoot decided to work with the architectural firm Urhahn to create a vision for the neighborhood. Urhahn is known for its approach to cooperating with residents (Uitermark and Bosker, 2014). Through meetings and focus groups with residents, they designed the plan 'City Wharf Oostenburg.' In the plan, they activated the entrepreneurial register by proposing incremental development of the area and using bottom-up initiatives and participatory tools to steer development. The entrepreneurial register was invoked to stimulate residents to take an active role in the development process. Due to the weak housing market, Stadgenoot divided the area into smaller lots. Small investors or residents could buy the lots and realize their projects within the larger urban development project.

For decades, the neighborhood organization the Eilandenoverleg (EO) has represented the residents of Oostenburg-Noord in planning processes. Initially, EO was content with the chosen development strategy. As a neighborhood organization, it attempted to define the residents' principles for the residents of Oostenburg-Noord. However, they mainly invoked the civic register by stressing the importance of decision-making power for residents and social housing. Through a letter to Stadgenoot, they noted the importance of high green ambitions for the area, the need for social housing, and their desire for space for small- and medium-sized businesses, creative entrepreneurs, and cultural activities (Eilandenoverleg, 2013). Moreover, EO proposed to Stadgenoot to organize public meetings to create guidelines for the development of the neighborhood. The public meetings should determine what would happen in the area. Stadgenoot agreed to the proposal of EO and organized four meetings in a nearby public venue. Thus, eventually, the parties agreed to define the residents' principles together. They organized four public meetings in a nearby venue. However, there were conflicting ideas about how the meetings would be organized and the role of EO. Here, we can see a clash between the entrepreneurial and civic registers. The public meetings were organized in small groups to make the meetings more dynamic, a way of organizing associated with the entrepreneurial register. A civil servant was very content with the workshops: "Look, they [notorious naysayers] could share their opinion, which is important, because you need to know what is going on in the neighborhood. But hearing the other stories, and we could do that through the meetings, went really, really well" (Civil servant 1, Amsterdam, 2018). A member of EO was more critical: "The themes were discussed in small groups. In those groups professionals [architects and developers] were quite dominant. The residents were underrepresented" (Resident 1, Amsterdam, 2017).

The formulated principles included making the areas near the water publicly accessible, limiting access for cars, creating green spaces, and developing a square for the neighborhood. Stadgenoot asked EO to respond to the principles during the last public meeting. In their response, EO criticized the way the meetings were organized. In their critique, they invoked the civic register. The members of EO argued that the meetings were attended by many civil servants, architects, and designers, but not necessarily neighborhood residents.

Moreover, the residents did not influence the topics that were discussed. They also criticized that structural issues were ignored by dividing the meetings into themes. EO pushed for the following issues: locating the high-rise buildings near the railroad, increasing the amount of social housing, building a noise barrier to limit the noise of the trains, and limiting the accessibility of cars in the area as much as possible. But there was also praise from EO. They thought the plans were promising and offered to cooperate with Stadgenoot (Eilandenoverleg, 2013).

Although EO and Stadgenoot had the same goal, they had contradictory assumptions about how the public meetings would be organized. Therefore, there was no clear agreement between the resident organization and the developer. The EO claimed the mantle of being the true spokespersons of the neighborhood through activating the civic register. Still, the public meetings showed different opinions about how the residents' principles should be defined. EO's asserting that professionals dominated the public meetings could be easily dismissed as arguments of 'nay-sayers'. Hence, EO could only influence the definition of the residents' principles in a limited way and did not achieve a strong position to negotiate with the developers or the municipality.

Stadgenoot and Rijksvastgoedbedrijf agreed that realizing social housing in Oostenburg-Noord was not their priority. "We concluded with each other that 20% social housing and 80% market rate housing would balance the housing stock in the neighborhood" (Civil servant 1, Amsterdam, 2018). Together, Stadgenoot and Rijksvastgoedbedrijf negotiated a development agreement with the municipality. The development agreement specified the parties' responsibilities for the project, including the amount of social housing and who was accountable for the public space. The agreement was unavailable to the public and EO did not participate in the negotiations.

After the development agreement was signed, the land use plan was created. Some of the residents' principles, as formulated by EO and the residents, were incorporated into this plan. The waterfront remained 70% publicly accessible, high-rise buildings near the railroad, and car parking facilities were limited. Moreover, the plan stressed the importance of high green ambitions and stimulated the development of a renewable energy cooperative for the neighborhood. Although these provisions are encouraged, they are not obligatory (Gemeente Amsterdam, 2016). Though some of the demands of EO were incorporated in the flexible land use plan, both EO and the developers still had conflicting assumptions about the amount of social housing needed for Oostenburg-Noord.

The lack of clarity about social housing became a conflict between the municipality, Stadgenoot, and EO. The municipality and Stadgenoot intended to develop 16% of the total land area into social housing (20% of the total housing units was reserved for social housing). "We ended up with 20% social housing and 80% market rate housing, to balance out the neighborhood" (the neighborhood has predominately social housing) (Civil servant 1, Amsterdam, 2018). A member of EO published an opinion piece in the local newspaper to criticize the low amount of land designated for social housing. Activating the civic register, EO argued that at least 35% of the total land area should be reserved for social housing. EO also reached out to politicians. "We had talks with them. Before every council meeting we sent them our written responses to new developments" (Resident 1, Amsterdam, 2017). Thus, EO argued that more social housing needed to be part of the residents' principles, while the housing association and the municipality argued that less social housing was needed. The housing association and the municipality invoked the market register in their argumentation. There was already enough supply of social housing in the area, and the demand for market-rate housing was high in Amsterdam.

However, in a turn of events, when the land use plan came to a vote in the municipal council, most politicians sided with the definition of residents' principles of EO. This meant that the land use plan demanded that at least 20% of the land be reserved for social housing. In comparison, the commissioner had already signed a development agreement that designated 16% of the total land for social housing. The disparity between the flexible land use plan and the development agreement was solved through an amendment to the development agreement. "We left the development agreement for what it was, we made an amendment, and that took into account the demands of the council. This was signed by the parties [developers and municipality] and approved by the council" (Civil servant 1, Amsterdam, 2018). The initial agreement for 16% of the total land for social housing was raised to 20%. The amendment fixed one of the contradictory assumptions between EO and the developers, although EO would still have preferred more social housing.

After the municipal council adopted the land use plan, the parties signed the amendment, and the Rijksvastgoedbedrijf decided to sell their land. The buyer of the land was a joint venture between the investor Stonewell and the developer VORM. VORM took the lead in negotiating and managing the project from the side of the joint venture. The tender process was not directed to deliver the interests of residents but was primarily focused on the highest price. "Only the price mattered, you didn't need to hand in a design, and there were no extra points for sustainability" (Developer 2, Amsterdam, 2018).

The conflict over social housing hurt the relation between EO and the developers. To prevent future conflict, Stadgenoot proposed to organize meetings between EO, the developers, and the municipality. In exchange for their consent, EO got access to the decision-making process of Stadgenoot, VORM, and the municipality. The EO used the meetings to pressure the developers to align with their definition of residents' principles, such as using renewable energy sources, increasing the size of the housing units, and building community facilities. By attending the meetings, EO and the developers started forming more or less enforceable agreements about the area's development. In this way, the residents' principles, as defined by EO, could materialize in more or less enforceable agreements. First of all, there was an agreement about the meetings. Stadgenoot organized the meetings, and EO and the other parties could set the agenda. This agreement was not enforceable but allowed EO to influence decision-making processes. In the meetings EO noted that they were especially concerned about the size of the apartments, the sustainability of the project, and the community facilities. Thus, secondly, an agreement about residents' principles, such as the size of the apartments, was formed by putting the topic on the meeting agenda. The developers were therefore encouraged to include a minimum size of the apartments into the sub-contracts to prevent micro-apartment development.

> We are going to look whether we can formulate rules for the land area designated for social housing, the division of the typology of the units, and the size of the units. I won't say that we will regulate it very narrowly, but we will look into it.
>
> (Developer 1, Amsterdam, 2017)

Those sub-contracts are enforceable.

Thirdly, an agreement about the residents' principles concerning high green ambitions was formed. The developers announced that the project would use renewable energy sources. Stadgenoot already wanted high green ambitions for the project, so they agreed when EO pressed for renewable energy sources. The influence of the EO on this agreement was mostly indirect, through agenda-setting.

> No, we did not listen very directly to them, but the fact that the residents were involved of course made the municipality and the housing association promise that we must do something about sustainability. And we must do something about social housing, or we would get in trouble. So only that is already influential.
>
> (Developer 3, Amsterdam, 2018)

Finally, a letter of intent was made about community facilities with residents. Three members of EO proposed the plan for the community facilities, which was eventually declined. Stadgenoot could assist the community center but would not cover all the costs. So the initiative takers needed to create a plan that proved to be financially sound. Because they lacked the expertise to design a professional plan, they applied for a subsidy to get professional help. With the subsidy they got funding to hire a consultant, who helped formulate a plan more in line with the developers' standards. With the improved plan, Stadgenoot agreed to sign an agreement to create the community center. In the agreement Stadgenoot agreed to financially support the community facility, but only if there were other financial supporters. This shows how much the entrepreneurial register dictates the actions of Stadgenoot. The housing association supports community initiatives but must be as financially viable as possible.

In the first phase of the interactions between the neighborhood organization and the developers, there were contradictory assumptions about the development process. The neighborhood organization assumed they would be a negotiating party and claimed the mantle of the true spokespersons of the neighborhood. However, they could not claim to be *the* representatives of the neighborhood because the housing association and municipality invited other actors to take on that role as well. Therefore, their position could be dismissed as the position of nay-sayers. Hence, the municipality and the developers signed a development agreement together without the involvement of residents. However, the residents pressured politicians to alter the land use plan to include more social housing. This shows that both residents and developers can use private and public laws to achieve their goals.

Moreover, it shows that contracts are increasingly important in urban development but are not set in stone and can be adjusted. Because of the conflict, the developers and the municipality changed their contract and added some of the terms of the residents into an amendment. Hereafter, the relations changed; through a couple of meetings, several agreements between the residents, the developers, and the municipality were made. The meetings show that relations can substitute written agreements and that the agreement can also change when the relations change. However, residents need to claim their position in order to be accepted as a negotiation party. Notably, agreements about the project's design, such as the public space, were easier than agreements on social housing.

7.3 Kingsbridge Armory

The Kingsbridge Armory is located in Kingsbridge Heights, which is in the northwest of the Bronx. The area is a working-class area with a diverse population. Over 40% of the residents are foreign-born, with large Caribbean, Central American, and East, South, and Southeast Asian communities. The neighborhood struggles with poverty, with around 30% of the residents living below the poverty line (Chen and Hu, 2024). The neighborhood has an active group of community activists who are united in the Northwest Bronx Community and Clergy Coalition (NBCCC). The NBCCC fights for racial justice, affordable housing, and economic opportunities in the neighborhood. The Kingsbridge Armory was built between 1912 and 1917 and used for military purposes. In 1996, the ownership was transferred to the city of New York. Since then, the building has largely been vacant.

At first, there was a proposal to develop the armory into a shopping mall. The borough president, Rubén Díaz Jr., vetoed this plan because he feared that it would lead to gentrification and the displacement of local businesses. He activated the civic register when he announced that " we've seen how the interests of the people have prevailed over corporate America, and boy does that feel good"(Goldenberg, 2009). In the 2010s, a unique approach was almost successful in transforming the Kingsbridge Armory, which took the concerns vis-à-vis gentrification seriously. The project would redevelop a former armory into the world's largest ice-skating rink through a community benefit agreement (CBA). The CBA detailed how community groups, local businesses, and residents would profit from the ice-skating center. The CBA included agreements to invest some of the profits in the neighborhood, provide living wages for employees, and procure from local entrepreneurs. The plan to develop an ice-skating center was not uncontroversial; residents in the neighborhood did not have a strong connection to ice skating. However, community intermediaries invoked a mix of the civic and market registers to justify the plan for an ice-skating center. "The CBA is designed so that local businesses could benefit from it" (Resident 29, New York, 2019). The most striking arrangement in the CBA was making sure that local residents would profit from the development project. In the CBA, this is done in three major ways. First, 51% of the jobs would be allocated to people from the neighborhood, and they would receive a living wage. Second, there would be a local procurement plan, and between 25% of the services and products will be locally procured. Third, the developers would invest a minimum of $8.000.000 in total and yearly 1% of annual gross ice rink rental revenue up to $25.000.000 and 2% of annual gross ice rink rental revenue exceeding $25.000.0000 into projects that are valued by the community. This ensures that neighborhood organizations will benefit from the development long after the construction is completed. These are enforceable agreements to make sure that the neighborhood would continuously profit from the development. The neighborhood organizations reasoned that by making sure that local people would be hired and local companies would be used for procurement, gentrification could be limited. Moreover, an arrangement was made to prioritize making use of the services of minority- or women-owned businesses. The CBA was signed in 2013, but the developer struggled with finding investors in the project. Therefore, the plan never materialized.

The NBCCC was one of the signees of the CBA. After it became clear that there would be no investors for developing an ice-skating hall, they were asked by the city of New York to help develop the armory. They were the co-organizers of the participatory process and helped develop the vision plan for the area. The participatory process was coordinated by the community working group. The community working group was co-chaired by the NBCCC leader Sandra Lobo and council member Pierina Sanchez. The working group consisted of various actors that played an active role in the neighborhood, from churches, to cultural groups, local business organizations, schools, labor unions, and elected officials. The NYCEDC, New York's development department, created, together with WXY studio and Hester Street Collaborative, a for-profit community intermediary, a project team to develop the plan.

The participatory process took nine months, and around 4,000 residents actively engaged in the participatory activities. The community work group organized public workshops, surveys, small group discussions, and discussions with industry representatives. Invoking the civic register and ensuring that the process was inclusive, the organizers analyzed the demographics of those who attended the workshop. Moreover, all workshops were bilingual (English and Spanish), to cater to the large Latino population in Kingsbridge Heights. This process led to the so-called 'guiding principles for the redevelopment of the Kingsbridge Armory,' which were summarized and explained in the Together for Kingsbridge Vision Plan. The guiding principles are:

1. Prioritize youth
2. Welcome older adults
3. Foster intergenerational relationships
4. Create jobs and wealth for existing workers and communities
5. Grow a regenerative local economy
6. Maximize community ownership
7. Put the Bronx on the map

The guiding principles highlight the wish that the redevelopment of Kingsbridge Armory would benefit both youth and older adults. The idea was that they would receive opportunities for work and education but that those opportunities shouldn't exclude older adults. Thus, job and vocational training should be both available for youth and older people. Next, it was very important that the redevelopment would benefit local residents. The fear of gentrification is strong in the neighborhood because the area is still relatively affordable compared to other places in

New York. Thus, residents should be prioritized when new employees are being hired; their new development should include contracting targeted at minority and woman-owned businesses and workforce training programs. Lastly, the guiding principles call for community ownership. This principle means that the residents should share in the revenue created in the development of the Amory. The plan is to attract activities that could create revenue for activities that need support but are important for the community. For example, the hall can be used for film or entertainment activities, which can help fund small business incubators or cultural activities. After the vision plan was finalized and endorsed by a wide variety of actors from Kingsbridge Heights in New York, the city and state of New York agreed to invest 200 million dollars in the redevelopment of the armory. This support from the city and the state of New York made it more likely that this time the project will be realized. The neighborhood organization decided to submit its own proposal in the RFP-process. According to the leader of NBCCC it was time that they would take the lead in the development process 'We've been fighting back for a really long time, it's time to fight forward' (Chen and Hu, 2024). However, the City of New York decided to go with a competing proposal. Sandro Lobo, the NWBCCC Executive Director and co-chair of the Together for Kingsbridge visioning process stated the following:

The City's vision calls for a 'redevelopment that creates quality jobs, supports career development, [and] elevates entrepreneurs.' So far, there is only a general list of intended future uses for the Armory, without any concrete information on the programming or partners who will help bring it to life and meet these goals. This is of concern to all of us who, after 25 years, want the Armory finally transformed into an economic engine that prepares people for good-paying jobs of today and tomorrow, and maps a path for the power and capital generated by the Bronx to support the Bronx. We are convening a Coalition of Accountability made up of faith, community, labor, and small businesses that will continually monitor and advocate for a project that is transparent and genuinely invests in the community that surrounds it. The coalition will center its work around four areas: good jobs, community ownership, anti-displacement, and environmental standards. It will also pursue a legally binding Community Benefits Agreement that ensures these core priorities become a reality (N.W.B.C.C.C, 2025).

This shows that the residents' principles are mostly translated into less enforceable agreements.

7.4 Codifying residents' principles

Residents' principles are presented in various ways: through manifestos, community criteria, guidelines, or a myriad of other forms. These principles present the needs and wishes of the neighborhood in a unifying and unequivocal way. As the cases of Neue Mitte Altona, Oostenburg-Noord, and Kingsbridge Armory show, this is not a straightforward process; the residents' principles are defined through a process of conflict, negotiation, and compromise. After the residents' principles are more or less defined, there is a process of codification. As Table 7.1 shows, some of

Table 7.1 Overview of codification of residents' needs

	Resident' principles	*Less enforceable agreements*	*More enforceable agreement*
Neue Mitte Altona	Self-build cooperatives		x
	Public park		x
	Accessibility for people with a disability	x	
	Preservation of historical buildings		x
	Participatory processes	x	
	Sustainable mobility		x
	Social housing		x
	Small-scale businesses		x
Oostenburg-Noord	Social housing		x
	Meetings between actors	x	
	Size of apartments		x
	High green ambitions	x	
	Community facility	x	
Kingsbridge Armory	Prioritize youth	x	
	Welcome older adults	x	
	Foster intergenerational relationships	x	
	Create jobs and wealth for existing workers and communities	x	
	Grow a regenerative local economy	x	
	Maximize community ownership	x	
	Put the Bronx on the map	x	

those principles end up in less enforceable agreements and some in more enforceable agreements. The more enforceable agreements are, the higher the likelihood that promises to residents in participatory processes will be realized.

7.5 The legal thread in urban politics

This chapter describes the legal thread that binds urban politics together. The legal thread is woven together with the moral and political threads to resolve public issues. The legal thread is used to stabilize relations between actors by making promises enforceable, which increases the probability that specific actions will occur. As the three different cases show, the legal thread is often spun from various legal tools. Those can be associated with public law, such as planning laws and land use plans, but increasingly they are based on private law. Development agreements are signed before land use plans are changed or participatory processes are organized. This makes development agreements one of the most consequential legal tools in current-day urban politics. Participatory processes are often summarized in residents' principles: a set of needs, aspirations, and goals that summarize the outcomes of participatory processes and public debate. The residents' principles seem to be unequivocal and coherent but often cover up the conflicting needs of residents. However, the residents' principles play an important role; they provide a framework for decision-making processes and provide legitimacy for the project.

In the case of Neue Mitte Altona there were conflicting residents' principles that were finalized after the municipality already signed an agreement with the developers. This limits the extent to which the residents' principles materialize. But, as the case of Oostenburg-Noord shows, development agreements are not set in stone and can be adjusted. After residents mobilized, some of their principles were implemented due to an adjustment in the development agreement and informal meetings with the developers. Lastly, the case of Kingsbridge Armory shows that community intermediaries can also take an important role in formulating the development agreement. This ensures that residents' principles are not only window dressing but also a strong framework for the development project. Moreover, agreements can be harnessed by residents to enforce their interests in the development project. Q8 in Neue Mitte Altona and EO in Oostenburg Noord used less enforceable agreements to make sure that some of their needs were realized. In Kingsbridge Armory, the residents first used a community benefit agreement and, thereafter, a request for proposal to make sure that the project would benefit the neighborhood. Those agreements are enforceable and give residents the most certainty that promises made to them in participatory processes will materialize. Interestingly, the Koordinerungsgremiem in Neue Mitte Altona declared the participatory process death, not unlike the participation strike in the K-Buurt, but was able to turn some of their interests into enforceable agreements.

References

The American Law Institute. 1981a. *Restatement (Second) of Contracts §1.*

The American Law Institute. 1981b. *Restatement (Second) of Contracts §2.*

Beck Online. 2019. "§ 165 Städtebauliche Entwicklungsmaßnahmen." https://beck-online.beck.de/.

Birzer, Markus, Martin Brinkmann, and Wolfgang Gessenharter. 2011. "Anlage B Zum Masterplan Mitte Altona Teil1: Burgerforderungen." *Hamburg.*

Chen, Stefanos, and Winnie Hu. 2024, January 19. "A Moonshot Plan to Fill a Cavernous Dilapidated Armory in the Bronx." *The New York Times.*

Commission on European Contract Law. 2002. *Principles of European Contract Law Art.* 2:101: (1).

Durkheim, E. 1984. *The Division of Labour in Society*. London: The MacMillan Press.
Eilandenoverleg. 2013. "Reactie Op Planvorming Oostenburg-Noord." *Amsterdam*.
Eisenberg, M.A. 2018. *Foundational Principles of Contract Law*. New York: Oxford University Press.
Franzén, M. 2005. "New Social Movements and Gentrification in Hamburg and Stockholm: A Comparative Study." *Journal of Housing and the Built Environment* 20: 51–77.
Freie und Hansestadt Hamburg. 2013. "Masterplan Mitte Altona: Fundamente Für Ein Neues Stück Stadt." *Hamburg*.
Gemeente Amsterdam. 2016. "Bestemmingsplan Stadswerf Oostenburg Toelichting." *Amsterdam*.
Goldenberg, S. 2009, December 14. "Council Rejects Kingsbridge Armory Development Plan." *New York Post*.
Koordinierungsgremium Mitte Altona. 2012. "Ein Moratorium Für Mitte Altona."
Koordinierungsgremium Mitte Altona. 2015. "Moratorium Altona." http://wiki.rechtaufstadt.net/index.php/Moratorium_Altona.
Macaulay, Stewart. 1963. "Non-Contractual Relations in Business: A Preliminary Study." *American Sociological Review* 28 (1): 55–67. https://doi.org/10.4324/9780429494338.
Macaulay, Stewart. 1985. "An Empirical View of Contract." *Wisconsin Law Review* 465: 465–82.
Savini, Federico. 2016. "Don't Blame Public Law: The Legal Articulation of Certainty in Amsterdam Land-Use Planning." *Town Planning Review* 87 (4): 459–79. https://doi.org/10.3828/tpr.2016.29.
N.W.B.C.C.C. 2025. "Statement From Northwest Bronx Community & Clergy Coalition on Kingsbridge Armory Developer Selection." 2025. https://www.northwestbronx.org/armory-announcement-statement.
Smits, J.M. 2014. *Contract Law A Comparative Introduction*. Cheltenham: Edward Elgar Publishing Limited.
Stapper, E.W. 2021, September. "Contracting with Citizens: How Residents in Hamburg and New York Negotiated Development Agreements." *Land Use Policy* 111: 105743. https://doi.org/10.1016/j.landusepol.2021.105743.
Stapper, E.W. 2022. "Private Ordering of Public Processes: How Contracts Structure Participatory Processes in Urban Development in Amsterdam and Hamburg." *Urban Studies* 59 (9): 1872–88. https://doi.org/10.1177/00420980211024144.
Steg, Arbos, Argus, and Evers & Küsser. 2012. *Vorbereitende Untersuchungen Mitte Altona*. Steg, Arbos Freiraumplanung, Argus Stadt- und Verkehrsplanung, Evers & Küssner Stadt Planer.
Uitermark, Justus, and Tjerk Bosker. 2014. "Wither the 'Undivided City'? An Assessment of State-Sponsored Gentrification in Amsterdam." *Tijdschrift Voor Economische En Sociale Geografie* 105 (2): 221–30. https://doi.org/10.1111/tesg.12072.
Weber, Max. 1978. *Economy and Society: An Outline of Interpretive Sociology*. Los Angeles and London: University of California Press.

8 Conclusion

This book has shown that the increased use of contracts, community intermediaries, and co-creation processes in urban politics is the result of the institutionalization and displacement of critiques from various urban actors. This has made urban politics more and more ordered through negotiation processes. This can be explained by both democratizing forces and processes of capital accumulation. **Chapter 1** described how urban actors embraced the idea that the governments were too bureaucratic and the commercial parties were too focused on profits to develop urban development projects according to the needs of society. The creativity, enthusiasm, and entrepreneurial spirit of neighborhood residents needed to be harnessed to successfully develop urban projects. This is not the result of improved planning methods focused on co-creation and 'bottom-up' practices, as some authors seem to argue (Albrechts, 2012; Durose and Richardson, 2015; Leino and Puumala, 2020; Torfing et al., 2019). Nor is it merely the result of neoliberal policy changes that seek to increase market profits by making residents responsible for development projects (Swyngedouw, 2005, 2007) or a post-political strategy to suppress conflict (Metzger et al., 2015; Rancière, 2010; Mouffe, 2011). Instead, this evolution reflects historical processes in which residents, commercial parties, and government agencies sought to reshape planning practices and administer institutional contradictions, such as the contradiction between democracy and capitalism. These planning methods are shaped by various urban actors (Artioli and Le Galès, 2025). The reshaping of planning practices often tilts in favor of commercial parties and government agencies, but residents are not powerless. Detailing how critiques are displaced, coopted, or compromised shows how urban processes are often working in favor of processes of capital accumulation but that this process is contingent. This shows that other ways of organizing cities are possible.

8.1 How morals, politics, and law shape urban politics

From the 1970s, there has been a plea to involve citizens more in urban development processes. This plea has been answered in different decades by giving citizens the right to participate, to see their involvement as market research, and to see their involvement as a responsibility. These transformations took a long time to crystallize. For example, activist movements in Hamburg claimed the right to make decisions about their neighborhood by occupying and repurposing abandoned

DOI: 10.4324/9781032712840-8

buildings in the 1970s. Two decades later, this led to the foundation of intermediary organizations such as Stattbau and Lawaetz Foundation to redevelop occupied or abandoned buildings (Scheller, 2020). These intermediaries served as buffers between the municipality and the activists, avoiding direct subsidies to squatters (Scheller and Thörn, 2018; Stattbau Hamburg, 2024). This led to the renovation of old buildings and the development of co-housing projects and was aligned with the new motto of the city of Hamburg *Unternehmen Hamburg* (enterprising Hamburg), which aimed to stimulate economic growth and attract middle- and high-income families to the city (Neumann, 2020; Novy and Colomb, 2013; Von Dohnanyi, 1983). However, not all the squatters decided to work with the municipality; the Rote Flora group refused to enter contractual agreements and demanded to be removed from the land use plan (Buchholz, 2016; Scheller, 2020). Thus, critiques of residents are sometimes compromised (working with intermediaries of the municipality), sometimes coopted (becoming the new motto of the city), and sometimes displaced (some projects have strong involvement of residents, but residents lack decision-making power on city-wide plans). Comparable processes have occurred in Amsterdam and New York, although residents of New York have a harder time challenging commercial parties or government agencies due to the lack of city-wide comprehensive planning policies and legislation.

This shows that the social fabric of cities is constantly changing. Likewise, the processes of urban politics and governance is never linear, nor complete (Le Galès and Vitale, 2013). These changes occur due to the contradictions between property and planning and capitalism and democracy that dominate urban politics (Foglesong, 1986; Stein, 2019; Young, 1990). Property owners are hostile toward actions that restrict their activities but require government interventions such as investments in infrastructure. Meanwhile, planning processes need to appear to be geared towards the common good to be considered legitimate. The contradiction between capitalism and democracy emerges because democracy provides legitimacy and public resources to the infrastructures that capitalism needs for its accumulation processes. However, whereas the logic of democracy needs majority decisions, the logic of capitalism bases decisions upon profits. As described in **Chapter 4**, these contradictions in planning institutions are never solved but are dealt with through displacements, co-options, or compromises. They create fault lines in urban politics, fault lines between residents and developers, politicians and investors, and activists and civil servants. The way in which actors deal with those fault lines, varies from city to city, from neighborhood to neighborhood, and from project to project. To illustrate, the residents of the Esso-Häuser in Hamburg had to leave their houses, which is a clear form of displacement. Moreover, the landowner tried to co-opt the position of residents by giving them a new contract with fewer rights. This was prevented, which resulted in a long participatory process and a compromise between residents, the developers, and the municipality. Residents had to agree to the realization of market-rate housing, but in exchange, they received social housing, affordable housing cooperatives, and spaces for cultural activities.

As described in **Chapter 3**, the administrations of Amsterdam, Hamburg, and New York deal with institutional contradictions by designing policies that are increasingly becoming more entrepreneurial, promoting the use of contracts, community intermediaries, and co-creation. Traditional public meetings, often seen as outdated, are being replaced by co-creation workshops, elected officials are seen as less in touch with the needs of residents than community intermediaries, and negotiated agreements are prioritized above public law. For example, in Hamburg, the government agency of Stattwerkstatt actively promotes co-creation, consultancy firms are increasingly hired to design participatory processes in Amsterdam, and community benefit agreements can circumvent part of the land use plan approval process in New York (Freie und Hansestadt Hamburg, 2020; New York City Bar, 2010; Stapper, 2021). These new policies are often a compromise between activist movements such as Recht auf Stadt in Hamburg and Housing Justice for All in New York, claiming more decision-making power and the right for self-organization and interests from commercial parties and government actors.

Institutional contradictions influence the way planning decisions are made. From decision to decision, there is a possibility to serve the interests of property owners or plan for the common good; there is a possibility to make democratic decisions or focus on profits. As presented in **Chapter 4**, when these moments of contention occur, actors fall back on so-called pragmatic registers. Pragmatic registers are arrangements that bring actors and objects together and organize collective action through morals, politics, and laws. Through pragmatic registers, actors can justify their actions and move from their specific experiences to general judgments. Moving from individual preferences toward general judgments—based on pragmatic registers—is important in order to mobilize support from diverse groups within the neighborhood and outside of the neighborhood. Neighborhood residents can be convinced by the argument that it is their right to make decisions, but this argument does not translate well in boardroom discussions about real estate investments. The argument that harnessing the creativity of residents will lead to better designed project is probably more convincing.

In this book, I have described three pragmatic registers that are prevalent in urban politics based on the work of Luc Boltanski, Laurent Thévenot, and Ève Chiapello: the civic, market, and entrepreneurial registers (Boltanski and Chiapello, 2005; Boltanski and Thévenot, 1991). The civic register's main organizing principle is the empowerment of residents; it aims to do this by portraying residents as activists fighting for their rights. The preferred method of making decisions is through democratic practices, and relations are stabilized through legislation. The market register bases its ordering on economic growth, balancing demand, and supply, and aiming for profits. Citizens are seen as clients, and decisions are made through competition and efficiency. The preferred legal methods for the market register are private law tools such as contracts. Lastly, the entrepreneurial register premises are based on innovation and creativity. Residents are entrepreneurs who can turn ideas into projects with enthusiasm and networking skills. Decisions are made through collaborations in projects that are articulated in more or less enforceable agreements. The civic register became omnipresent in urban politics during the 1970s and the 1980s, the market register between the 1980s and 2000s, and the entrepreneurial register from the 2010s onward. The registers are omnipresent in urban politics but never omnipotent. Because urban politics is a complex network of different actors and objects that are interdependent on each other, registers are often compromised with each other. To realize a development project, commercial parties might activate the market register, but municipal policies push for the entrepreneurial register, and residents invoke the civic register. The outcome is a compromise between those registers, creating variations from project to project. Thus, pragmatic registers weave morals, politics, and law together to overcome the fault lines. Pragmatic registers are not outside forces that determine the actions of actors and objects. They are relational, embedded, and embodied; they are frameworks for coordinating collective action. Contracts embody the world of deal-making and are heavily associated with the market register. But they can also serve as community benefit agreements, mediating a compromise with the civic register. Post-its signal a creative way of brainstorming; they are deeply intertwined with the entrepreneurial register. But when they structure discussions leading to neighborhood votes, they enable a compromise with the civic register. As actors working for the common good, civil servants are strongly related to the civic register. However, constrained by city budgets, they frequently invoke the market register. Therefore, I use the metaphor of the thread to describe how they connect actors and objects with each other.

As described in **Chapter 6**, the political thread plays an important role in organizing decision-making processes in those moments of contention, publics forms. Publics are the spaces in which decisions are made about how to coordinate collective action and where critiques can be voiced about planning practices. Publics function as the spaces where the contradictions between planning and property and democracy and capitalism are negotiated by forging justification for collective action. Public officials—civil servants, politicians, and judges—play an important role in creating publics. They decide when to pull specific issues into the public sphere. Public officials can be pressured to open a public, but well-established actors such as big landowners can do this more easily than loosely organized residents. The example of Essex Crossing in New York showed that affluent homeowners were able to open and close the public easier than the representatives of Puerto Rican, Black, and Asian communities. This does not imply that underprivileged residents are always in this position. For example, the citizens of the K-Buurt in Amsterdam were able to start a public debate about the future of their neighborhood. They achieved this by skillfully using media and influencing politicians. Within the public, there is debate about how to organize collective action. Different actors voice their critiques about what is happening in their neighborhood in order to influence planning decisions. For example, the residents of the Northwest Bronx voiced the critique that most development projects result in gentrification and that the redevelopment of the Kingsbridge Armory should prevent gentrification.

In this process, as described in **Chapter 5**, the moral thread plays an important role in deciding what is valuable and what is not valuable. This provides a coordination mechanism in which collective action can occur. Through this process, actors and objects are imbued with worthiness. This relates to valuing what parts of a development project are important and who can be the true spokesperson of the neighborhood. Valuing which parts of a development project are important can range from the design of the housing and the accessibility of infrastructure to the construction of playgrounds. In the Essex Crossing project in New York, it took almost 40 years before a compromise could be reached. Market-rate housing was allowed in exchange for affordable housing and other promises to neighborhood residents. The process of valuing results in a set of unified and unequivocal set of principles that summarize the needs of residents. I refer to those needs as the residents' principles. Those residents' principles can come in the form of a manifesto, which happened in Neue Mitte Altona in Hamburg, a neighborhood code as developed for the Esso-Häuser in Hamburg, or community guidelines, which were formulated in the Essex Crossing project in New York. Moreover, an important element of the debate is the discussion of who is allowed to speak as the representative for the residents. This culminates in some actors claiming the mantle of being the true spokesperson of the neighborhood. It is important to note that valuing processes need to be tested to reality. As noted in **Chapter 4**, the residents and activists involved in the Esso-Häuser actively resisted the notion of the owners that the Esso-Häuser needed to be demolished. The residents and activists valued the building as a center of neighborhood life that needed to be renovated and the owners as a building that was deteriorating. In the end, the building needed to be evacuated because the building's structure was deemed to be collapsing. This shows that processes of valuation are always embedded in the material world.

Throughout the process of valuing, eventually, actors can agree to a particular way forward. As described in **Chapter 6**, this course of action is stabilized through the legal thread. The legal thread is used to stabilize relations between actors by making promises enforceable. This ensures that certain actions will occur. Although this can happen through both public and private law, it is increasingly achieved through private law arrangements such as development agreements. Private law provides actors with the ability to make project-specific agreements and gives them thus more flexibility in the design of a development project. However, public and private law are deeply entangled, and development agreements are always framed through public laws such as land use plans. In the end, if the moral, political, and legal threads are woven together, there is certainty for all the actors, and it is possible to undertake collective action. The divisions caused by the hermeneutic contradictions are temporarily overcome.

Institutional contradictions are increasingly being dealt with through the activation of the entrepreneurial register in Amsterdam, Hamburg, and New York. This explains the increased use of contracts, community intermediaries, and co-creation in urban planning and the transformation of urban politics. Government agencies and developers enter (contractual) agreements to realize development projects. As these agreements precede the ability of residents to get involved, they, therefore, also structure participatory processes. Those participatory processes are increasingly organized along the principles of co-creation; residents discuss in small groups elements of the design, put Post-its on a wall of ideas, or engage in Lego-design sessions. This unlocks the creativity of residents but also limits central discussions to discuss structural issues such as the lack of social housing. Next, community intermediaries—such as consultancy firms or neighborhood organizations—often either organize the participatory processes or strongly influence them. This creates tension about the question of who represents residents in these processes: elected officials, civil servants, neighborhood organizations, or activists? In order to claim the mantle of being the true spokesperson of the neighborhood, actors need to earn the worthiness of being the true spokespersons of the neighborhood. The combination of signing agreements before participation is organized, co-creation processes preventing discussions about structural problems, and the struggle to be seen as worthy to represent the neighborhood limits the ability of residents to bend development projects towards their needs.

However, the case studies described in this book show that astute residents can mobilize support from the media, politicians, and courts to position themselves as co-negatives of agreements. Increasingly, this happens in the form of neighborhood codes, community criteria, and civic codes, summarized in this book as resident principles. Contracts can be co-negotiated by residents in such a way that they hold parties accountable for delivering promises to the neighborhood, even to reduce social inequalities. But it should be noted that these case studies are unique cases—selected because they show how residents can influence more or less enforceable agreements.

The increased activation of the entrepreneurial register and the increased use of contracts, community intermediaries, and co-creation processes have four major consequences for urban politics. First, social inequalities—related but not determined by race, class, and other privileges—are reproduced. Those already well-positioned in society can better navigate participatory processes and often labyrinthine rules and regulations. The ability to speak up during a co-creation session or to think about legal language in contracts is not equally distributed in society. As the residents of the K-Buurt in Amsterdam have shown in Chapter 5, less privileged people often have more difficulty in getting their needs realized. Civil servants and consultants tend to express themselves in a professional language that is more familiar to higher-educated residents. This is even more the case for legal documents. Moreover, for working people, it might be hard to reserve time to attend a participation meeting. Second, residents who can successfully participate in development processes are deemed good citizens, implicitly devaluing those who cannot participate or do not participate in the right way. As the residents of the Koordineriungsgremium and Q8 have shown in Hamburg, participating in a more activist way versus a more entrepreneurial way can lead to different outcomes. There is a struggle for who can claim the mantle of being the true spokesperson in every participatory process. Neighborhood residents have to earn the worthiness of representing the neighborhood, whereas developers and civil servants inherently have a position at the negotiation table. Third, community intermediaries, such as neighborhood organizations or for-profit consultancy firms, increasingly organize participatory processes. Although they do not determine what happens in those processes, the design does structure the context in which decisions are being made. They can undermine the position of elected officials who are not always involved in the design and the process of participation. This results in unclarity about who can make decisions about development projects: the people active in the participatory process or elected officials? Fourth, contracts are not simply a reflection of social and political systems. Residents who can navigate contractual negotiations and direct municipal resources toward their goals play a major role. Moreover, prioritizing contracts over public laws as the foundation for decision-making fragments urban policy. This can lead to projects where residents are empowered, benefiting the entire neighborhood, and others where residents have limited influence. Hence, contracts are more than the sum of their parts; they can transform the social and political system in which they are embedded.

8.2 A new register gaining traction

As this book has shown, institutional contradictions are temporarily overcome through the employment of civic, market, and entrepreneurial registers. These registers originate from particular critiques of actors within society. In the last decade, concerns about climate change have led to large demonstrations across the world, including in Amsterdam, Hamburg, and New York. During climate marches, people demanded stronger climate action from decision-makers. The Paris Climate Agreement was signed in 2015 and requires its signees to draw up plans to keep the earth from heating more than 1.5 degrees Celsius (United Nations, 2015). This has led to large-scale climate plans such as the European Green Deal and the Inflation Reduction Act (European Commission, 2019; The White House, 2024), influencing planning practices in Amsterdam, Hamburg, and New York. Whereas Amsterdam and Hamburg already had goals to become more sustainable cities, Amsterdam and New York aim to become climate neutral in 2050 and Hamburg in 2045. That is a strong shift in ambition. These decarbonization goals are already influencing participatory processes. Policy goals such as the decentralization of (carbon-neutral) energy production require collaboration with residents. There is a certain tension between the need to decarbonize quickly and the often slow processes of working with residents. However, in densely populated cities in Europe and North America, participatory processes will be needed to create support for these policies.

In Amsterdam, the 'climate roadmap' describes participation as a communication and activation tool for decreasing Amsterdam's dependency on fossil fuels for heating (Gemeente Amsterdam, 2020, p. 72). Next, participation is a tool to increase local ownership over decentralized carbon-neutral energy production (Gemeente Amsterdam, 2020, p. 131). Moreover, wind turbine projects need participation from residents as early as possible (Gemeente Amsterdam, 2020, p. 190). In Hamburg, the city-wide climate plan was discussed through an online participatory process. The municipality wrote policy papers with their envisioned key climate goals, which were discussed in online meetings (Freie und Hansestadt Hamburg, 2024). There was also outreach to NGOs, businesses, and climate scientists, who were described as important stakeholders in achieving climate neutrality (Freie und Hansestadt Hamburg, 2024). The City of Yes carbon neutrality plan in New York notes the importance of working with various actors, such as neighborhood organizations and alliances, to achieve its goals. However, participation does not seem to be an important element of the plan. The Climate Mobilization Act, which requires large buildings to cut their carbon emissions or refine fines, notes the responsibilities of tenants to reduce their emissions as well (City of New York, 2024).

In 2000, Thévenot, Moody, and Lafaye described the green register (Thévenot et al., 2000). The register's main organizing principle is environmental friendliness, with valued actors such as environmentalists and valued objects such as pristine wilderness, healthy environments, and natural habitats. Future generations and the protection of ecosystems play an important role in justifying actions (Thévenot et al., 2000). Based on the current developments in Amsterdam, Hamburg, and New York, participatory processes related to climate policies are mostly used to activate residents to take on responsibilities. This shows that many planning practices will probably activate a compromise between the entrepreneurial and green registers. Public laws will be used to force actors to strive for climate neutrality, whereas agreements will be used to foster collaboration.

However, it is also possible that a new register will emerge that seems related but is distinct from the green register. This could be comparable to the distinction between the market and entrepreneurial register. Both registers are oriented toward justifications based on supply and demand. However, the market register values profits, and the entrepreneurial register innovation. This register could have as its main principle carbon neutrality rather than a focus on environmental friendliness. Valued actors will be climate scientists, entrepreneurs, and activists. Whereas most actions will be centered on objects such as carbon, methane, and nitrogen, the register will prioritize the prevention of global warming over protecting wilderness areas. This register could be called the carbon register because justifications for actions are given based on whether carbon emissions increase or decrease. Public laws that prioritize decarbonization will be the preferred way of using laws. But time will tell whether such a register will emerge.

8.3 A research agenda

Participatory processes have been extensively examined in urban studies, while community intermediaries have received less attention, and contracts, in particular, remain significantly understudied. I argue that urban studies need to take contracts seriously. Rather than dismissing them as private sector tools designed to enforce the interest of commercial parties, social scientists must study how contractual relations form and change over time. Being aware of unequal power relations is necessary, but the assumption that urban elites are always the dominant forces behind contracts does not hold up to empirical scrutiny. Studying the details and nuances of contractual processes gives us insight into how actors' reflexive engagement with structural features can lead to new political and sociological imaginaries.

I conclude by posing three questions for future research. This book has shown that contractual relations are formed through political action and appeals to moral standards. The actors who are able to claim the mantle of true spokespersons can powerfully influence how contractual relations materialize. Researchers of urban development should therefore ask:

1. Which groups claim the mantle of being the true spokesperson of the neighborhood?

   Valuable sources to answer this question include newspaper articles, policy documents, and interviews. By analyzing how different moral registers are invoked over time, it becomes clear which groups can claim the mantle of being true spokespersons. It also helps to understand how citizens' principles are formulated and how the capitalist-democracy tension is administered. What is the relation between representatives and the represented? Which actors are seen as worthy, and which actors are devalued? Understanding how, when, and who claims the mantle of the true representative gives us insight into which actors are recognized and accepted as co-negotiators of agreements and which actors are excluded from negotiations. My research focused on critical cases where residents were co-negotiators. Future research could compare typical and atypical cases to study how moral and political boundaries between actors are drawn.

   Next, this book has shown that contracts are prioritized over public planning laws to determine how development projects will be designed. However, contracts are not set in stone, and they can be adjusted. There are often multiple legal tools used to steer the actions of actors, ranging from binding contracts to less enforceable neighborhood codes, community criteria, or civic codes to planning laws. Scrutinizing how these legal tools are being employed and how to serve the interests of different actors is an important research area. It is important to study these tools not as static instruments but as embedded in relations and changing over time. Therefore, urban study scholars should explore the following questions:
2. How do public and private legal tools function in practice, and how do their use and significance evolve over time?

   This question can be best answered by studying the content of legal tools and interviewing actors. Interviews can shed light on how contracts and public laws are used to coordinate the actions of actors. Moreover, interviews can help to understand what kind of unwritten agreements are used to foster cooperation between actors. This will furnish insight into how different legal tools are used to achieve the goals of different actors. To what extent do non-enforceable agreements complement or even supplement enforceable agreements? Do contractual relations change over time? How do contracts and planning laws interact with each other? It will show how legal tools create hierarchies between actors and whose interests are privileged in agreements.
3. How are agreements with residents monitored and enforced?

   Participatory processes have been common practices in cities in North America and Europe since the 1970s. They have been academically studied and scrutinized. However, there is a lack of research on how promises made during participatory processes are being monitored and enforced. Alongside studying written agreements, interviews should provide insight into how agreements work and how benefits accrue to residents. Can agreements help to prevent gentrification? Can customized contracts strengthen the influence of residents over their neighborhoods? Both the potential of contracts to empower communities and to depoliticize issues should be investigated.

8.4 A policy agenda

This book has examined how cities are increasingly ordered through negotiation, valuing contracts, community intermediaries, and co-creation processes. This book has also shown that these processes have the risk of reproducing social inequalities; not all urban actors are well-positioned to use negotiations to their advantage. But above all, this book has highlighted the power of law. Agreements are often signed before participation is organized, which constrains the ability of residents to influence development projects. However, the projects studied in this book also portray that agreements can be harnessed to advance the goals of residents. The municipality of Hamburg promotes this idea by using a transparency portal and making all contracts available for the public to read. The projects of Neue Mitte Altona and Kingsbridge Armory show that neighborhood residents can creatively use contracts to structurally benefit the neighborhood. Although the participatory process of Neue Mitte Altona was heavily criticized, the development agreement included a clause that controlled rent for shop owners. Although the project never materialized, the community benefit agreement of Kingsbridge Armory included a clause that neighborhood organizations would yearly receive a percentage of the revenue from the main business operator in the project.

This kind of clause shows that contracts can be used to let residents structurally benefit from developments in their neighborhood, and planners should take note. Moreover, the outcomes of participatory processes were translated into development agreements in projects such as Essex Crossing and the Esso-Häuser, which are good practices to show what happens with residents' input on plans. However, next to better contracting practices, public laws should also be strengthened to address the position of residents. The 'participatie verordening' in Amsterdam regulates how residents are involved in planning practices, even giving residents so-called neighborhood rights. But public laws could also be designed to create resident committees that monitor development processes, ensuring that promises to the neighborhood will be realized.

Next to better use of laws, it is important that participatory processes should be repoliticized. Elected officials play a limited role in those processes—especially in Amsterdam and Hamburg—which makes civil servants and community intermediaries responsible for making and explaining political decisions to residents. Participatory processes are a great space to discuss politics, and elected officials should explain political decisions there. This is important for two reasons. First, sometimes, decisions are important for the city but less important or difficult for the neighborhood. Those decisions need to be explained. Second, not all residents have the time or ability to be active during participatory processes. This has the risk of reproducing social inequalities. Elected officials are often present or represented at community board meetings or participatory processes in New York. This is a practice that politicians from Amsterdam and Hamburg can learn from. Next to a better representation from elected officials, those who organize participatory processes should aim for a diverse representation. The case of the Esso-Häuser in Hamburg had so-called 'plan buddies' who reached out to underrepresented groups. The active involvement of a neighborhood organization in the K-Buurt ensured that groups that normally do not attend participatory meetings became actively involved. Centrally organized entities, such as the Office of Neighborhood Strategies or Stadtwerkstatt, should evaluate participatory processes based on how represented they are and how the outcomes of participatory processes are incorporated into development agreements.

References

Albrechts, L. 2012. "Reframing Strategic Spatial Planning by Using a Coproduction Perspective." *Planning Theory* 12 (1): 46–63. https://doi.org/10.1177/1473095212452722.
Artioli, Francesca, and Patrick Le Galès. 2025. "Metropolitan Governance as Organised Anarchy: The Case of the Paris Region." *Cities* 158: 105607. https://doi.org/10.1016/j.cities.2024.105607.
Boltanski, Luc, and Eve Chiapello. 2005. *The New Spirit of Capitalism*. London, UK: Verso.
Boltanski, Luc, and Laurent Thévenot. 1991. *On Justification: Economies of Worth*. Princeton: Princeton University Press.
Buchholz, Tino. 2016. *Struggling for Recognition and Affordable Housing in Amsterdam and Hamburg*. Groningen: University of Groningen.
City of New York. 2024. "Climate Mobilization Act." https://council.nyc.gov/data/green/.
Durose, C., and L. Richardson. 2015. *Designing Public Policy for Co-Production*. Bristol: Policy Press.
European Commission. 2019. *The European Green Deal*. Brussels: European Commission.
Foglesong, R.E. 1986. *Planning the Capitalist City: The Colonial Era to the 1920s*. Princeton: Princeton University Press.
Freie und Hansestadt Hamburg. 2020. "Was Will Die Stadwerkstatt."
Freie und Hansestadt Hamburg. 2024. "Gemeinsam Für Eine Klimafreundliche Stadt." https://www.hamburg.de/politik-und-verwaltung/behoerden/bukea/themen/klimaschutz/klimaplan-und-klimaschutzgesetz/onlinebeteiligungklimaplan−169878.
Gemeente Amsterdam. 2020. "Nieuw Amsterdams Klimaat." *Gemeente Amsterdam*.
Le Galès, Patrick, and Tommaso Vitale. 2013. "Governing the Large Metropolis. A Research Agenda." https://doi.org/10.31235/osf.io/95zsc.
Leino, H., and E. Puumala. 2020. "What Can Co-Creation Do for the Citizens? Applying Co-Creation for the Promotion of Participaiton in Cities." *Environment and Planning C: Politics and Space* 39 (4): 781–99.
Metzger, Jonathan, Phil Allmendinger, and Stijn Oosterlynck. 2015. "The Contested Terrain of European Territorial Governance." In *Planning Against the Political: Democratic Deficits in European Territorial Governance*, edited by Jonathan Metzger, Phil Allmendinger, and S. Oosterlynck, 1–29. New York and London: Routledge.
Mouffe, Chantal. 2011. *On the Political. On the Political*. New York: Routledge. https://doi.org/10.4324/9780203870112.
Neumann, Arndt. 2020. "From Fordist to Neo-Liberal Urban Spaces in Times of de-Industrialization: A Conceptual Frame for a Complex Relationship." *Urban History* 47 (2): 220–35. https://doi.org/10.1017/S0963926819000233.
New York City Bar. 2010. "The Role of Community Benefit Agreements in New York City´s Land Use Process."

Novy, Johannes, and Claire Colomb. 2013. "Struggling for the Right to the (Creative) City in Berlin and Hamburg: New Urban Social Movements, New 'Spaces of Hope'?" *International Journal of Urban and Regional Research* 37 (5): 1816–38. https://doi.org/10.1111/j.1468–2427.2012.01115.x.

Rancière, J. 2010. *Dissensus: On Politics and Aesthetics*. Edited by Steven Corcoran. New York: Continumm International Publishing Group.

Scheller, David. 2020. "Hamburg: Housing Movements and Local Government." In *Contemporary Co-Housing in Europe: Towards Sustainable Cities?*, edited by Pernilla Hagbert, Henrik Gutzon Larsen, Håkan Thörn, and Cahtrin Wasshede, 57–74. Routledge.

Scheller, David, and Håkan Thörn. 2018. "Governing 'Sustainable Urban Development' Through Self-Build Groups and Co-Housing: The Cases of Hamburg and Gothenburg." *International Journal of Urban and Regional Research* 42 (5): 914–33. https://doi.org/10.1111/1468–2427.12652.

Stapper, E.W. 2021, September. "Contracting with Citizens: How Residents in Hamburg and New York Negotiated Development Agreements." *Land Use Policy* 111: 105743. https://doi.org/10.1016/j.landusepol.2021.105743.

Stattbau Hamburg. 2024. "Die Entsehung van STATTBAU Und Die Instrumente Alternativer Sanierung in Hamburg." https://stattbau-hamburg.de/wp-content/uploads/2021/02/STATTBAU-Geschichte-der-Entstehung.pdf.

Stein, S. 2019. *Capital City: Gentrification and the Real Estate State*. London and New York: Verso.

Swyngedouw, Erik. 2005. "Governance Innovation and the Citizen: The Janus Face of Governance-Beyond-the-State." *Urban Studies* 42 (11): 1991–2006.

Swyngedouw, Erik. 2007. "The Post-Political City: Re-Imagining Democracy in the Neoliberal City." In *Urban Politics Now*, edited by BAVO. Rotterdam: NAi Publishers.

Thévenot, Laurent, Michael Moody, and Claudette Lafaye. 2000. "Forms of Valuing Nature: Arguments and Modes of Justification in French and American Environmental Disputes." In *Rethinking Comparative Cultural Sociology: Repertoires of Evaluation in France and the United States*, edited by Laurent Thévenot and Michele Lamont, 229–73. Cambridge: Cambridge University Press.

Torfing, J.B., E. Sorensen, and A. Roiseland. 2019. "Transforming the Public Sector into an Arena for Co-Creation: Barriers, Drivers, Benefits and Ways Forward." *Administration & Society* 51 (5): 795–825.

United Nations. 2015. *Paris Agreement*.

Von Dohnanyi, Klaus. 1983. "Unternehmen Hamburg." http://www.ueberseeclub.de/resources/Server/pdf-Dateien/1980-1984/vortrag-1983-11-29Dr.%20Klaus%20von%20Dohnanyi.pdf.

The White House. 2024. "Inflation Reducation Act." https://www.whitehouse.gov/cleanenergy/inflation-reduction-act-guidebook/.

Young, Iris Marion. 1990. *Justice and the Politics of Difference*. New York: Princeton University Press.

Appendix I

Interviewees

Case	*Interviewee*	*Date*
Community intermediaries	Community intermediary 1	2017
	Community intermediary 2	2017
	Community intermediary 3	2017
	Community intermediary 4	2017
	Community intermediary 5	2017
	Community intermediary 6	2017
	Community intermediary 7	2017
	Community intermediary 8	2017
	Community intermediary 9	2017
	Community intermediary 10	2017
	Community intermediary 11	2017
	Community intermediary 12	2017
	Community intermediary 13	2017
	Community intermediary 14	2017
	Community intermediary 15	2017
	Community intermediary 16	2017
	Community intermediary 17	2017
	Community intermediary 18	2017
	Community intermediary 19	2017
	Community intermediary 20	2017
Oostenburg	Resident 1	2017
	Politician 1	2018
	Entrepreneur 1	2018
	Civil Servant 1	2018
	Community intermediary 21	2018

(*Continued*)

(Continued)

Case	*Interviewee*	*Date*
	Resident 2	2018
	Resident 3	2018
	Developer 1	2017
	Resident 4	2018
	Resident 5	2018
	Resident 6	2018
	Politician 1	2018
	Developer 2	2018
	Developer 3	2018
Zeeburgerpad	Resident 7	2017
	Resident 8	2017
	Resident 9	2017
	Community intermediary 22	2017
	Politician 2	2017
	Resident 10	2017
	Resident 11	2017
	Resident 12	2017
	Politician 3	2017
	Politician 4	2017
	Civil servant 2	2017
	Resident 13	2018
K-Buurt	Civil servant 3	2017
	Civil servant 4	2017
	Civil servant 5	2017
	Resident 14	2017
	Resident 15	2017
	Politician 5	
Haventraatterrein	Developer 4	2017
	Civil servant 6	2017
	Civil servant 7	2017
Landtong Nieuwe Meer	Resident 16	2017
	Resident 17	2017
	Resident 18	2017
Hamburg general	Resident 19	2017
	Civil servant 8	2018
	Academic 1	2018

(Continued)

(Continued)

Case	*Interviewee*	*Date*
Mitte Altona	Community intermediary 23	2018
	Civil servant 9	2018
	Politician 6	2018
	Civil servant 10	2018
	Politician 7	2018
	Politician 8	2018
	Civil servant 11	2018
	Community intermediary 24	2018
	Resident 20	2018
	Resident 21	2018
	Resident 22	2018
	Resident 23	2018
	Resident 24	2018
PlanBude	Civil servant 12	2018
	Politician 9	2018
	Civil servant 13	2018
	Community intermediary 25	2018
	Community intermediary 26	2018
Gängeviertel	Resident 25	2018
	Resident 26	2018
	Community intermediary 27	2018
	Community intermediary 28	2018
Kingsbridge Armory	Resident 27	2018
	Civil servant 14	2019
	Civil servant 15	2018
	Resident 28	2019
	Resident 29	2019
	Resident 30	2018
Essex Crossing	Academic 2	2018
	Resident 31	2018
	Community intermediary 29	2018
	Resident 32	2019
	Developer 5	2019
	Resident 33	2019
Jerome Avenue	Resident 34	2019
Sendero Verde	Civil servant 16	2019
Columbia CBA	Resident 35	2019

(*Continued*)

(Continued)

Case	*Interviewee*	*Date*
The Peninsula	Developer 6	2019
	Developer 7	2018
	Resident 36	2019
New York general	Resident 37	2019
	Civil servant 17	2019
	Academic 3	2019
	Academic 4	2019
	Academic 5	2019
	Academic 6	2019
	Academic 7	2019

Appendix II

News articles

	Project	*Paper*	*Title*	*Date*	*Author*	*Words*
1	Kingsbridge Armory	*Daily News*	Duty calls at armory. City calls for plans on building overdue for revamp	27-September-2006	Bill Egbert	432
2	Kingsbridge Armory	*The New York Times*	An armory, long furlough, soon to get its orders	5-November-2006	Jennifer Bleyer	718
3	Kingsbridge Armory	*Daily News*	Task force sounds off: City drops gag order on armory plans, and local leaders say it's all good	15-May-2007	Bill Egbert	406
4	Kingsbridge Armory	*The New York Times*	A neighborhood in waiting—Correcting appended	12-August-2007	Jake Mooney	1564
5	Kingsbridge Armory	*The New York Times*	Yet again, a majestic armory contemplates its future	28-October-2007	Gregory Beyer	289
6	Kingsbridge Armory	*Daily News*	Ups and downs in Bronx: Boro dug in as major changes got underway	30-December-2007	Bob Kappstatter	1076
7	Kingsbridge Armory	*Daily News*	Related wins armory rehab project	21-March-2008	Bill Egbert	408
8	Kingsbridge Armory	*The New York Post*	Mall of duty- Armory's $310 million retail rehab	21-April-2008	Tom Topousis	376
9	Kingsbridge Armory	*The New York Times*	City says the Kingsbridge Armory will become a shopping center	22-April-2008	Timothy Williams	912
10	Kingsbridge Armory	*Daily News*	Coalition waging battle with armory developer for Kingsbridge benefits	25-April-2008	Bill Egbert	329
11	Kingsbridge Armory	*The New York Times*	Bronx groups demand a voice in a landmark's revival	25-June-2008	Terry Pristin	1233

(*Continued*)

(Continued)

	Project	Paper	Title	Date	Author	Words
12	Kingsbridge Armory	*Daily News*	Shopping for approval. Public hearing on Kingsbridge Armory mall plan	2-October-2008	Bill Egbert	458
13	Kingsbridge Armory	*Daily News*	Battle brewing over tax break for armory developer	10-March-2009	Bill Egbert	404
14	Kingsbridge Armory	*Daily News*	Small biz owners fight bx. Big-box store plan	16-July-2009	Albor Ruiz	569
15	Kingsbridge Armory	*Daily News*	Armory goes to people: Public hearing on controversial plan to be held tonight	27-July-2009	Mike Jaccarino	290
16	Kingsbridge Armory	*Daily News*	An armory food fight: Public hearings focuses on massive market plan	10-September-2009	Bill Egbert	425
17	Kingsbridge Armory	*The New York Times*	Proposed supermarket divides Bronx community	30-September-2009	Terry Pristin	1293
18	Kingsbridge Armory	*The New York Times*	Planners accept proposal for mall at Bronx Armory	20-October-2009	Sam Dolnick	634
19	Kingsbridge Armory	*The New York Times*	Coalition vows wage fight over Kingsbridge Armory mall proposal	17-November-2009	Sam Dolnick	1082
20	Kingsbridge Armory	*Daily News*	Wages stall mall: Bloomy nixes armory projects pay mandate	18-November-2009	Frank Lombardi	513
21	Kingsbridge Armory	*Daily News*	Build bridge to good Bronx jobs	19-November-2009	Errol Louis	630
22	Kingsbridge Armory	*Daily News*	Armory plan standoff, council panel set to kill deal if builder won't pay living wage	23-November-2009	Bill Egbert	365
23	Kingsbridge Armory	*The New York Times*	Voting 45–1, council rejects $310 million plan for mall at Bronx armory	15-December-2009	Sam Dolnick	882
24	Kingsbridge Armory	*The New York Post*	A Bronx bummer—Mike's armory plan shot down	15-December-2009	Sally Goldenberg	374
25	Kingsbridge Armory	*Daily News*	Council armory assault nixes bx. Shopping mall	15-December-2009	Frank Lambardi	373

(Continued)

(Continued)

	Project	*Paper*	*Title*	*Date*	*Author*	*Words*
26	Kingsbridge Armory	*Daily News*	Kissing jobs goodbye	15-December-2009	Editorial	504
27	Kingsbridge Armory	*The New York Post*	Mike's call to armory—will veto council's vote to kill 1200 jobs	16-December-2009	David Sefiman	453
28	Kingsbridge Armory	*The New York Times*	A stimulus that's short of stimulating	16-December-2009	Jim Dwyer	733
29	Kingsbridge Armory	*The New York Post*	Lunatics in charge—council's mad Kingsbridge vote	17-December-2009	Steve Cuozzo	774
30	Kingsbridge Armory	*The New York Post*	Mike rips blunder in the Bronx	17-December-2009	David Seifman	150
31	Kingsbridge Armory	*The New York Post*	Kingsbridge Commissar	18-December-2009	-	413
32	Kingsbridge Armory	*The New York Times*	Council overrides veto, blocking plan for armory mall	22-December-2009	Sam Dolnick	538
33	Kingsbridge Armory	*Daily News*	Council gives 'Bah! Humbug!' to Mike vetoes	22-December-2009	Erin Einhorn and Frank Lombardi	494
34	Kingsbridge Armory	*The New York Post*	'No jobs': A promise he'll keep	23-December-2009	-	203
35	Kingsbridge Armory	*Daily News*	Bad job on jobs	24-December-2009	Editorial	434
36	Kingsbridge Armory	*Daily News*	Diaz maps plan for Bronx of the future	26-February-2010	Bob Kappstatter	599
37	Kingsbridge Armory	*Daily News*	Ruben's second thoughts	11-March-2010	Editorial	161
38	Kingsbridge Armory	*Daily News*	Armory task force	24-March-2010	Bill Egbert	388
39	Kingsbridge Armory	*The New York Post*	Empty Armory Haunting Ambitious Bronx Beep	28-March-2010	David Seifman	271

(Continued)

(Continued)

	Project	Paper	Title	Date	Author	Words
40	Kingsbridge Armory	*Daily News*	This domino must not fall	3-April-2010	Editorial	464
41	Kingsbridge Armory	*Daily News*	An armory tug of war: Plan to move new schools in and boot military units stalls	7-April-2010	Brendan Brosh and Daniel Beekman	423
42	Kingsbridge Armory	*Daily News*	Domino Effect	10-April-2010	Editorial	379
43	Kingsbridge Armory	*The New York Times*	Community pacts questioned in the zoning process	28-April-2010	Terry Pristing	1336
44	Kingsbridge Armory	*The New York Times*	Wage proposal for workers at subsidized projects may prompt a fight at city hall	24-May-2010	Sam Dolnick	631
45	Kingsbridge Armory	*Daily News*	Living wage kills projects, Bloomy says	25-May-2010	Erin Einhorn	246
46	Kingsbridge Armory	*Daily News*	Churches fighting for living wages	10-October-2010	Albor Ruiz	543
48	Kingsbridge Armory	*The New York Post*	In the Bronx, an empty sore instead of jobs	12-December-2010	Candice M. Glove	471
49	Kingsbridge Armory	*Daily News*	Diaz jobs the Bronx	14-December-2010	Editorial	399
50	Kingsbridge Armory	*Daily News*	Don't gimme shelter. Beep rips Mike's Wakefield bid	17-December-2010	Mike Jac-carino and Kate Lucadamo	358
51	Kingsbridge Armory	*The New York Post*	I'll be savior of armory—Rolls-Royce Rev.'s Bx. Conversion BID	21-June-2011	David Seifman	468
52	Kingsbridge Armory	*Daily News*	BEEP's taking heat on armory report	30-June-2011	Bob Kappstatter	743
53	Kingsbridge Armory	*The New York Post*	Deal near after armory debacle	12-January 2012	David Seifman	558

(Continued)

(Continued)

	Project	*Paper*	*Title*	*Date*	*Author*	*Words*
54	Kingsbridge Armory	*The New York Times*	As wage concerns ebb, Bronx armory push is revived	12-January-2012	Kate Taylor and David W. Chen	753
55	Kingsbridge Armory	*Daily News*	Setting the state Diaz's state of borough will boast development	23-February-2012	Daniel Beekman	567
56	Kingsbridge Armory	*Daily News*	Rodeo is a-coming'! Cowboys will gallop into vacant armory	6-March-2012	Daniel Beekman	491
57	Kingsbridge Armory	*Daily News*	What a n-ice idea! Kingsbridge Armory rink on the mark	21-March-2012	Daniel Beekman	423
58	Kingsbridge Armory	*Daily News*	Beep's power play. Diaz push to turn armory into ice center	24-August-2012	Tanyanika Samuels	442
59	Kingsbridge Armory	*The New York Times*	Ice center with 9 rinks is proposed for Bronx armory	24-August-2012	Winnie Hu	575
60	Kingsbridge Armory	*The New York Post*	Diaz in the penalty box	29-August-2012	Editorial	361
61	Kingsbridge Armory	*Daily News*	Cooler than ice: Legends urge hip-hop museum in place of sports center	18-September-2012	Daniel Beekman	453
62	Kingsbridge Armory	*Daily News*	Risky propositions	24-September-2012	Editorial	519
63	Kingsbridge Armory	*Daily News*	Cheers and jeers at forum: One would-be armory developer attended 2nd meet, another didn't	19-October-2012	Daniel Beekman	443
64	Kingsbridge Armory	*Daily News*	Forgotten armory Diaz nearly omits mega-project from boro address	20-February-2013	Denis Slattery	441
65	Kingsbridge Armory	*Daily News*	Armory plans to be unveiled	22-April-2013	Tanyanika Samuels	356
66	Kingsbridge Armory	*The New York Times*	Plan for ice center in Bronx armory moves forward	24-April-2013	Winnie Hu	780

(Continued)

(Continued)

	Project	Paper	Title	Date	Author	Words
67	Kingsbridge Armory	*Daily News*	Worth the skate armory set to become Kingsbridge national ice center	25-April-2013	Jennifer H. Cunning-ham	379
68	Kingsbridge Armory	*Daily News*	Cut from same blade green-friendly both inside & out at Kingsbridge ice center	2-June-2013	Jennifer H. Cunning-ham	448
69	Kingsbridge Armory	*Daily News*	Ice, Ice, Baby! CB7 backs massive skating palace planned for Kingsbridge Armory	19-September-2013	Jennifer H. Cunning-ham	502
70	Kingsbridge Armory	*The New York Times*	Scrutiny over Bronx councilman's demands for ice center plan	22-November-2013	Winnie Hu	1014
71	Kingsbridge Armory	*The New York Times*	City council approves an ice center for the Bronx	11-December-2013	Winnie Hu	672
72	Kingsbridge Armory	*The New York Times*	Plans for huge ice center in Bronx stall	7-June-2014	Winnie Hu	543
73	Kingsbridge Armory	*The New York Times*	Plan to build ice center in the Bronx stalls amid a feud	9-June-2014	Winnie Hu	541
75	Kingsbridge Armory	*Daily News*	Ice cold move: Rink developer pulls out of festival promise	19-June-2014	Jennifer H. Cunning-ham	442
76	Kingsbridge Armory	*Daily News*	Real cold news armory neighbors hit with big rent hikes	21-July-2014	Pete Barrett	414
77	Kingsbridge Armory	*Daily News*	Bid to thaw armory cold war	7-October-2014	Ben Kochman	269
79	Kingsbridge Armory	*Daily News*	Rant and rave pol rips dance party planned for Armory	15-October-2014	Denis Slattery	486

(Continued)

(Continued)

	Project	*Paper*	*Title*	*Date*	*Author*	*Words*
80	Kingsbridge Armory	*Daily News*	Thinking rink developer, city ink Kingsbridge Armory deal	17-October-2014	Ben Kochman	324
81	Kingsbridge Armory	*Daily News*	Let Bill build	27-September-2015	Editorial	475
82	Kingsbridge Armory	*The New York Post*	DeB puts messier dream on ice	4-April-2016	Rich Clader	445
83	Kingsbridge Armory	*Daily News*	A Kingsbridge too far	10-April-2016	Editorial	448
84	Kingsbridge Armory	*The New York Times*	Bronx ice center plan hangs in the balance	11-April-2016	Charles V. Bagli	1171
85	Kingsbridge Armory	*Daily News*	Messier's slapshot over rink	13-April-2016	Denis Slattery	205
86	Kingsbridge Armory	*The New York Post*	Messier fires $lap (slap) shot at de Blasio	13-April-2016	Rich Clader	108
87	Kingsbridge Armory	*The New York Times*	A lawsuit, then a compromise offer on a stalled Bronx ice center plan	14-April-2016	Charles v. Bagli	719
88	Kingsbridge Armory	*The New York Times*	After suit, city offers developer a compromise on a stalled Bronx ice center plan	15-April-2016	Charles v. Bagli	719
89	Kingsbridge Armory	*The New York Post*	Prayers for pucks Messier in Bronx rink plea	6-May-2016	Rich Calder	296

Nr	*Project*	*Paper*	*Title*	*Date*	*Author*	*Words*
1	Essex Crossing	*The New York Times*	Two slum areas will be vacated	27-01-1957	-	-
2	Essex Crossing	*The New York Times*	Perspectives: Changeover in the housing agency; Putting a Dinkins imprint on a Koch plan	27-01-1957	Alan Oser	-
3	Ess2x Crossing	*The New York Times*	City planner aid 3 slum projects	18-06-1957	-	-
4	Essex Crossing	*The New York Times*	Co-ops approved for Seward Park	15-08-1957	-	-
5	Essex Crossing	*The New York Times*	Renewal is voted in east side area	23-06-1965	-	-
6	Essex Crossing	*The New York Times*	State pays $2.6 million on Seward Park project	19-06-1967	-	-
7	Essex Crossing	*The New York Times*	Neighborhoods: Chinatown is troubled by new influx	16-06-1970	-	-
8	Essex Crossing	*The New York Times*	Housing complex slated for Seward Park in '73	31-08-1971	Lauri Johnston	-
9	Essex Crossing	*The New York Times*	Letters to the editor	11-03-1973	-	-
10	Essex Crossing	*The New York Times*	Housing for Jews upheld by court	13-09-1973	Steven Weisman	-
11	Essex Crossing	*The New York Times*	Activities of Grand Street settlement reflect diversity of neighborhood	5-12-1973	Grace Lichtenstein	-
12	Essex Crossing	*The New York Times*	Low-Rent units on Delancy St. are voted down	25-04-1980	Joyce Purnick	-

(Continued)

(Continued)

Nr	*Project*	*Paper*	*Title*	*Date*	*Author*	*Words*
13	Essex Crossing	*The New York Times*	New money, people and ideas alter Chinatown of tradition	28-12-1981	Edward Gargan	-
14	Essex Crossing	*The New York Times*	Koch jeered on housing at town hall meeting	30-04-1982	-	-
15	Essex Crossing	*The New York Times*	Bias is admitted by New York City in public housing	01-06-1992	Robert Pear	-
16	Essex Crossing	*The New York Times*	A privatization plan challenges cooperative's long held idealism	10-10-1996	Steven Greenhouse	-
17	Essex Crossing	*The New York Times*	Free market comes to Lower East Side: As co-op price caps are lifted, some residents are wary of change	15-06-2000	Tina Kelley	-
18	Essex Crossing	*Daily News*	A plaque for your woes developers vs. LES locals on new housing mega-complex	15-06-2000	Michael Gartland	437
19	Essex Crossing	*The New York Times*	Neighborhood report; Lower east side; A park carved from Tenements still goes begging 100 years later	1-04-2001	Denny Lee	-
20	Essex Crossing	*The New York Times*	Neighborhood report: Lower East Side; A plan for five vacant lots gets plenty of vacant stares	30-11-2003	Steve Kurutz	-
21	Essex Crossing	*The New York Times*	Forty years of growth, except where it was expected	27-08-2007	David Gonzalez	-

(Continued)

(Continued)

Nr	*Project*	*Paper*	*Title*	*Date*	*Author*	*Words*
22	Essex Crossing	*The New York Times*	Agreement seems near on long-stalled Lower East Side project	15-12-2010	Cara Buckly	-
23	Essex Crossing	*The New York Times*	Board backs development of site on Lower East side with housing	25-01-2011	Cara Buckley	-
24	Essex Crossing	*The New York Times*	City plans redevelopment for vacant area in lower Manhattan	17-09-2013	Charles Bagli	-
25	Essex Crossing	*Daily News*	Grower East Side Bloomy's $1b superproject even includes a farm	19-09-2013	Mara Gay	411
26	Essex Crossing	*The New York Times*	They kept a lower East Side lot vacant for decades	23-03-2014	Russ Buettner	2705
27	Essex Crossing	*The New York Times*	Forgotten but not gone	15-03-2015	Ginia Bellafante	932
28	Essex Crossing	*The New York Times*	A newer Lower East Side	26-06-2015	Ronda Kaysen	679
29	Essex Crossing	*The New York Times*	Where gritty meets trendy	3-05-2016	Julie Besonen	1383
30	Essex Crossing	*The New York Times*	Essex Crossing, a renewal project 60 years in the making: Works in progress	15-06-2017	Helene Stapinski	961
31	Essex Crossing	*The New York Times*	Urban renewal 60 years in the making	18-06-2017	Helen Stapinski	880
32	Essex Crossing	*The New York Times*	Fight to save a cherished urban garden moves to court	8-03-2019	Luis Ferré-Sadurní	1419

(Continued)

(Continued)

Nr	*Project*	*Paper*	*Title*	*Date*	*Author*	*Words*
33	Essex Crossing	*The New York Times*	New York marketplace embraces its immigrant past; Square feet	2-05-2019	Jon Hurdle	1377
34	Essex Crossing	*The New York Times*	Brand-new melting pot on the Lower East Side	3-05-2019	Jon Hurdle	1265
35	Essex Crossing	*The New York Times*	New Essex Street market opens in an enormous new space; Off the menu	14-05-2019	Florence Fabricant	1274
36	Essex Crossing	*The New York Times*	New Essex Street market opens in an enormous new space	15-05-2019	Florence Fabricant	1324
37	Essex Crossing	*The New York Times*	New food halls sprout up in New York City: Front burner	3-09-2019	Florence Fabricant	731
38	Essex Crossing	*The New York Times*	New food halls sprout up in New York City: Front burner	3-09-2019	Florence Fabricant	731
39	Essex Crossing	*The New York Times*	New food halls sprout up in New York City	4-09-2019	Florence Fabricant	670
40	Essex Crossing	*The New York Times*	Essex crossing is the anti-Hudson Yards: Critic's notebook	7-11-2019	Michael Kimmelman	1925
41	Essex Crossing	*The New York Times*	It's vast, varied, even virtuous	11-11-2019	Michael Kimmelman	1834
42	Essex Crossing	*The New York Times*	I.C.P. to reopen at Essex Crossing	14-01-2020	James Estrin	494
43	Essex Crossing	*The New York Times*	Photography center at Essex Crossing	15-01-2020	James Estrin	491

(Continued)

Nr	Project	Paper	Title	Date	Author	Words
1	Neue Mitte Altona	*Taz, die Tageszeitung*	Traumen ist erlaubt: Mitte Altona mit einem Bürgerforum beginnt die Planung für das Gelände nördlich des Bahnhofs Altona. Sozial und ökologisch stellen die Anwohner sich ihre Nachbarschaft vor	07-June-2010	Sven-Michael Veit	581
2	Neue Mitte Altona	*Welt am Sonntag*	Die neue Mitte Altona nimmt Gestalt an	21-November-2010	Olaf Dittmann	148
3	Neue Mitte Altona	*Taz, die Tageszeitung*	Beteiligte wollen bremsen; Stadt Entwicklung Anwohner und Initiativen fordern ein Moratorium für die Planung zur Neuen Mitte Altona.	2-February-2012	Lena Kaiser	430
4	Neue Mitte Altona	*Taz, die Tageszeitung*	Votum für Planung stopp: Neue Mitte Altona das Bürgerforum entscheidet sich mit großer Mehrheit für ein Moratorium	04-february-2012	-	303
5	Neue Mitte Altona	*Taz, die Tageszeitung*	Vorbild Ottensen: Planung Rot-Grün in Altona verlangt sozialen mix für Neue Mitte	28-April-2012	-	99
6	Neue Mitte Altona	*Taz, die Tageszeitung*	Lieber nochmal rechnen; Stadt Entwicklung bevor die Planungen zum groß Projekt Neue Mitte Altona endgültig festgezurrt werden, prüft die Stadt die Finanzierungsmodalitäten	6-July-2012	Lena Kaiser	482
7	Neue Mitte Altona	*Taz, die Tageszeitung*	Bahn frei für die Mitte Altona; Stadtentwicklung Deutsche Bahn geht die Verlagerung des Bahnhofs Altona an.	9-July-2012	Sven-Michael Veit	422
8	Neue Mitte Altona	*Taz, die Tageszeitung*	Verschenkte Chance; Kommentar: Lena Kaiser über die Neue Mitte Altona	16-August-2012	Lena Kaiser	216

(Continued)

(Continued)

Nr	*Project*	*Paper*	*Title*	*Date*	*Author*	*Words*
9	Neue Mitte Altona	*Taz, die Tageszeitung*	Wem gehört Altona; Neue Mitte was auf dem Gelände nördlich des Altonaer Bahnhofs entstehen soll, ist nicht heraus; Während die Eigentümer Gewerbeflachen favorisieren, fordert eine Initiativen sozialen Wohnungsbau	23-August-2012	Lena Kaiser	438
10	Neue Mitte Altona	*Taz, die Tageszeitung*	ECE darf planen und bauen; Stadtplanung Senat und Projektentwickler einig über Konzept für Neue Mitte Altona.	12-September-2012	Marco Carini	400
11	Neue Mitte Altona	*Taz, die Tageszeitung*	Wir brauchen Platz; Stadt Entwicklung das Netzwerk autofreie Mitte Altona will im Planungsprozess mitmischen	03-June-2013	-	390
12	Neue Mitte Altona	*Die Welt*	Harte Kritik an Neuer Mitte Altona: Internes Behördenpapier: Stadt plant ungesunde und minderwertige Wohnbebauung	20-June-2013	Axel Tiedemann	473
13	Neue Mitte Altona	*Taz, die Tageszeitung*	Neue Mitte in der Bandschleife; Stad 13Entwicklung Die Bahn verschiebt die Entscheidung über den Umzug des Bahnhofs Altona und blockiert damit die plane für die Neue Mitte	9-September-2013	Kai Von Appen	652
14	Neue Mitte Altona	*Die Welt*	Gelände für Neue Mitte Altona kontaminiert; 3500 Wohnungen sollen hier entstehen	20-September-2013	Nina Paulsen	245
15	Neue Mitte Altona	*Die Welt*	Mitte Altona: Weitere Verzögerungen; Die Stadt verhandelt noch mit Investoren.	8-October-2013	Iris Hellmuth	482
16	Neue Mitte Altona	*Die Welt*	Altona verkauft Schulhofe für den Wohnungsbau: mehr als 1000 neue Wohnungen geplant	9-december-2013	Axel Tiedemann	283
17	Neue Mitte Altona	*Taz, die Tageszeitung*	Neue Mitte kann losgehen; Altona der Senat einigt sich mit Grundstückseigentümern auf Grundlagen für das größte bau Projekt nach der Hafencity	18-December-2013	Marco Carini	515

(*Continued*)

(Continued)

Nr	*Project*	*Paper*	*Title*	*Date*	*Author*	*Words*
18	Neue Mitte Altona	*Die tageszeitung*	Schone Neue Mitte Altona: Bauprojekt Senat und Grundstückseigentümer einigen sich, Kritiker vermissen Transparenz	27-December-2013	-	612
19	Neue Mitte Altona	*Taz, die Tageszeitung*	Bahn verspätet sich weiter; Altona über dem Umzug des Bahnhofs wird später entscheiden. Bauprojekt Neue Mitte auf der Kippe	18-February-2014	-	321
20	Neue Mitte Altona	*Taz, die Tageszeitung*	Bahn frei für Neue Mitte Altona	02-July-2014	Lena Kaiser	548
21	Neue Mitte Altona	*Spiegel Online*	Hamburgs neuer Hauser	30-July-2014	Franziska Bossy	542
22	Neue Mitte Altona	*Taz, die Tageszeitung*	Neue Mitte Altona	31-July-2014	-	92
23	Neue Mitte Altona	*Taz, die Tageszeitung*	Neue Mitte Altona kriegt Profil: Wettbewerb Oberbau Direktor stellt entwurfe ersten Bauabschnitt vor.	31-July-2014	Marco Carini	464
24	Neue Mitte Altona	*Taz, die Tageszeitung*	Bahn frei für neue Wohnformen; Wohnprojekte I Hamburg fordert Baugemeinschafen, indem es 20 Prozent des städtischen Baulandes reserviert, auf dem Wohnungen entstehen.	13-September-2014	Hannes Stepputat	572
25	Neue Mitte Altona	*Taz, die Tageszeitung*	Noch ein Schulhof auf dem Dach; Enge die Neue Stadteilschule in Mitte Altona soll Park- und Dachflachen als Schulhof nutzen.	15-October-2014	Kaija Kutter	610
26	Neue Mitte Altona	*Suddeutsche Zeiting*	Mix aus Denkmalern und Neubauten: Hamburg bekommt nach der Hafencity ein weiteres städtebauliches Groß Project—das Stadtviertel Neue Mitte Altona	24-Oktober-2014	Sabine Richter	1081

(Continued)

(Continued)

Nr	*Project*	*Paper*	*Title*	*Date*	*Author*	*Words*
27	Neue Mitte Altona	*Die Welt*	Start für einen neuen Stadtteil: Spatenstich für die Neue Mitte Altona—mittelfristig Söllen hier 2fast 3500 Wohnungen entstehen	19-November-2014	Axel Tiedemann	535
28	Neue Mitte Altona	*Die Welt*	Bahn frei für die Große Neue Mitte Altona: Vertrag zur Bahnhof-Verlegung unterzeichnet.	20-December-2014	Axel Tiedemann	840
29	Neue Mitte Altona	*Die Welt*	Start für das neue Altona: Bauarbeiten für Hamburgs zweitgrößtes Bau Projekt beginnen	25-February-2016	Eva Eusterhus	932
30	Neue Mitte Altona	*Zeit Online*	Wie viel Grün Bekommt das neue Altona? Die ersten Wohnungen von Mitte Altona werden gebaut—doch wird es in Hamburgs zweitgrößten wohn Projekt auch grün geben?	25-February-2016	Mark Spörrle	2267
31	Neue Mitte Altona	*Handelsblatt*	Immobilienprojekt Neue Mitte Altona; Vorbildliche Inklusion in Hamburg	3-November-2016	Reiner Reichel	1006
32	Neue Mitte Altona	*Bild*	Die größten bau Projekte der Stadt von oben: Aussicht auf 4581 Wohunungen	29-August-2018	Michaela Klauer	386
33	Neue Mitte Altona	*Welt online*	Bezirkschefin Liane Melzer; In dieser Art zu bauen liegt die Zukunft	13-January-2019	Eva Eusterhus	1352
34	Neue Mitte Altona	*Die Welt*	In dieser Art zu bauen liegt die Zukunft: Altona boomt, kaum ein andere Bezirk scheibt so viele Groß Projekte an.	14-January-2019	Eva Eusterhus	1293
35	Neue Mitte Altona	*Hamburger Mogenpost*	Neue Mitte Altona: Manhattan lasst Grüßen	27-December-2019	-	711
36	Neue Mitte Altona	*Hamburger Morgenpost*	Neue Mittel Altona: Autoarmes Quartier7gescheitert? Stadt setzt neue Regeln durch	21-April-2020	Mike Schlink	494

Nr	Project	Paper	Title	Date	Author	Words
1	Paloma Viertel	*Immobilien Zeitung*	City Nord Hamburg; Zum 50. Geburtstag nur noch wenige Plätze frei	26-February-2009	-	1604
2	Paloma Viertel	*Die Welt*	Verjüngskur für das Esso-Haus; Einstige Kozernzentrale in der City Nord wird für 25 Millionen Euro saniert—Hotelneubau geplant	13-October-2009	Gisela Schütte	439
3	Paloma Viertel	*Taz, die Tageszeitung*	Kampf um St. Pauli; Gentrifizierung auf dem Areal der "Esso Häuser" am Speilbudenplatz könnte die Politik eine der letzten Chancen nutzen, der Yuppisierung van St. Pauli etwas entgegenzusetzen	22-September-2010	Lena Kaiser	564
4	Paloma Viertel	*Taz, die Tageszeitung*	Büroturm im Sperrgebiet; Wohnungsmangel 6000 Menschen demonstrieren in Hamburg gegen leer stand.	25-October-2010	Lena Kaiser and Kai von Appen	767
5	Paloma Viertel	*Taz, die Tageszeitung*	Unter Konsensdruck; Abriss Das Areal der "Esso Häuser" am Spielbudenplatz ist umkämpft.	22-Novemer-2010	Lena Kaiser	506
6	Paloma Viertel	*Taz, die Tageszeitung*	Esso-Häuser: Abriss rückt näher; Gentrifizierung Der Investor, der über die Zukunft der "Esso Häuser" am Speilbudenplatz 7entscheidet, hält Abriss der Häuser für sinnvoll	17-May-2011	Lena Kaiser	509

(*Continued*)

(Continued)

Nr	*Project*	*Paper*	*Title*	*Date*	*Author*	*Words*
7	Paloma Viertel	*Taz, die Tageszeitung*	Verdrängt wird niemand; St. Pauli an den Esso-Häusern am Spielbudenplatz scheiden sich die Geister	23-May-2011	Lena Kaiser	655
8	Paloma Viertel	*Taz, die Tageszeitung*	Charme verliert gegen Geld; Reeperbahn Investor beendet die Gespräche mit der Initiative für den Erhalt der "Esso Häuser" und will einen Neubau am Spielbudenplatz.	8-February-2012	Janis Dietz	529
9	Paloma Viertel	*Taz, die Tageszeitung*	Kein Abriss ohne Kompromiss; Esso Häuser Nach dem Alleingang der Bayerischen Hausbau, den Dialog mit der Anwohner-Initiative aufzukündigen, stellen sich Bezirkspolitiker von GAL und SPD quer	10-February-2012	Lena Kaiser	518
10	Paloma Viertel	*Taz, die Tageszeitung*	Esso-Initiative Außen vor; Stadtentwicklung der Investor Bayerische Hausbau will exklusiv mit seinen Mieter Innen sprechen	19-March-2012	KNÖ	292
11	Paloma Viertel	*Taz, die Tageszeitung*	Tauziehen um Erhalt der Esso-Häuser geht weiter; Gentrificizerung Stadt will Gutachten bezahlen.	13-October-2012	LKA	325
12	Paloma Viertel	*Die Welt*	Umstrittenes Gutachten auf Staatskosten zu Esso-Häusern; Stadt 13zahlt für weitere Ex14pertise zum Zustand der Gebäude am Spielbudenplatz	11-January-2013	Ulrich Gassdorf	882

(Continued)

(Continued)

Nr	*Project*	*Paper*	*Title*	*Date*	*Author*	*Words*
13	Paloma Viertel	*Welt Online*	Esso-Häuser; Gutachten auf Staatskosten sorgt für Streit	11-January-2013	Ulrich Gassdorf	904
14	Paloma Viertel	*Die Welt*	Prominente Abrissgegner; Persönlichkeiten aus Wirtschaft und Kultur machen sich in einem gemeinsamen Manifest für den Erhalt der maroden Esso-Häuser an der Reeperbahn stark	11-June-2013	Ulrich Gassdorf; Marlies Fischer	665
15	Paloma Viertel	*Die Welt*	Umstrittene Esso-Häuser offenbar stark baufällig; Gutachten wird Donnerstag veröffentlicht	12-June-2013	Ulrich Gassdorf	203
16	Paloma Viertel	*Die Welt*	Mieter der Esso-Häuser erhalten Recht auf Rückkehr; Bayerische Hausbau will Ersatzwohnungen auf St. Pauli stellen.	20-July-2013	Anne Fuchs; Charlotte Gerling; Friederike Ulrich	733
17	Paloma Viertel	*Taz, die Tageszeitung*	Esso-Häuser kommen weg; Gentrifizierung die Bayerische Hausbau hat die Abriss des Komplexes an der Reeperbahn beantragt, der Bezirksamtsleiter sieht dagegen kein Mittel	16-August-2013	Carsten Bisping	486
18	Paloma Viertel	*Die Welt*	Abriss der Esso-Häuser wird wohl genehmigt; Hitziges Informationstreffen mit Anwohnern	25-August-2013	-	297
19	Paloma Viertel	*Welt am Sonntag*	Karriere in der Mitte der Stadt; Bezirksamtsleiter Andy Grote ist seit 15 Monaten Herr über den Kiez und die Innenstadt.	25-August-2013	Ulrich Gassdorf	1200

(Continued)

(Continued)

Nr	*Project*	*Paper*	*Title*	*Date*	*Author*	*Words*
20	Paloma Viertel	*Die Welt*	Es ist ein totaler Schlamassel; Ein Streitgespräch über die Zukunft der Esso-Häuser an der Reeperbahn.	30-August-2013	Ulrich Gassdorf and Daniel Szewczyk	1962
21	Paloma Viertel	*Taz, die Tageszeitung*	Zukunft für Clubs ungewiss; Esso-Häuser Clubs sollten zu gleichen Konditionen zurückkehren, aber davon ist jetzt keine Rede mehr	27-September-2013	Dominik Brück	299
22	Paloma Viertel	*Die Welt*	Esso-Häuser: Steg soll Umzug leiten; Noch wohnen 90 Parteien im Abbruchhaus	30-August-2013	Ulrich Gassdorf	173
23	Paloma Viertel	*Die Welt*	Hamburg Kompakt; Reeperbahn: Mieterinitiative zeigt Besitzer der Esso-Häuser an	9-October-2013	-	606
24	Paloma Viertel	*Spiegel Online*	Polizei evakuiert Esso-Häuser wegen Einsturzgefahr	15-December-2013	-	379
25	Paloma Viertel	*Welt Online*	Hamburg; Einsturzgefahr—Häuser auf Reeperbahn evakuiert	15-December-2013	-	335
26	Paloma Viertel	*Welt Online*	Hamburg; Solidaritäts-Demo für Mieter der "Esso-Häuser"	16-December-2013	Daniel Schäfer, Axel Tiede-mann, André Zand-Vakili and Michaela Klauer	843
27	Paloma Viertel	*Die Welt*	Einsturzgefahr: Esso-Häuser über Nacht evakuiert; Weil Gebäude plötzlich schwankt, müssen Bewohner ihre Wohnungen über-stürzt verlassen	16-December-2013	Daniel Schäfer, André Zand-Vakili and Axel Tiedemann	629

(*Continued*)

(Continued)

Nr	*Project*	*Paper*	*Title*	*Date*	*Author*	*Words*
28	Paloma Viertel	*Spiegel Online*	Hamburger Esso-Häuser sind unbewohnbar	17-December-2013	-	365
29	Paloma Viertel	*Taz, die Tageszeitung*	Weihnachten im Hostel; Alle raus! Die maroden Esso-Häuser an der Hamburger Reeperbahn sind am Wochenende evakuiert worden	18-December-2013	Marta Popowska	692
30	Paloma Viertel	*Die Welt*	Esso-Häuser: Ehemalige Bewohner erheben schwere Vorwürfe; Viele der 91 Betroffenen werden die Weihnachtstage in Hotels verbringen	19-December-2013	Denis Fengler	780
31	Paloma Viertel	*Welt Online*	Nach Evakuierung; Mieter der "Esso-Häuser" erheben schwere Vorwürfe	19-December-2013	Denis Fengler	796
32	Paloma Viertel	*Taz, die Tageszeitung*	Wer ist schuld?; Esso-Häuser nach der Evakuierung der maroden Gebäude müsse die Eigentümerin Bayerische Hausbau belangt und nicht belohnt werden, findet die Initiative Esso-Häuser	19-December-2013	Lena Kaiser	501
33	Paloma Viertel	*Die Zeit*	Rettet den Schmuddel!; In Hamburg eskaliert ein Streit um Wohnhäuser auf St. Pauli.	19-December-2013	Maximilian Probst	462
34	Paloma Viertel	*Taz, die Tageszeitung*	Touri36st in der eigenen Stadt; Umzug Andreas Sidiropoulos ist einer der Bewohner der Esso-Häuser, die ihre Wohnung wegen akuter Einsturzgefahr verlassen mussten.	24-December-2013	Ilka Kreutzträger	775

(Continued)

(Continued)

Nr	*Project*	*Paper*	*Title*	*Date*	*Author*	*Words*
35	Paloma Viertel	*Die Welt*	Esso-Häuser: Montag beginnt Räumung; Bewohner dürfen nicht selbst Kisten packen	26-August-2014	Friederike Ulrich	246
36	Paloma Viertel	*Die Welt*	Angriff auf die Polizei: St. Pauli stellt sich gegen die Gewalttäter; Initiative überreicht gemeinsame Erklärung.	3-January-2014	Denis Fengler	819
37	Paloma Viertel	*Die Welt*	Geheimpapier: Staatsschutz warnt vor weiteren linksradikalen Anschlägen; Szene ist nacht Polizei-Einschätzung durch Auseinandersetzung um Rote Flora, Esso-Häuser und Flüchtlinge gewaltbereiter geworden	6-January-2014	André Zand-Vakili	669
38	Paloma Viertel	*Taz, die Tageszeitung*	Umzug ins Zwischelager; Evakuierung Die Bewohner der Hamburger Esso-Häuser packen ihre Sachen.	6-January-2014	Janto Rössner	510
39	Paloma Viertel	*Zeit Online*	Ach wie schön lebt es sich in der Gefahrenzone; Polizisten im Ganzkörperpanzer, 40Polizeisporter auf Spähfahrt und mittendrin im Hamburger Gefahrengebiet: 50.000 Bewohner.	8-January-2014	Jan Feitag	1105
40	Paloma Viertel	*Die Welt*	Stadt im Fokus; Esso-Häuser; Abbruch der Esso-Häuser unter Auflagen	17-January-2014	-	265

(Continued)

(Continued)

Nr	*Project*	*Paper*	*Title*	*Date*	*Author*	*Words*
41	Paloma Viertel	*Welt Online*	Reeperbahn; Geisterbau- Esso-Häuser sind fast komplett geräumt	17-January-2014	-	335
42	Paloma Viertel	*Spiegel Online*	Eine Stadt schreit sich an	20-January-2014	Fabian Reinbold	997
43	Paloma Viertel	*Die Welt*	Hamburg Kompakt; St. Pauli: Viele Ex-Esso haus-bewohner noch ohne Ersatzwohnung	8-February-2014	-	500
44	Paloma Viertel	*Welt Online*	Hamburger Reeperbahn; Abriss der berühmten Kiez-Tankstelle hat begonnen	13-February-2014	-	400
45	Paloma Viertel	*Taz, die Tageszeitung*	Mut zur Lücke; Verhärtete Fronten die Bayerische Hausbau erhöht den Druck; Sie will die "Esso-Häuser" am Speilbudenplatz auf St. Pauli zwar in Kürze abreißen, aber nur neu bauen, wen die SPD von ihrer Forderung abrückt, dass dort zur Hälfte Sozialwohnungen gebaut werden sollen	21-February-2014	Lena Kaiser	645
46	Paloma Viertel	*Welt Online*	Hamburg; Investor droht mit riesiger Baulücke auf Esso-Areal	21-February-2014	-	357
47	Paloma Viertel	*Die Welt*	Esso-Häuser: Investor setzt Bezirk Mitte unter Druck; Bayerische Hausbau will das Ensemble abreißen, aber nicht die geforderte Menge Sozialwohnungen bauen	22-February-2014	Axel Tiedemann	798

(Continued)

(Continued)

Nr	*Project*	*Paper*	*Title*	*Date*	*Author*	*Words*
48	Paloma Viertel	*Die Welt*	Esso-Häuser: Neubau ungewiss; Investor und Bezirk streiten um Quote	14-March-2014	-	144
49	Paloma Viertel	*Taz, die Tageszeitung*	Eine gewisse Blockade; Esso Häuser Die Bayerische Hausbau hat angedroht, am Spielbudenplatz nicht neu zu bauen.	18-March-2014	Lena Kaiser	680
50	Paloma Viertel	*Die Welt*	Grüne: Stadt soll Esso-Häuser kaufen; Eigentümer Bayerisch Hausbau lehnt ab.	8-April-2014	Ulrich Gassdorf	397
51	Paloma Viertel	*Welt Online*	Bürgerbeteiligung; Esso-Häuser-Initiative pocht auf Mitspracherecht	24-April-2014	-	606
52	Paloma Viertel	*Taz, die Tageszeitung*	Ein Container für Ideen; Stadtentwicklung Bürgerinitiativen fordern ein Mitspracherecht bei der Planung der Esso Häuser	25-April-2014	Stef	306
53	Paloma Viertel	*Die Welt*	Anwohner wollen selbst Ideen für Neubau auf Esso-Areal entwickeln; Initiative fordert verbindliches 54Mitspracherecht bei der Planung	25-April-2014	Daniel Schäfer	754
54	Paloma Viertel	*Taz, die Tageszeitung*	Abriss—und dann?; Gentrifizierung I Das Ende der Esso-Häuser rückt näher, die Diskussion, was aus dem Gelände wird, ist noch nicht vorbei	10-May-2014	Meret Michel	714

(*Continued*)

(Continued)

Nr	Project	Paper	Title	Date	Author	Words
55	Paloma Viertel	*Taz, die Tageszeitung*	Gewalt ohne Folgen; Gentrifizierung II Die Esso-Häuser-Security ging einen Bezirkspolitiker der Piraten körperlich an—doch die Staatsanwaltschaft winkt ab	10-May-2014	KVA	428
56	Paloma Viertel	*Taz, die Tageszeitung*	Die Esso-Häuser	10-May-2014	-	115
57	Paloma Viertel	*Welt Online*	Reeperbahn; Esso-Häuser-Investor bietet Kompromiss an	30-May-2014	Ulrich Gassdorf	902
58	Paloma Viertel	*Die Welt*	Stadt im Fokus; Esso-Häuser: Pauli-Initiative will Investor-Angebot prüfen	31-May-2014	-	153
59	Paloma Viertel	*Die Welt*	Teure Bürgerbeteiligung bei Neubau auf Esso-Gelände; Mitte stellt Beteiligungsverfahren für fast 100.000 euro vor.	23-July-2014	Insa Gall and Ulrich Gassdorf	761
60	Paloma Viertel	*Taz, die Tageszeitung*	Vorschläge in Lego; Planbude die Anwohner können jetzt mitbestimmen, was auf dem Areal der ehemaligen Esso-Häuser gebaut wird.	30-October-2014	Katharina Schipkowski	534
61	Paloma Viertel	*Immobilien Zeitung*	Hamburg: 60% geförderte Wohnungen für Esso-Häuser Areal	20-May-2015	Friedhelm Feldhaus	609
62	Paloma Viertel	*Immobilien Zeitung*	Bayerische Hausbau knackt den St.-Pauli-Code	28-May-2015	-	657

(*Continued*)

(Continued)

Nr	*Project*	*Paper*	*Title*	*Date*	*Author*	*Words*
63	Paloma Viertel	*Taz, die Tageszeitung*	Esso-Häuser: Alle voll des Lobes; Stadentwicklung Städtebaulicher Wettbewerb für Grundstück am Spielbudenplatz endet mit einstimmiger Jury-Entscheidung.	24-September-2015	Gernot Knodler	466
64	Paloma Viertel	*Die Welt*	Niederländer planen Dachgärten auf Esso-Areal; Siegerentwurf des städtebaulichen Wettbewerbs zur Gestaltung des Geländes auf St. Pauli gekürt	24-September-2015	Jannik Schappert	802
65	Paloma Viertel	*Welt Online*	Hamburg; Niederländer planen Dachgärten auf Esso-Areal	24-September-2015	Jannik Schappert	803
66	Paloma Viertel	*Immobilien Zeitung*	NL und BeL setzen den St.-Pauli-Code um	1-October-2015	-	279
67	Paloma Viertel	*Taz, die Tageszeitung*	Esso-Areal wird beplant; Bürgerwerkstatt Neubebauung des Esso-Areals am Spielbudenplatz nimmt konkrete Formen an	20-July-2016	-	216
68	Paloma Viertel	*Die Welt*	Der St. Pauli-Code steht; Stadt und Investor präsentieren die Architektur der neuen Esso-Häuser	24-September-2016	Maritn Emermacher	843

(Continued)

(Continued)

Nr	*Project*	*Paper*	*Title*	*Date*	*Author*	*Words*
69	Paloma Viertel	*Hamburger Morgenpost*	So cool werden die neuen Esso-Häuser; St. Pauli Live-Clubs, XXL-Balkon, Basketball-Platz auf dem Dach—und rund 200 Wohnungen.	24-September-2016	Ankea Janssen	434
70	Paloma Viertel	*Zeit Online*	170.000 Euro im Müll; Was jedes Jahr so in den Hamburger Mülleimern landet.	26-September-2016	Mark Spörrle	3044
71	Paloma Viertel	*Zeit Online*	Wie sollen die neuen Esso-Häuser heißen?; Der Neubau bracht einen Namen—"Esso" darf nicht darin vorkommen	19-April-2017	Mark Spörrle	2801
72	Paloma Viertel	*Welt Online*	Reeperbahn; Aus dem Ex-Esso-Areal wird das Paloma Viertel	30-May-2017	-	171
73	Paloma Viertel	*BILD*	Wo die Esso-Häuser standen, entsteht jetzt das Paloma Viertel; So wird der Kiez zusammengewürfelt	31-May-2017	Jörg Köhnmann	333
74	Paloma Viertel	*Hamburger Morgenpost*	Neubau heißt Paloma-Viertel	31-May-2017	Mike Schlink	82
75	Paloma Viertel	*Taz, die Tageszeitung*	Irgendwann loslassen können; Abgang nach 18 Jahren im Amt ist für Hamburgs Oberbaudirektor Jörn Walter nächste Woche Schluss.	3-July-2017	Lena Kaiser, Gernot Knödler	1661

(*Continued*)

(Continued)

Nr	*Project*	*Paper*	*Title*	*Date*	*Author*	*Words*
76	Paloma Viertel	*Bild*	Quartier auf Esso-Häuser-Gelände fertig zusammengewürfelt; La Paloma, Oje	8-October-2017	Jörg Köhnemann	249
77	Paloma Viertel	*Welt Online*	Esso-Häuser; So geht es im Paloma-Viertel auf dem Kiez weiter	8-May-2018	-	617
78	Paloma Viertel	*Taz, die Tageszeitung*	Es wird sozial; Die Nachfolge der Esso-Häuser am Spielbudenplatz nimmt Form an: Viel geförderter Wohnraum soll ab 2019 gebaut werden.	9-May-2018	Philipp Steffens	514
79	Paloma Viertel	*Immobilien Zeitung*	Prozess zum Paloma-Viertel ist als Schablone ungeeignet	17-May-2018	-	375

Nr	*Project*	*Paper*	*Title*	*Date*	*Author*	*Words*
1	Oostenburg-Noord	*Het Parool*	Het Storkterrein als voorstelling	29-09-2001	Peter van Brummelen	759
2	Oostenburg-Noord	*Het Parool*	Niet veel Amsterdammers	30-07-2004	Lodewijk Bakker	716
3	Oostenburg-Norord	*Het Parool*	Brieven	8-05-2016	Jeroen Verhulst	474
4	Oostenburg-Noord	*NRC Handelsblad*	Oostelijke Eilanden Masterplan marineterrein: bekijk de eilanden als geheel, er valt zoveel te winnen	24-03-2018	Rob van Dijk, Marius Ernsting, and Lex Gründeman	416
5	**Oostenburg-Noord**	*Het Parool*	Oostenburg kann best wat steun gebruiken	14-06-2018	-	461

Nr	*Project*	*Paper*	*Title*	*Date*	*Author*	*Words*
1	K-Buurt	*Het Parool*	Je moet het op een leuke manier brengen	22-05-2024	Bart van Zoelen	875
2	K-Buurt	*Het Parool*	Neem inwoners van Zuidoost serieus en behoud metrolijnen	13-02-2024	Jim Haijen, Manoah Salampessy, Rebecca Pabó	706
3	K-Buurt	*Het Parool*	K-Buurt: onbetwist inspraakfenomeen	10-09-2018	Patrick Meershoek	633
4	K-Buurt	*Het Parool*	Betrokken bewoners K-Buurt vangen bot	10-05-2017	Patrick Meershoek	570
5	K-Buurt	*Het Parool*	K-Buurt ziet wens in vervulling gaan	30-03-2017	Partick Meershoek	577
6	K-Buurt	*Het Parool*	Meer woningen of een bruisend, gezellig plein?	20-09-2016	-	483
7	K-Buurt	*Het Parool*	Woningbouw komt, Kempering gaat	21-09-2016	Patrick Meershoek	426
8	K-Buurt	*Het Parool*	We trekken alles uit de kast, we gaan het doel halen	31-10-2022	Tim Wagemakers	758

Index

Note: Numbers in **bold** indicate a table.

Kolibri 360 GmbH
Ferdinand-Jühlke-Straße 7
99095 Erfurt, Deutschland
produktsicherheit@kolibri360.de